the doctrine of LAW & GRACE *unfolded*

GREAT CHRISTIAN BOOKS
LINDENHURST, NEW YORK

the doctrine of LAW & GRACE unfolded

JOHN BUNYAN

A GREAT CHRISTIAN BOOKS publication
Great Christian Books is an imprint of Rotolo Media
160 37th Street Lindenhurst, New York 11757 (631) 956-0998
www.GreatChristianBooks.com
email: mail@greatchristianbooks.com
Smooth Stones taken from Ancient Brooks
ISBN 978-1-61010-037-3

©2014 Rotolo Media / Great Christian Books

All rights reserved under International and Pan-American Copyright Conventions. No part of this book maybe reproduced in any form, or by any means, electronic or mechanical, including photocopying, and informational storage and retrieval systems without the expressed written permission from the publisher, except in the case of brief quotations embodied in articles or reviews or promotional/advertising/catalog materials. For additional information or permissions, address all inquiries to the publisher.

Bunyan, John, 1628–1688
The Doctrine of Law and Grace Unfolded / by John Bunyan
p. cm.
A "A Great Christian Book" book
GREAT CHRISTIAN BOOKS a division of Rotolo Media
ISBN 978-1-61010-037-3
Recommended Dewey Decimal Classifications: 200, 230
Suggested Subject Headings:
1. Religion—Christian literature—Christian theology
2. Christianity—The Bible—Covenant theology
I. Title

The book and cover design for this title are by Michael Rotolo. It is typeset in the Minion typeface by Adobe Inc. and is quality manufactured in the United States on acid-free paper stock. To discuss the publication of your Christian manuscript or out-of-print book, please contact Great Christian Books.

Manufactured in the United States of America

CONTENTS

The Editor's Preface ... 9
The Author's Preface ... 11

THE FIRST DOCTRINE—OF THE LAW

The Text Opened and the Doctrines Laid Down ... 25
Some Are Under The Law— The Covenant of Works ... 27
The Covenant of Works: What It Is & When It Was Given ... 28
What It Is To Be Under The Covenant of Works ... 34
Who They Are That Are Under The Covenant of Works ... 54
What Men May Attain To Under The Covenant of Works ... 62

THE SECOND DOCTRINE—OF GRACE

The People of God Are Not Under The Law But Under Grace—The New Covenant ... 85
The Doctrine Proved ... 87
The New Covenant is Free and Unchangeable ... 90
Who and How Men Are Brought Into The New Covenant ... 136
The Privileges of The New Covenant ... 160
Use and Examination About The Old Covenant ... 170
The Use of The New Covenant ... 182
A Word of Advice ... 186
The Unpardonable Sin ... 198
Objections Answered for the Comfort of Those Who Would have Their Part in The New Covenant ... 207
Footnotes ... 223

THE DOCTRINE OF LAW AND GRACE UNFOLDED

BY JOHN BUNYAN

OR, A DISCOURSE TOUCHING THE LAW AND GRACE; THE NATURE OF THE ONE, AND THE NATURE OF THE OTHER; SHOWING WHAT THEY ARE, AS THEY ARE THE TWO COVENANTS; AND LIKEWISE, WHO THEY BE, AND WHAT THEIR CONDITIONS ARE, THAT BE UNDER EITHER OF THESE TWO COVENANTS.

Wherein, for the better understanding of the reader, there are several questions answered touching the law and grace, very easy to be read, and as easy to be understood, by those that are the sons of wisdom, the children of the second covenant.

> "For the law made nothing perfect, but the bringing in of a better hope did; by the which we draw nigh unto God."
> —HEBREWS 7:19

> "Therefore we conclude that a man is justified by faith without the deeds of the law." —ROMANS 3:28

> "To him (therefore) that worketh not, but believeth on Him that justifieth the ungodly, his faith is counted for righteousness." —ROMANS 4:5

THE EDITOR'S PREFACE

It is difficult to understand those peculiar trials which called forth the mighty energies of Bunyan's mind, unless we are acquainted with the times in which he lived. The trammels of statecraft and priestcraft had been suddenly removed from religion, and men were left to form their own opinions as to rites and ceremonies. In this state of abrupt liberty, some wild enthusiasts ran into singular errors; and Bunyan's first work on "Gospel Truths" was published to correct them. Then followed that alarm to thoughtless souls—"A Few Sighs from Hell"; and, in 1659, as a further declaration of the most important truths of revelation, this work on the two covenants was sent forth to chastise error, and comfort the saints of God. It was published many times during the author's life; and since then, to a late period, very large impressions have been circulated. Upon a subject of such vast importance—upon which hangs all our eternal interests—all our indescribable joys or sorrows in a future and never-ending state—the requirements of our Creator—and His gracious provision of pardoning mercy, upon our failing to keep His Law—these are subjects of intense interest. How important is it that all our researches into these solemn realities should be guided simply by the revealed will of God! That was the fountain at which Bunyan drunk in all his knowledge; and with simplicity, and most earnest desire to promote the glory of God in the salvation of sinners, he here gives the result of his patient, prayerful, painful investigation. The humble dependence upon Divine mercy which the author felt is very striking. He was sensible of his lack of formal education; "no vain, whimsical, scholar-like terms"—no philosophy from Plato or Aristotle. He felt, as to human teaching, his weakness, but proved that, "when he was weak, then was he strong." He claimed an interest in the fervent prayers of his fellow saints—"My heart is vile, the devil lieth at watch, trust myself I dare not; if God do not help me, my heart will deceive me." This was the proper spirit in which to enter upon so solemn a subject; and the aid he sought was vouchsafed to him, and appears throughout this important work.

His first object is to define what is the Law, a strict obedience to which is exacted upon all mankind. It was given to Adam, and was afterwards more fully developed upon Mount Sinai. It commands implicit, universal, perfect obedience, upon pain of eternal ruin. He shows us that man, under the influence of that law, and while a stranger to the Law of Grace, may repent and reform his conduct, become a member of a Christian church, be a virgin waiting for his Lord, "but not step even upon the lowest round of the ladder that reacheth to heaven." While man is a stranger to the new birth, "his destiny is the lion's den; yea, worse than that, to be thrown into Hell to the very devils." Bunyan in this, as well as all other of his works, is awfully severe upon those who say, "Let us sin that grace may abound," perverting the consolatory doctrine of Divine grace to their souls" destruction. "What! because Christ is a Savior, wilt thou be a sinner! because His grace abounds, therefore thou wilt abound in sin! O wicked wretch! rake Hell all over, and surely I think thy fellow will scarce be found. If Christ will not serve their turn, but they must have their sins too, take them, Devil; if Heaven will not satisfy them, take them, Hell; devour them, burn them, Hell!" "Tell the hogs of this world what a hog-sty is prepared for them, even such an one as a God hath prepared to put the devil and his angels into."

To the distressed, sin-beaten Christian, this book abounds with consolation, and instructions how to overcome the devices of Satan, who will plant the Ten Commandments, like ten great guns, to destroy thy hopes. "Learn to outshoot the devil in his own bow, and to cut off his head with his own sword. Doth Satan tell thee thou prayest but faintly and with cold devotions? Answer him, I am glad you told me, I will trust the more to Christ's prayers, and groan, sigh, and cry more earnestly at the Throne of Grace." To such readers as have been driven to the verge of despair by a fear of having committed the unpardonable sin, here is strong consolation, and a very explicit scriptural definition of that awful crime. Want of space prevents me adding more than my earnest desire that the reading of this treatise may be productive of solid peace and comfort.

THE AUTHOR'S PREFACE TO THE READER

Dear Reader,

If at any time there be held forth by the preacher the freeness and fullness of the Gospel, together with the readiness of the Lord of Peace to receive those that have any desire thereto, presently it is the spirit of the world to cry out, Sure this man disdains the law, slights the law, and counts that of none effect; and all because there is not, together with the Gospel, mingled the doctrine of the law, which is not a right dispensing of the Word according to truth and knowledge. Again; if there be the terror, horror, and severity of the law discovered to a people by the servants of Jesus Christ, though they do not speak of it to the end people should trust to it, by relying on it as it is a covenant of works; but rather that they should be driven further from that covenant, even to embrace the tenders and privileges of the second, yet, poor souls, because they are unacquainted with the natures of these two covenants, or either of them, therefore, "they say," "Here is nothing but preaching of the law, thundering of the law"; when, alas, if these two be not held forth—to wit, the Covenant of Works and the Covenant of Grace, together with the nature of the one and the nature of the other—souls will never be able either to know what they are by nature or what they lie under. Also, neither can they understand what grace is, nor how to come from under the law to meet God in and through that other most glorious covenant, through which and only through which, God can communicate of Himself grace, glory, yea, even all the good things of another world.

I, having considered these things, together with others, have made bold to present yet once more to thy view, my friend, something of the mind of God, to the end, if it shall be but blessed to thee, thou mayest be benefited thereby; for verily these things are not such as are ordinary and of small concernment, but do absolutely concern thee to know, and that experimentally too, if ever thou do partake of the glory of God through Jesus Christ, and so escape the terror and insupportable vengeance that will otherwise come upon thee through His justice, because of thy living and dying in thy transgressions against the Law of God. And therefore, while thou livest here below, it is thy duty, if thou wish thyself happy for the time to come, to give up thyself to the studying of these two covenants treated of in the ensuing discourse; and so to study them until thou, through grace, do not only get the notion of the one and of the other in thy head, but until thou do feel the very power, life, and glory of the one and of the other: for take this for granted, he that is dark as touching the scope, intent, and nature of the law, is also dark as to the scope, nature, and glory of the Gospel; and also he that hath but a notion of the one, will barely have any more than a notion of the other.

And the reason is this: because so long as people are ignorant of the nature of the law, and of their being under it—that is, under the curse and condemning power of it, by reason of their sin against it—so long they will be careless, and negligent as to the inquiring after the true knowledge of the Gospel. Before the commandment came—that is, in the spirituality of it—Paul was alive—that is, thought himself safe; which is clear, (Romans 7:9-10, compared with Philippians 3:5-11, etc). But when that came, and was indeed discovered unto him by the Spirit of the Lord, then Paul dies (Romans 7) to all his former life (Philippians 3) and that man which before could content himself to live, though ignorant of the Gospel, cries out now, "I count all things but loss for the excellency of the knowledge of Christ Jesus my Lord" (verse 8). Therefore, I say, so long they will be ignorant of the nature of the Gospel, and how glorious a thing it is to be found within the bounds of it; for we use to say, that man that knoweth not himself to be sick, that man will not look out for himself a physician; and this Christ knew full well when He saith, "The whole have no need of the physician, but the sick";[1] that is, none will in truth desire the physician unless they know they be sick. That man also that hath got but a notion of the law—a notion, that is, the knowledge of it in the head, so as to discourse and talk of it—if he hath not felt the power of it, and that effectually too, it is to be feared will at the best be but a notionist in the Gospel; he will not have the experimental knowledge of the same in his heart; nay, he will not seek nor heartily desire after it; and all because, as I said before, he hath not experience of the wounding, cutting, killing nature of the other.

I say, therefore, if thou wouldst know the authority and power of the Gospel, labor first to know the power and authority of the law; for I am verily persuaded that the want of this one thing—namely, the knowledge of the law, is one cause why so many are ignorant of the other. That man that doth know the law doth not know in deed and in truth that he is a sinner; and that man that doth not know he is a sinner, doth not know savingly that there is a Savior.

Again; that man that doth not know the nature of the law, that man doth not know the nature of sin; and that man that knoweth not the nature of sin, will not regard to know the nature of a Savior; this is proved (John 8:31-36). These people were professors, and yet did not know the truth—the Gospel; and the reason was, because they did not know themselves, and so not the law. I would not have thee mistake me, Christian reader; I do not say that the law of itself will lead any soul to Jesus Christ; but the soul being killed by the law, through the operation of its severity seizing on the soul, then the man, if he be enlightened by the Spirit of Christ to see where remedy is to be had, will not, through grace, be contented without the real and saving knowledge through faith of Him.

If thou wouldst, then, wash thy face clean, first take a glass and see where it is dirty; that is, if thou wouldst indeed have thy sins washed away by the blood of Christ, labor first to see them in the glass of the law, and do not be afraid to see thy besmeared condition, but look on every spot thou hast; for he that looks on the foulness of his face by the *halves*, will wash by the halves; even so, he that looks on his sins by the halves, he will seek for Christ by the halves. Reckon thyself, therefore, I say, the biggest sinner in the world, and be persuaded that there is none worse than thyself; then let the guilt of it seize on thy heart, then also go in that case and condition to Jesus Christ, and plunge thyself into His merits and the virtue of His blood; and after that, thou shalt speak of the things of the law and of the Gospel experimentally, and the very language of the children of God shall feelingly drop from thy lips, and not till then (James 1).

Let this therefore learn thee thus much: he that hath not seen his lost condition hath not seen a safe condition; he that did never see himself in the devil's snare, did never see himself in Christ's bosom. "This my Son was dead, and is alive again: he was lost, and is found." "Among whom we also had our conversation in time past."[2] "But now are (so many of us as believe) returned unto" Jesus Christ, "the" chief "Shepherd and Bishop of your souls."

I say, therefore, if thou do find in this treatise, in the first place, something touching the nature, end, and extent of the law, do not thou cry out, therefore, all of a sudden, saying, "Here is nothing but the terror, horror, and thundering sentences of the law."

Again; if thou do find in the second part of this discourse something of the freeness and fullness of the Gospel, do not thou say neither, "Here is nothing but grace, therefore, surely, an undervaluing of the law." No; but read it quite through, and so consider of it; and I hope thou shalt find the two covenants—which all men are under, either the one or the other—discovered, and held forth in their natures, ends, bounds, together with the state and condition of them that are under the one, and of them that are under the other.

There be some that through ignorance do say how that such men as preach terror and amazement to sinners are beside the book, and are ministers of the letter—the law, and not of the Spirit—the Gospel; but I would answer them, citing them to the Sixteenth of Luke, from the nineteenth verse to the end; and (1 Corinthians 6:9-10; Galatians 3:10; Romans 3:9-19) only this caution I would give by the way, how that they which preach terror to drive souls to the obtaining of salvation by the works of the law, that preaching is not the right Gospel preaching; yet when saints speak of the sad state that man are in by nature, to discover to souls their need of the Gospel, this is honest preaching, and he that doth do so, he doth the work of a Gospel minister (Romans 3:9-25).

Again, there are others that say, because we do preach the free, full, and exceeding grace discovered in the Gospel, therefore we make void the law; when indeed, unless the Gospel be held forth in the glory thereof without confusion, by mingling the Covenant of Works therewith, the law can not be established. "Do we then make void the law through faith," or preaching of the Gospel; nay, stay, saith Paul, "God forbid: yea, we establish the law" (Romans 3:31).

And verily, he that will indeed establish the law, or set it in its own place, for so I understand the words, must be sure to hold forth the Gospel in its right colour and nature; for if a man be ignorant of the nature of the Gospel and the Covenant of Grace, they, or he, will be very apt to remove the law out of its place, and that because they are ignorant, not knowing "what they say, nor whereof they affirm."

And let me tell you, if a man be ignorant of the Covenant of Grace, and the bounds and boundlessness of the Gospel, though he speak and make mention of the name of the Father, and of the Son, and also of the name of the new covenant, and the blood of Christ, yet at this very time, and in these very words, he will preach nothing but the law, and that as a Covenant of Works.

Reader, I must confess it is a wonderfully mysterious thing, and he had need have a wiser spirit than his own that can rightly set these two covenants in their right places, that when he speaks of the one he doth not jostle the other out of its place. O, to be so well enlightened as to speak of the one—that is, the law—for to magnify the Gospel; and also to speak of the Gospel so as to establish, and yet not to idolise, the law, nor any particular thereof! It is rare, and to be heard and found but in very few men's breasts.

If thou shouldst say, What is it to speak to each of these two covenants so as to set them in their right places, and also to use the terror of the one so as to magnify and advance the glory of the other? To this I shall answer also, read the ensuing discourse, but with an understanding heart, and it is like thou wilt find a reply therein to the same purpose, which may be to thy satisfaction.

Reader, if thou do find this book empty of fantastic expressions, and without light, vain, whimsical, scholar-like terms, thou must understand it is because I never went to school to Aristotle, or Plato, but was brought up at my father's house, in a very mean condition, among a company of poor countrymen. But if thou do find a parcel of plain, yet sound, true, and home sayings, attribute that to the Lord Jesus His gifts and abilities, which He hath bestowed upon such a poor creature as I am and have been. And if thou, being a seeing Christian, dost find me coming short, though rightly touching at some things, attribute that either to my brevity, or, if thou wilt, to my weaknesses, for I am full of them. A word or two more, and so I shall have done with this.

First. And the first is, Friend, if thou do not desire the salvation of thy soul, yet I pray thee to read this book over with serious consideration; it may be it will stir up in thee some desires to look out after it, which at present thou mayest be without.

Secondly, If thou dost find any stirrings in thy heart by thy reading such an unworthy man's works as mine are, be sure that in the first place thou give glory to God, and give way to thy convictions, and be not too hasty in getting them off from thy conscience; but let them so work till thou dost see thyself by nature void of all graces, as faith, hope, knowledge of God, Christ, and the Covenant of Grace.

Thirdly, Then, in the next place, fly in all haste to Jesus Christ, thou being sensible of thy lost condition without Him, secretly persuading of thy soul that Jesus Christ standeth open-armed to receive thee, to wash away thy sins, to clothe thee with His righteousness, and is willing, yea, heartily willing, to present thee before the presence of the glory of God and among the innumerable company of angels with exceeding joy. This being thus, in the next place, do not satisfy thyself with these secret and first persuasions, which do or may encourage thee to come to Jesus Christ; but be restless till thou dost find by blessed experience the glorious glory of this the second covenant extended unto thee, and sealed upon thy soul with the very Spirit of the Lord Jesus Christ. And that thou mayest not slight this my counsel, I beseech thee, in the second place, consider these following things:

First, If thou dost get off thy convictions, and not the right way (which is by seeing thy sins washed away by the blood of Jesus Christ), it is a question whether ever God will knock at thy heart again or no; but rather say, such an one "is joined to idols, let him alone" (Hosea 4:17). Though he be in a natural state, "let him alone." Though he be in or under the curse of the law, "let him alone." Though he be in the very hand of the devil, "let him alone." Though he be a-going post-haste to Hell, "let him alone." Though his damnation will not only be damnation for sins against the law, but also for slighting the Gospel, yet "let him alone." My Spirit, My ministers, My Word, My grace, My mercy, My love, My pity, My common providences, shall no more strive with him; "let him alone." O sad! O miserable! who would slight convictions that are on their souls, which (if not slighted) tend so much for their good?

Secondly, If thou shalt not regard how thou do put off convictions, but put them off without the precious blood of Christ being savingly applied to thy soul, thou art sure to have the mis-spending of that conviction to prove the hardening of thy heart against the next time thou art to hear the Word preached or read. This is commonly seen, that those souls that have not regarded those convictions that are at first set upon their spirits, do commonly, and that by the just judgments of God upon them, grow more hard, more senseless, more seared and sottish in their spirits; for some, who formerly would quake and weep, and relent under the hearing of the Word, do now for the present sit so senseless, so seared, and hardened in their consciences, that certainly if they should have hell-fire thrown in their faces, as it sometimes cried up in their ears, they would scarce be moved; and this comes upon them as a just judgment of God (2 Thessalonians 2:11-12).

Thirdly, If thou do slight these, or those convictions that may be set upon thy heart by reading of this discourse, or hearing of any other good man preach the Word of God sincerely, thou wilt have the stifling of these or those convictions to account and answer for at the day of judgment; not only thy sins, that are commonly committed by thee in thy calling and common discourse, but thou shalt be called to a reckoning for slighting convictions, disregarding of convictions, which God useth as a special means to make poor sinners see their lost condition and the need of a Savior. Now here I might add many more considerations besides these, to the end thou mayest be willing to tend and listen to convictions; as,

First, Consider thou hast a precious soul, more worth than the whole world; and this is commonly worked upon, if ever it be saved, by convictions.

Secondly, This soul is for certain to go to Hell, if thou shalt be a slighter of convictions.

Thirdly, If that go to Hell, thy body must go thither too, and then never to come out again. "Now consider this, ye that" are apt to "forget God," and His convictions, "lest He tear you in pieces, and there be none to deliver" (Psalms 50:22).

But if thou shalt be such an one that shall, notwithstanding thy reading of thy misery, and also of God's mercy, shall persist to go on in thy sins, know, in the first place, that here thou shalt be left, by the things that thou readest, without excuse; and in the world to come thy damnation will be exceedingly aggravated for thy not regarding of them, and turning from thy sins, which were not only reproved by them, but also for rejecting of that Word of Grace that did instruct thee how and which way thou shouldst be saved from them. And so farewell; I shall leave thee, and also this discourse, to God, who I know will pass a righteous judgment both upon that and thee. I am yours, though not to serve your lusts and filthy minds, yet to reprove, instruct, and, according to that proportion of faith and knowledge which God hath given me, to declare unto you the way of life and salvation. Your judgings, railings, surmisings, and disdaining of me, that I shall leave till the fiery judgment comes, in which the offender shall not go unpunished, be he you or me; yet I shall pray for you, wish well to you, and do you what good I can. And that I might not write or speak in vain, Christian, pray for me to our God with much earnestness, fervency, and frequently, in all your knockings at our Father's door, because I do very much stand in need thereof; for my work is great, my heart is vile, the devil lieth at watch, the world would fain be saying, "Aha, aha, thus we would have it";

and of myself, keep myself I can not; trust myself I dare not; if God do not help me, I am sure it will not be long before my heart deceive me, and the world would have their advantage of me, and so God be dishonored by me, and thou also ashamed to own me. O, therefore, be much in prayer for me, thy fellow! I trust, in that glorious grace that is conveyed from Heaven to sinners, by which they are not only sanctified here in this world, but shall be glorified in that which is to come; unto which, the Lord of His mercy bring us all.

—JOHN BUNYAN

THE DOCTRINE OF THE LAW AND GRACE UNFOLDED

OR,

A DISCOVERY OF THE LAW AND GRACE; THE NATURE OF THE ONE, AND THE NATURE OF THE OTHER, AS THEY ARE THE TWO COVENANTS, ETC.

These are several titles which are set over the several TRUTHS contained in this book, for the sooner finding of them—

THE FIRST PART

1. The words of the text opened, and the doctrines laid down—that there are some that are under the law, e.g. under the Covenant of Works.
2. What the Covenant of Works is, and when it is given.
3. What it is to be under the Covenant of Works.
4. Who they are that are under the Covenant of Works.
5. What men may attain to that are under this Covenant of Works.

THE SECOND PART

1. The doctrine proved.
2. The New Covenant made with Christ.
3. The conditions of the New Covenant.
4. The suretiship of Christ.
5. Christ the messenger of the New Covenant.
6. Christ the sacrifice of the New Covenant.
7. Christ the High Priest of the New Covenant.
8. Christ completely fulfilled the conditions of the New Covenant.
9. The Covenant of Grace unchangeable; the opposers answered.
10. Who, and how men are actually brought into the New Covenant.
11. A word of experience.
12. The privileges of the New Covenant.
13. Two hell-bred objections answered.
14. A use of examination about the Old Covenant.
15. A legal spirit.
16. The use of the New Covenant.
17. The unpardonable sin.
18. Objections answered for their comfort who would have their part in the New Covenant.

"FOR YE ARE NOT UNDER THE LAW, BUT UNDER GRACE."
—Romans 6:14

THE WORDS OF THE TEXT OPENED, AND THE DOCTRINES LAID DOWN

In the three former chapters, the Apostle is pleading for the salvation of sinners by grace without the works of the law, to the end he might confirm the saints, and also that he might win over all those that did oppose the truth of this doctrine, or else leave them the more without excuse; and that he might so do, he taketh in hand, first, to show the state of all men naturally, or as they come into the world by generation, saying, in the Third Chapter, "There is none righteous, no, not one; there is none that understandeth; there is none that doeth good," etc. As if he had said, It seems there is a generation of men that think to be saved by the righteousness of the law; but let me tell them that they are much deceived, in that they have already sinned against the law; for by the disobedience of one, many, yea all, were brought into a state of condemnation (Romans 5:12-20). Now, in the Sixth Chapter he doth, as if he had turned him round to the brethren, and said, My brethren, you see now that it is clear and evident that it is freely by the grace of Christ that we do inherit eternal life. And again, for your comfort, my brethren, let me tell you that your condition is wondrous safe, in that you are under grace; for, saith he, "Sin shall not have dominion over you"; that is, neither the damning power, neither the filthy power, so as to destroy your souls: "For ye are not under the law"; that is, you are not under that that will damn you for sin; "but" you are "under grace," or stand thus in relation to God, that though you have sinned, yet you shall be pardoned. "For ye are not under the law, but under grace." If any should ask what is the meaning of the word "under," I answer, it signifieth, you are not held, kept, or shut up by it so as to appear before God under that administration, and none but that; or thus, you are not now bound by the authority of the law to fulfil it and obey it, so as to have no salvation without you so do; or thus, if you transgress against any one tittle of it, you by the power of it must be condemned. No, no, for you are not so under it; that is, not thus under the law. *Again*, "For ye are not under the law." What is meant by this word "law"? The word "law," in Scripture, may be taken more ways than one, as might be largely cleared. There is the law of faith, the law of sin, the law of men, the law of works, otherwise called the Covenant of Works, or the first or old covenant. "In that He saith a new *covenant*," which is the grace of God, or commonly called the Covenant of Grace, "He hath made the first old," that is, the Covenant of Works, or the law (Hebrews 8:13). I say, therefore, the word "law" and the word "grace," in this Sixth of the Romans, do hold forth the two covenants which all men are under; that is, either the one or the other. "For ye are not under the law"—that is, you to whom I do now write these words, who are and have been effectually brought into the faith of Jesus, you are not under the law, or under the Covenant of Works. He doth not, therefore, apply these words to all, but to some, when he saith, "But ye"; mark, *ye, ye* believers, *ye* converted persons, *ye* saints, *ye* that have been born. (YE) "for ye are not under the law," implying others are that are in their natural state, that have not been brought in to the Covenant of Grace by faith in Jesus Christ.

The words, therefore, being thus understood, there is discovered these two truths in them—DOCTRINE FIRST. That there are some in Gospel times that are under the Covenant of Works. DOCTRINE SECOND. That there is never a believer under the law, as it is the Covenant of Works, but under grace through Christ. "For ye," you believers, you converted persons, ye "are not under the law but under grace"; or, for you are delivered and brought into or under the Covenant of Grace.

THE FIRST DOCTRINE

THERE ARE SOME THAT ARE UNDER THE LAW, OR UNDER THE COVENANT OF WORKS

For the first, THAT THERE ARE SOME THAT ARE UNDER THE LAW, OR UNDER THE COVENANT OF WORKS, see, I pray you, that Scripture in the Third of the Romans, where the Apostle, speaking before of sins against the law, and of the denunciations thereof against those that are in that condition, he saith, "What things soever the law saith, it saith to them who are under the law"; mark, "it saith to them who are under the law, that every mouth may be stopped, and all the world become guilty before God" (Romans 3:19). That is, all those that are under the law as a Covenant of Works, that are yet in their sins, and unconverted, as I told you before. Again he saith, "But if ye be led by the Spirit, ye are not under the law" (Galatians 5:18). Implying again, that those which are for sinning against the law, or the works of the law, either as it is the old covenant, these are under the law, and not under the Covenant of Grace. Again he saith, "For as many as are of the works of the law are under the curse" (Galatians 3:10). That is, they that are under the law are under the curse; for mark, they that are under the Covenant of Grace are not under the curse. Now, there are but two covenants, therefore, it must needs be that they that are under the curse are under the law, seeing those that are under the other covenant are not under the curse, but under the blessing. "So, then, they which be of faith are blessed with faithful Abraham," but the rest are under the law (Galatians 3:9).

Now I shall proceed to what I do intend to speak unto. FIRST. I shall show you what the Covenant of Works, or the law, is, and when it was first given, together with the nature of it. SECOND. I shall show you what it is to be under the law, or Covenant of Works, and the miserable state of all those that are under it. THIRD. I shall show you who they are that are under this covenant, or law. FOURTH. I shall show you how far a man may go and yet be under this covenant, or law.

WHAT THE COVENANT OF WORKS IS, AND WHEN IT WAS GIVEN

I. WHAT THIS COVENANT OF WORKS IS, AND WHEN IT WAS GIVEN

What This Covenant Is

The Covenant of Works or the law, here spoken of, is the law delivered upon Mount Sinai to Moses, in two tables of stone, in ten particular branches or heads; for this see Galatians 4. The Apostle, speaking there of the law, and of some also that through delusions of false doctrine were brought again, as it were, under it, or at least were leaning that way (verse 21) he saith, As for you that desire to be under the law, I will show you the mystery of Abraham's two sons, which he had by Hagar and Sarah; these two do signify the two covenants; the one named Hagar signifies Mount Sinai, where the law was delivered to Moses on two tables of stone (Exodus 24:12; 34:1; Deuteronomy 10:1). Which is that, that whosoever is under, he is destitute of, and altogether without the grace of Christ in his heart at the present. "For I testify again to every man," saith he, speaking to the same people, that "Christ has become of no effect unto you, whosoever of you are justified by the law," namely, that given on Mount Sinai—"ye are fallen from grace" (Galatians 5:3-4). That is, not that any can be justified by the law; but this meaning is, that all those that seek justification by the works of the law, they are not such as seek to be under the second covenant, the Covenant of Grace.

Also the Apostle, speaking again of these two covenants, saith, "But if the ministration of death," or the law, for it is all one, "written and engraven in stones," mark that, "was glorious, how shall not the ministration of the Spirit," or the Covenant of Grace, "be rather glorious?" (2 Corinthians 3:7-8). As if he had said, It is true, there was a glory in the Covenant of Works, and a very great excellency did appear in it—namely, in that given in the stones on Sinai—yet there is another covenant, the Covenant of Grace, that doth exceed it for comfort and glory.

When It Was Given

But, though this law was delivered to Moses from the hands of angels in two tables of stones, on Mount Sinai, yet this was not the first appearing of this law to man; but even this in substance, though possibly not so openly, was given to the first man, Adam, in the Garden of Eden, in these words: "And the LORD God commanded the man, saying, Of every tree of the garden thou mayest freely eat: but of the tree of the knowledge of good and evil, thou shalt not eat of it; for in the day that thou eatest thereof thou shalt surely die" (Genesis 2:16-17). Which commandment then given to Adam did contain in it a forbidding to do any of those things that was and is accounted evil, although at that time it did not appear so plainly, in so many particular heads, as it did when it was again delivered on Mount Sinai; but yet the very same. And that I shall prove thus:

God commanded Adam in Paradise to abstain from all evil against the first covenant, and not from some sins only; but if God had not commanded Adam to abstain from the sins spoken against in the Ten Commandments, He had not commanded to abstain from all, but from some; therefore it must needs be that He then commanded to abstain from all sins forbidden in the law given on Mount Sinai. Now that God commanded to abstain from all evil or sin against any of the Ten Commandments, when He gave Adam the command in the garden, it is evident that He did punish the sins that were committed against those commands that were then delivered on Mount Sinai, before they were delivered on Mount Sinai, which will appear asfolloweth:

The First, Second, and Third Commandments were broken by Pharaoh and his men; for they had false gods which the Lord executed judgment against (Exodus 12:12); and blasphemed their true God (Exodus 5:2) which escaped not punishment (Exodus 7:17-25). For their gods could neither deliver themselves nor their people from the hand of God; but "in the thing wherein they dealt proudly, He was above them" (Exodus 18:11).

Again; some judge that the Lord punished the sin against the Second Commandment, which Jacob was in some measure guilty of in not purging his house from false gods, with the defiling of his daughter Dinah (Genesis 34:2).

Again; we find that Abimelech thought the sin against the Third Commandment so great, that he required no other security of Abraham against the fear of mischief that might be done to him by Abraham, his son, and his son's son, but only Abraham's oath (Genesis 21:23). The like we see between Abimelech and Isaac (Genesis 31:53). The like we find in Moses and the Israelites, who durst not leave the bones of Joseph in Egypt, because of the oath of the Lord, whose name, by so doing, would have been abused (Exodus 13:19).

And we find the Lord rebuking His people for the breach of the Fourth Commandment (Exodus 16:27-29).

And for the breach of the Fifth, the curse came upon Ham (Genesis 9:25-27). And Ishmael dishonoring his father in mocking Isaac was cast out, as we read (Genesis 21:9-10). The sons-in-law of Lot for slighting their father perish in the overthrow of Sodom (Genesis 19:14).

The Sixth Commandment was broken by Cain, and so dreadful a curse and punishment came upon him that it made him cry out, "My punishment is greater than I can bear" (Genesis 4:13).

Again; when Esau threatened to slay his brother, Rebecca sent him away, saying, "Why should I be deprived also of you both in one day?" hinting unto us, that she knew murder was to be punished with death (Genesis 27:45) which the Lord Himself declared likewise to Noah (Genesis 9:6).[3] Again; a notable example of the Lord's justice in punishing murder we see in the Egyptians and Pharaoh, who drowned the Israelites' children in the river (Exodus 1:22); and they themselves were drowned in the sea (Exodus 14:27).

The sin against the Seventh Commandment was punished in the Sodomites, etc., with the utter destruction of their city and themselves (Genesis 19:24-25). Yea, they suffer "the vengeance of eternal fire" (Jude 7). Also the male Shechemites, for the sin committed by Hamor's son, were all put to the sword (Genesis 34:25-26).

Our first parents sinned against the Eighth Commandment in taking the forbidden fruit, and so brought the curse on themselves and their posterity (Genesis 3:16). Again; the punishment due to the breach of this Commandment was by Jacob accounted death (Genesis 31:30-32). And also by Jacob's sons (Genesis 44:9-10).

Cain sinning against the Ninth Commandment as in Genesis 4:9, was therefore cursed as to the earth (Verse 11). And Abraham, though the friend of God, was blamed for false-witness by Pharaoh, and sent out of Egypt (Genesis 12:18-20) and both he and Sarah reproved by Abimelech (Genesis 20:9-10, 16).

Pharaoh sinned against the Tenth Commandment, and was therefore plagued with great plagues (Genesis 12:15, 17). Abimelech coveted Abraham's wife, and the Lord threatened death to him and his, except he restored her again; yea, though he had not come near her, yet for coveting and taking her the Lord fast closed up the wombs of his house (Genesis 20:3, 18).

Further Arguments

I could have spoken more fully to this, but that I would not be too tedious, but speak what I have to say with as much brevity as I can. But before I pass it, I will besides this give you an argument or two more for the further clearing of this, that the substance of the law delivered on Mount Sinai was, before that, delivered by the Lord to man in the garden. As, first, "death reigned over them that had not sinned after the similitude of Adam's transgression"—that is, though they did not take the forbidden fruit as Adam did; but had the transgression been no other, or had their sin been laid to the charge of none but those that did eat of that fruit, then those that were born to

Adam after he was shut out of the garden had not had sin, in that they did not actually eat of that fruit, and so had not been slaves to death; but, in that death did reign from Adam to Moses, of from the time of his transgression against the first giving of the law, till the time the law was given on Mount Sinai, it is evident that the substance of the Ten Commandments was given to Adam and his posterity under that command, "Eat not of the tree that is in the midst of the garden." But yet, if any shall say that it was because of the sin of their father that death reigned over them, to that I shall answer, that although original sin be laid to the charge of his posterity, yet it is also for their sins that they actually committed that they were plagued. And again, saith the Apostle, "For where no law is, *there* is no transgression" (Romans 4:15). For "sin is not imputed when there is no law; nevertheless death reigned from Adam to Moses." saith he (Romans 5:13,14). But if there had been no law, then there had been no transgression, and so no death to follow after as the wages thereof; for death is the wages of sin (Romans 6:23) and sin is the breach of the law; an actual breach in our particular persons, as well as an actual breach in our public person (1 John 3:4).[4]

Again; there are no other sins than those against that law given on Sinai, for the which those sins before mentioned were punished; therefore the law given before by the Lord to Adam and his posterity is the same with that afterwards given on Mount Sinai. Again; the conditions of that on Sinai and of that in the garden are all one; the one saying, "Do this and live," the other saying the same. Also judgment denounced against men in both kinds alike; therefore this law it appeareth to be the very same that was given on Mount Sinai.

Again; the Apostle speaketh but of two covenants—to wit, grace and works—under which two covenants all are; some under one, and some under the other. Now this to Adam is one, therefore that on Sinai is one, and all one with this; and that this is a truth, I say, I know, because the sins against that on Sinai were punished by God for the breech thereof before it was given there; so it doth plainly appear to be a truth; for it would be unrighteous with God for to punish for that law that was not broken; therefore it was all one with that on Sinai.

Now the law given on Sinai was for the more clear discovery of those sins that were before committed against it; for though the very substance of the Ten Commandments were given in the garden before they were received from Sinai, yet they lay so darkly in the heart of man, that his sins were not so clearly discovered as afterwards they were; therefore, saith the Apostle, the law was added (Galatians 3:19). Or, more plainly, given on Sinai, on tables of stone, "that the offence might abound"—that is, that it might the more clearly be made manifest and appear (Romans 5:20).

Again; we have a notable resemblance of this at Sinai, even in giving the law; for, first, the law was given twice on Sinai, to signify that indeed the substance of it was given before. And, secondly, the first tables that were given on Sinai were broken at the foot of the mount, and the others were preserved whole, to signify that though it was the true law that was given before, with that given on Sinai, yet it was not so easy to be read and to be taken notice of, in that the stones were not whole, but broken, and so the law written thereon somewhat defaced and disfigured.

OBJECTION: But if any object and say, though the sins against the one be the sins against the other, and so in that they do agree, yet it doth not appear that the same is therefore the same Covenant of Works with the other.

ANSWER: That which was given to Adam in Paradise you will grant was the Covenant of Works; for it runs thus: Do this and live; do it not and die; nay, "Thou shalt surely die." Now there is but one Covenant of Works. If therefore I prove that that which was delivered on Mount Sinai is the Covenant of Works, then all will be put out of doubt. Now that this is so it is evident:

1.) Consider the two covenants are thus called in Scripture, the one the administration of death, and the other the administration of life; the one the Covenant of Works, the other of grace; but that delivered on Sinai is called the ministration of death; that, therefore, is the Covenant of Works. "But if," saith he, "the ministration of death, written *and* engraven on stones was glorious." (2 Corinthians 3:7)

2.) The Apostle, writing to the Galatians, doth labor to beat them off from trusting in the Covenant of Works; but when he comes to give a discovery of that law or covenant—he laboring to take them off from trusting in it—he doth plainly tell them it is that which was given on Sinai (Galatians 4:24-25). Therefore that which was delivered in two tables of stone on Mount Sinai, is the very same thing that was given before to Adam in Paradise, they running both alike; that in the garden saying, Do this and live; but in the day thou eatest thereof—or dost not do this—thou shalt surely die.

And so is this on Sinai, as is evident when he saith, "the man which doeth those things shall live by them" (Romans 10:5). And in case they break them, even any of them, it saith, "Cursed is every one that continueth not in all things which are written in the (whole) book of the law to do them" (Galatians 3:10). Now this being thus cleared, I shall proceed.

WHAT IT IS TO BE UNDER THE COVENANT OF WORKS

II. A SECOND THING TO CONSIDER:

To show what it is to be under the law as it is *a Covenant of Works*; **to which I shall speak, and that thus:**

To be under the law as it is a Covenant of Works, is to be bound, upon pain of eternal damnation, to fulfil, and that completely and continually, every particular point of the Ten Commandments, by doing them—Do this, and then thou shalt live; otherwise, "cursed *is* every one that continueth not in all," in every particular thing or "things which are written in the book for the law to do them" (Galatians 3:10). That man that is under the first covenant stands thus, and only thus, as he is under that covenant, or law. Poor souls, through ignorance of the nature of that Covenant of Works, the law that they are under, they do not think their state to be half so bad as it is; when, alas! there is none in the world in such a sad condition again besides themselves; for, indeed, they do not understand these things. He that is under the law, as it is a Covenant of Works, is like the man that is bound by the law of his king, upon pain of banishment, or of being hanged, drawn, and quartered, not to transgress any of the commandments of the king; so here, they that are under the Covenant of Works, they are bound, upon pain of eternal banishment and condemnation, to keep within the compass of the law of the God of Heaven. The Covenant of Works may, in this case, be compared to the laws of the Medes and Persians, which being once made, can not be altered. Daniel 6:8. You find that when there was a law made and given forth that none should ask a petition of any, God or man, but of the king only; this law being established by the king (verse 9). Daniel breaking of it, let all do whatever they can, Daniel must go into the lions' den (verse 16). So here, I say, there being a law given, and sealed with the Truth and the Word of God—how that "the soul that sinneth, it shall die" (Ezekiel 18:4). Whosoever doth abide under this covenant, and dieth under the same, they must and shall go into the lion's den; yea, worse than that, for they shall be thrown into Hell, to the very devils.

But to speak in a few particulars for thy better understanding herein, know:

FIRST. That the Law of God, or Covenant of Works, doth not contain itself in one particular branch of the law, but doth extend itself into many, even into all the Ten Commandments, and those ten into very many more, as might be showed; so that the danger doth not lie in the breaking of one or two of these ten only, but it doth lie even in the transgression of any one of them. As you know, if a king should give forth ten particular commands to be obeyed by his subjects upon pain of death; now if any man doth transgress against any one of these ten, he doth commit treason, as if he had broke them all, and lieth liable to have the sentence of the law as certainly passed on him as if he had broken every particular of them.

SECOND. Again; you know that the laws being given forth by the king, which if a man keep and obey for a long time, yet if at the last he slips and breaks those laws, he is presently apprehended, and condemned by that law. These things are clear as touching the Law of God, as it is a Covenant of Works. If a man doth fulfil nine of the Commandments, and yet breaketh but one, that being broken will as surely destroy him and shut him out from the joys of Heaven as if he had actually transgressed against them all; for indeed, in effect, so he hath. There is a notable Scripture for this in the Epistle of James, Second Chapter, at the tenth verse, that runs thus: "For whosoever shall keep the whole law, and yet offend in one point, he is guilty of all"—that is, he hath in effect broken them all, and shall have the voice of them all cry out against him. And it must needs be so, saith James, because "He that said," or that law which said, "Do not commit adultery, said also, Do not kill. Now, if thou commit no adultery, yet if thou kill, thou art become a transgressor of the law" (Verse 11). As thus; it may be thou didst never make to thyself a god of stone or wood, or at least not to worship them so greatly and so openly as the heathen do, yet if thou hast stolen, born false witness, or lusted after a woman in thy heart (Matthew 5:28) thou hast transgressed the law, and must for certain, living and dying under that covenant, perish for ever by the law; for the law hath resolved on that before-hand, saying, "Cursed is every one that continueth not in ALL things"; mark, I pray you, "in all things"; that is the Word, and that seals the doctrine.

THIRD. Again; though a man doth not covet, steal, murder, worship gods of wood and stone, etc., yet if he do take the Lord's name in vain, he is for ever gone, living and dying under that covenant. "Thou shalt not take the name of the LORD thy God in vain"; there is the command. But how if we do? Then he saith, "the LORD will not hold him guiltless that taketh His name in vain." No; though thou live as holy as ever thou canst, and walk as circumspectly as ever any did, yet if thou dost take the Lord's name in vain, thou art gone by that covenant: "For I will not," mark "I will not," let him be in never so much danger, "I will not hold him guiltless that taketh My name in vain" (Exodus 20:7). And so likewise for any other of the ten, do but break them, and thy state is irrecoverable, if thou live and die under that covenant.

FOURTH. Though thou shouldest fulfil this covenant, or law, even all of it, for a long time, ten, twenty, forty, fifty, or threescore years, yet if thou do chance to slip and break one of them but once before thou die, thou art also gone and lost by that covenant; for mark, "Cursed is every one that continueth not in all things," that continueth not in ALL things, mark that, "which are written in the book of the law to do them." But if a man doth keep all the Law of God his whole lifetime, and only sin one time before he dies, that one sin is a breach of the law, and he hath not continued in doing the things contained therein. For, so to continue, according to the sense of this Scripture, is to hold on without any failing, either in thought, word, or deed; therefore, I say, though a man doth walk up to the law all his lifetime, but only at the very last sin one time before he die, he is sure to perish for ever, dying under that covenant. For, my friends, you must understand that the Law of God is "yea," as well as the Gospel; and as they that are under the Covenant of Grace shall surely be saved by it, so, even so, they that are under the Covenant of Works and the law, they shall surely be damned by it, if continuing there. This is the Covenant of Works and the nature of it—namely, not to abate anything, no, not a mite, to him that lives and dies under it; "I tell thee," saith Christ, "thou shalt not depart thence," that is, from under the curse, "till thou hast paid the very last mite." (Luke 12:59)

FIFTH. Again; you must consider that this law doth not only condemn words and actions, as I said before, but it hath authority to condemn the most secret thoughts of the heart, being evil; so that if thou do not speak any word that is evil, as swearing, lying, jesting, dissembling, or any other word that tendeth to, or savoreth of sin, yet if there should chance to pass but one vain thought through thy heart but once in all thy lifetime, the law taketh hold of it, accuseth, and also will condemn thee for it. You may see one instance for all in (Matthew 5:27-28) where Christ saith, that though a man doth not lie with a woman carnally, yet if he doth but look on her, and in his heart lust after her, he is counted by the law, being rightly expounded, such an one that hath committed the sin, and thereby hath laid himself under the condemnation of the law. And so likewise of all the rest of the commands; if there be any thought that is evil do but pass through thy heart, whether it be against God or against man in the least measure, though possibly not discerned of thee, or by thee, yet the law takes hold of thee therefore, and doth by its authority, both cast, condemn, and execute thee for thy so doing. "The thought of foolishness is sin" (Proverbs 24:9).

SIXTH. Again; the law is of that nature and severity, that it doth not only inquire into the generality of thy life as touching several things, whether thou art upright there or no; but the law doth also follow thee into all thy holy duties, and watcheth over thee there, to see whether thou dost do all things aright there—that is to say, whether when thou dost pray thy heart hath no wandering thoughts in it; whether thou do every holy duty thou doest perfectly without the least mixture of sin; and if it do find thee to slip, or in the least measure to fail in any holy duty that thou dost perform, the law taketh hold on that, and findeth fault with that, so as to render all the holy duties that ever thou didst unavailable because of that. I say, if, when thou art a hearing, there is but one vain thought, or in praying, but one vain thought, or in any other thing whatsoever, let it be civil or spiritual, one vain thought once in all thy lifetime will cause the law to take such hold on it, that for that one thing it doth even set open all the floodgates of God's wrath against thee, and irrecoverably by that covenant it doth bring eternal vengeance upon thee; so that, I say, look which ways thou wilt, and fail wherein thou wilt, and do it as seldom as ever thou canst, either in civil or spiritual things, as aforesaid—that is, either in the service of God, or in thy employments in the world, as thy trade or calling, either in buying or selling any way, in anything whatsoever; I say, if in any particular it find thee tardy, or in the least measure guilty, it calleth thee an offender, it accuseth thee to God, it puts a stop to all the promises thereof that are joined to the law, and leaves thee there as a cursed transgressor against God, and a destroyer of thy own soul.[5]

Here I would have thee, by the way, for to take notice, that it is not my intent at this time to enlarge on the several commands in particular—for that would be very tedious both for me to write and thee to read; only thus much I would have thee to do at the reading hereof—make a pause, and sit still one quarter of an hour, and muse a little in thy mind thus with thyself, and say, Did I ever break the law; yea or no? Had I ever, in all my lifetime, one sinful thought passed through my heart since I was born; yea or no? And if thou findest thyself guilty, as I am sure thou canst not otherwise choose but do, unless thou shut thy eyes against thy every day's practice, then, I say, conclude thyself guilty of the breach of the first covenant. And when that this is done, be sure, in the next place, thou do not straightway forget it and put it out of thy mind, that thou art condemned by the same covenant; and then do not content thyself until thou do find that God hath sent thee a pardon from Heaven through the merits of our Lord Jesus Christ, the mediator of the second covenant. And if God shall but give thee a heart to take this my counsel, I do make no question but these words spoken by me, will prove an instrument for the directing of thy heart to the right remedy for the salvation of thy soul.

Thus much now touching the law, and the severity of it upon the person that is found under it, having offended or broken any particular of it, either in thought, word, or action; and now, before I do proceed to the next thing, I shall answer four objections that do lie in my way, and also, such as do stumble most part of the world.

FOUR OBJECTIONS

OBJECTION #1: But you will say, Methinks you speak very harsh; it is enough to daunt a body. Set the case, therefore, that a man, after he hath sinned and broken the law, repenteth of his wickedness and promiseth to do so no more, will not God have mercy then, and save a poor sinner then?

ANSWER #1: I told you before, that the covenant, once broken, will execute upon the offender that which it doth threaten to lay upon him; and as for your supposing that your repenting and promising to do so no more may help well, and put you in a condition to attain the mercy of God by the law, these thoughts do flow from gross ignorance both of the nature of sin, and also of the nature of the justice of God. And if I were to give you a description of one in a lost condition for the present, I would brand him out with such a mark of ignorance as this is.

ANSWER #2: (The first answer is expounded by the second). The law, as it is a Covenant of Works, doth not allow of any repentance unto life to those that live and die under it; for the law being once broken by thee, never speaks good unto thee, neither doth God at all regard thee, if thou be under that covenant, notwithstanding all thy repenting and also promises to do so no more. No, saith the law, thou hast sinned, therefore I must curse thee; for it is My nature to curse, even, and nothing else but curse, every one that doth in any point transgress against Me (Galatians 3:10). They brake My covenant "and I regarded them not, saith the Lord" (Hebrews 8:9). Let them cry, I will not regard them; let them repent, I will not regard them; they have broken My covenant, and done that in which I delighted not; therefore, by that covenant I do curse, and not bless; damn, and not save; frown, and not smile; reject, and not embrace; charge sin and not forgive it. They brake My covenant "and I regarded them not"; so that I say, if thou break the law, the first covenant, and thou being found there, God looking on thee through that, He hath no regard on thee, no pity for thee, no delight in thee.

OBJECTION #2: But hath not the law promises as well as threatenings? saying, "The man which doeth these things shall live," mark, he shall live, "by them," or in them (Romans 10:5; Galatians 3:12).

ANSWER: First, To break the Commandments is not to keep or fulfil the same; but thou hast broken them, therefore the promise doth not belong to thee by that covenant. Second, The promises that are of the law are conditional, and so not performed unless there be a full and continual obedience to every particular of it, and that without the least sin. "Do this"—mark, do this—and afterwards thou shalt live; but if thou break one point of it once in all thy life, thou hast not done the law; therefore the promises following the law do not belong unto thee if one sin hath been committed by thee. As thus, I will give you a plain instance—"Set the case, there be a law made by the king, that if any man speak a word against him he must be put to death, and this must not be revoked, but must for certain be executed on the offender; though there be a promise made to them that do not speak a word against him, that they should have great love from him; yet this promise is nothing to the offender; he is like to have no share in it, or to be ever the better for it; but contrariwise, the law that he hath offended must be executed on him; for his sin shutteth him out from a share of, or in, the promises." So it is here, there is a promise made indeed, but to whom? Why, it is to none but those that live without sinning against the law; but if thou, I say, sin one time against it in all thy lifetime, thou art gone, and not one promise belongs to thee if thou continue under this covenant. Methinks the prisoners at the bar, having offended the law, and the charge of a just judge towards them, do much hold forth the law, as it is a Covenant of Works, and how it deals with them that are under it. The prisoner having offended, cries out for mercy; Good, my lord, mercy, saith he, pray, my lord, pity me. The judge saith, What canst thou say for thyself that sentence of death should not be passed upon thee? Why, nothing but this, I pray my lord be merciful. But he answers again, Friend, the law must take place, the law must not be broken. The prisoner saith, Good, my lord, spare me, and I will never do so any more. The judge, notwithstanding the man's outcries and sad condition, must, according to the tenor of the law, pass judgment upon him, and the sentence of condemnation must be read to the prisoner, though it makes him fall down dead to hear it, if he executes the law as he ought to do. And just thus it is concerning the Law of God.

OBJECTION #3: Ay, but sometimes, for all your haste, the judge doth also give some pardons, and forgives some offenders, notwithstanding their offences, though he be a judge.

ANSWER: It is not because the law is merciful, but because there is manifested the love of the judge, not the love of the law. I beseech you to mark this distinction; for if a man that hath deserved death by the law be, notwithstanding this, forgiven his offence, it is not because the law saith, "spare him"; but it is the love of the judge or chief magistrate that doth set the man free from the condemnation of the law. But mark; here the law of men and the Law of God do differ; the law of man is not so irrevocable; but if the Supreme please he may sometimes grant a pardon without satisfaction given for the offence; but the Law of God is of this nature, that if a man be found under it, and a transgressor, or one that hath transgressed against it, before that prisoner can be released there must be a full and complete satisfaction given to it, either by the man's own life or by the blood of some other man; for "without shedding of blood is no remission" (Hebrews 9:22); that is, there is no deliverance from under the curse of the Law of God; and therefore, however the law of man may be made of none effect sometimes by showing mercy without giving of a full satisfaction, yet the Law of God can not be so contented, nor at the least give way, that the person offending that should escape the curse and not be damned, except some one do give a full and complete satisfaction to it for him, and bring the prisoner into another covenant—to wit, the Covenant of Grace, which is more easy, and soul-refreshing, and sin-pardoning.

I say, therefore, you must understand that if there be a law made that reaches the life, to take it away for the offence given by the offender against it, then it is clear that if the man be spared and saved, it is not the law that doth give the man this advantage, but it is the mere mercy of the king, either because he hath a ransom or satisfaction some other way, or being provoked thereto out of his own love to the person whom he saveth. Now, thou also having transgressed and broken the Law of God, if the law be not executed upon thee, it is not because the law is merciful, or can pass by the least offence done by thee, but thy deliverance comes another way; therefore, I say, however it be by the laws of men where they be corrupted and perverted, yet the Law of God is of that nature, that if it hath not thy own blood or the blood of some other man—for it calls for no less, for to ransom thee from the curse of it, being due to thee for thy transgression, and to satisfy the cries, the doleful cries, thereof, and ever for to present thee pure and spotless before God, notwithstanding this fiery law—thou art gone if thou hadst a thousand souls; for "without shedding of blood there is no remission" (Hebrews 9:22); no forgiveness of the least sin against the law.

OBJECTION #4. But, you will say, "I do not only repent me of my former life, and also promise to do so no more, but now I do labor to be righteous, and to live a holy life; and now, instead of being a breaker of the law, I do labor to fulfil the same. What say you to that?"

ANSWER: Set the case, thou couldst walk like an angel of God; set the case, thou couldst fulfil the whole law, and live from this day to thy life's end without sinning in thought, word, or deed, which is impossible; but, I say, set the case it should be so, why, thy state is as bad, if thou be under the first covenant, as ever it was. For, first, I know thou darest not say but thou hast at one time or other sinned; and if so, then the law hath condemned thee; and if so, then I am sure that thou, with all thy actions and works of righteousness, canst not remove the dreadful and irresistible curse that is already laid upon thee by that law which thou art under, and which thou hast sinned against; though thou livest the holiest life that any man can live in this world, being under the law of works, and so not under the Covenant of Grace, thou must be cut off without remedy; for thou hast sinned, though afterwards thou live never so well.

The reasons for this that hath been spoken are these:

First, The nature of God's justice calls for it—that is, it calls for irrecoverable ruin on them that transgress against this law; for justice gave it, and justice looks to have it completely and continually obeyed, or else justice is resolved to take place, and execute its office, which is to punish the transgressor against it. You must understand that the justice of God is as unchangeable as His love; His justice can not change its nature; justice it is, if it be pleased; and justice it is, if it be displeased. The justice of God in this case may be compared to fire; there is a great fire made in some place; if thou do keep out of it, it is fire; if thou do fall into it, thou wilt find it fire; and therefore the Apostle useth this as an argument to stir up the Hebrews to stick close to Jesus Christ, lest they fall under the justice of God by these words, "For our God is a consuming fire" (Hebrews 12:29); into which, if thou fall, it is not for thee to get out again, as it is with some that fall into a material fire; no, but he that falls into this, he must lie there for ever; as it is clear where he saith, "Who among us shall dwell with everlasting burnings, and with devouring fire?" (Isaiah 33:14). For justice once offended knoweth not how to show any pity or compassion to the offender, but runs on him like a lion, takes him by the throat, throws him into prison, and there he is sure to lie, and that to all eternity, unless infinite satisfaction be given to it, which is impossible to be given by any of us the sons of Adam.

Secondly, The faithfulness of God calls for irrecoverable ruin to be poured out on those that shall live and die under this covenant. If thou, having sinned but one sin against this covenant, and shouldst afterwards escape damning, God must be unfaithful to Himself and to His Word, which both agree as one. First, he would be unfaithful to Himself; to Himself, that is, to His justice, holiness, righteousness, wisdom, and power, if He should offer to stop the running out of His justice for the damning of them that have offended it. And secondly, He would be unfaithful to His Word, His written Word, and disown, deny, and break that, of which He hath said, "It is easier for Heaven and earth to pass, than one tittle of the law to fail," or be made of none effect (Luke 16:17). Now, if He should not, according to His certain declarations therein, take vengeance on those that fall and die within the threat and sad curses denounced, in that His Word could not be fulfilled.

Thirdly, Because otherwise he would disown the sayings of His Prophets, and gratify the sayings of His enemies; His Prophets say He will take vengeance; His enemies say He will not; His Prophets say He will remember their iniquities, and recompense them into their bosom; but His enemies say they should do well, and they shall have peace, though they walk after the imaginations of their own hearts, and be not so strict as the Word commands, and do not as it saith (Deuteronomy 29:19-20). But let me tell thee, hadst thou a thousand souls, and each of them was worth a thousand worlds, God would set them all on a light by fire, if they fall within the condemnings of His Word, and thou die without a Jesus, even the right Jesus; "for the Scriptures can not be broken." What! dost thou think that God, Christ, Prophets, and Scriptures, will all lie for thee? and falsify their words for thee? It will be but ill venturing thy soul upon that.

And the reasons for it are these: First, Because God is God; and secondly, Because man is man.

First, Because God is perfectly just and eternally just, perfectly holy and eternally holy, perfectly faithful and eternally faithful; that is, without any variableness or shadow of turning, but perfectly continueth the same, and can not as well cease to be God as to alter or change the nature of His Godhead. As He is thus the perfection of all perfections, He gave out His Law to be obeyed; but if any offend it, then they fall into the hands of this His eternal justice, and so must drink of His irrevocable wrath, which is the execution of the same justice. I say, this being thus, the law being broken, justice takes place, and so faithfulness followeth to see that execution be done, and also to *testify that He is true, and doth denounce His unspeakable, insupportable, and unchangeable* vengeance on the party offending.

Secondly, Because thou art not as infinite as God, but a poor created weed, that is here today and gone tomorrow, and not able to answer God in His essence, being, and attributes; thou art bound to fall under Him, for thy soul or body can do nothing that is infinite in such a way as to satisfy this God, which is an infinite God in all His attributes.

Misery of Man by This Law

But to declare unto you the misery of man by this law to purpose, I do beseech you to take notice of these following particulars, besides what has been already spoken: First, I shall show the danger of them by reason of the law, as they come from Adam; Second, as they are in their own persons particularly under it.

First, The Danger of Them by Reason of the Law, As They Come from Adam

1.) As they come from Adam, they are in a sad condition, because he left them a broken covenant. Or take it thus: because they, while they were in him, did with him break that covenant. O! this was the treasure that Adam left to his posterity; it was a broken covenant, insomuch that death reigned over all his children, and doth still to this day, as they come from him, both natural and eternal death (Romans 5). It may be, drunkard, swearer, liar, thief, thou dost not think of this.

2.) He did not only leave them a broken covenant, but also made them himself sinners against it. He (Adam) made them sinners—"By one man's disobedience many were made sinners" (Romans 5:19). And this is worse than the first.

3.) Not only so, but he did deprive them of their strength, by which at first they were enabled to stand, and left them no more than dead men. O helpless state! O how beggarly and miserable are the sons of Adam!

4.) Not only so, but also before he left them he was the conduit pipe through which the devil did convey off his poisoned spawn and venom nature into the hearts of Adam's sons and daughters, by which they are at this day so strongly and so violently carried away, that they fly as fast to Hell, and the devil, by reason of sin, as chaff before a mighty wind.

5.) In a word, Adam led them out of their paradise, that is one more; and put out their eyes, that is another; and left them to the leading of the devil. O sad! Canst thou hear this, and not have thy ears to tingle and burn on thy head? Canst thou read this, and not feel thy conscience begin to throb and dag? If so, surely it is because thou art either possessed with the devil, or besides thyself.

Second, The Cause of Their Being in a Sad Condition, *Which is by Reason of Their Being in Their Particular Persons Under It*

1.) Therefore, they that are under the law, they are in a sad condition, because they are under that which is more ready, through our infirmity, to curse than to bless; they are under that called the ministration of condemnation, that is, they are under that dispensation, or administration, whose proper work is to curse and condemn, and nothing else (2 Corinthians 3).

2.) Their condition is sad who are under the law, because they are not only under that ministration that doth condemn, but also that which doth wait an opportunity to condemn; the law doth not wait that it might be gracious, but it doth wait to curse and condemn; it came on purpose to discover sin, "The law entered," saith the Apostle, "that the offence might abound" (Romans 5:20) or appear indeed to be that which God doth hate, and also to curse for that which hath been committed; as he saith, "Cursed is every one that continueth not in all things which are written in the book of the law to do them" (Galatians 3:10).

3.) They are in a sad condition, because that administration they are under that are under the law doth always find fault with the sinner's obedience as well as his disobedience, if it be not done in a right spirit, which they that are under that covenant can not do, by reason of their being destitute of faith; therefore, I say, it doth control them, saying, "This was not well done, this was done by the halves, this was not done freely, and that was not done perfectly, and out of love to God." And hence it is that some men, notwithstanding they labor to live as holy as ever they can according to the law, yet they do not live a peaceable life, but are full of condemnings, full of guilt and torment of conscience, finding themselves to fail here, and to fall short there, omitting this good which the law commands, and doing that evil which the law forbids, but never giveth them one good word for all their pains.

4.) They that are under the law are in a sad condition, because they are under that administration that will never be contented with what is done by the sinner. If thou be under this covenant, work as hard as thou canst, the law will never say, "Well done"; never say, "My good servant"; no; but always it will be driving thee faster, hastening of thee harder, giving thee fresh commands, which thou must do, and upon pain of damnation not to be left undone. Nay, it is such a master that will curse thee, not only for thy sins, but also because thy good works were not so well done as they ought to be.

5.) They that are under this covenant or law, their state is very sad, because this law doth command impossible things of him that is under it; and yet doth but right in it, seeing man at the first had in Adam strength to stand, if he would have used it, and the law was given them, as I said before, when man was in his full strength; and therefore no inequality if it commands the same still, seeing God that gave thee strength did not take it away. I will give you a similitude for the clearing of it. Set the case that I give to my servant ten pounds, with this charge, Lay it out for my best advantage, that I may have my own again with profit; now if my servant, contrary to my command, goeth and spends my money in a disobedient way, is it any inequality in me to demand of my servant what I gave him at first? Nay, and though he have nothing to pay, I may lawfully cast him into prison, and keep him there until I have satisfaction. So here; the law was delivered to man at the first when he was in a possibility to have fulfilled it; now, then, though man have lost his strength, yet God is just in commanding the same work to be done. Ay, and if they do not do the same things, I say, that are impossible for them to do, it is just with God to damn them, seeing it was they themselves that brought themselves into this condition; therefore, saith the Apostle, "What things soever the law (or commands) saith, it saith to them who are under the law; that every mouth may be stopped, and all the world may become guilty before God" (Romans 3:19). And this is thy sad condition that art under the law (Galatians 3:10).

But if any should object, and say, But the law doth not command impossible things of natural man:

I should answer in this case as the Apostle did in another very much like unto it, saying, "Understanding neither what they say, nor whereof they affirm." For doth not the law command thee to love the Lord thy God with all thy soul, with all they strength, with all thy might, etc., and can the natural man do this? How can those that are accustomed to do evil, do that which is commanded in this particular? "Can the Ethiopian change his skin, or the leopard his spots?" (Jeremiah 12:23).

Doth the law command thee to do good, and nothing but good, and that with all thy soul, heart, and delight? which the law as a Covenant of Works calleth for; and canst thou, being carnal, do that? But there is no man that hath understanding, if he should hear thee say so, but would say that thou wast either bewitched or stark mad.

6.) They that are under the law are in a sad condition, because that though they follow the law, or Covenant of Works; I say, though they follow it, it will not lead them to Heaven; no, but contrariwise, it will lead them under the curse. It is not possible, saith Paul, that any should be justified by the law, or by our following of it; for by that "is the knowledge of sin," and by it we are condemned for the same, which is far from leading us to life, being the ministration of death (2 Corinthians 3). And again; "Israel, which followeth after the law of righteousness, hath not attained to the law of righteousness.

Wherefore? Because *they sought it* not by faith, but by the law, and by the works thereof" (Romans 9:30-32).

7.) They that are under the law are in a sad condition, because they do not know whether ever they shall have any wages for their work or no; they have no assurance of the pardon of their sins, neither any hopes of eternal life; but poor hearts as they are, they work for they do not know what, even like a poor horse that works hard all day, and at night hath a dirty stable for his pains; so thou mayest work hard all the days of thy life, and at the day of death, instead of having a glorious rest in the Kingdom of Heaven, thou mayest, nay, thou shalt, have for thy sins the damnation of thy soul and body in Hell to all eternity; forasmuch, as I said before, that the law, if thou sinnest, it doth not take notice of any good work done by thee, but takes its advantage to destroy and cut off thy soul for the sin thou hast committed.

8.) They that are under the law are in a sad condition, because they are under that administration; upon whose souls God doth not smile, they dying there; for the administration that God doth smile upon His children through, is the Covenant of Grace, they being in Jesus Christ, the Lord of life and consolation; but contrariwise to those that are under the law; for they have His frowns, His rebukes, His threatenings, and with much severity they must be dealt withal—"For they continued not in My covenant, and I regarded them not, saith the Lord" (Hebrews 8:9).

9.) They are in a sad condition, because they are out of the faith of Christ; they that are under the law have not the faith of Christ in them; for that dispensation which they are under is not the administration of faith. The law is not of faith, saith the Apostle (Galatians 3:12).

10.) Because they have not received the Spirit; for that is received by the hearing of faith, and not by the law, nor the works thereof (Galatians 3:2).

11.) In a word, if thou live and die under that covenant, Jesus Christ will neither pray for thee, neither let thee have one drop of His blood to wash away thy sins, neither shalt thou be so much as one of the least in the Kingdom of Heaven; for all these privileges come to souls under another covenant, as the Apostle saith—"For such are not under the law, but under grace"—that is, such as have a share in the benefits of Jesus Christ, or such as are brought from under the first covenant into the second; or from under the law into the grace of Christ's Gospel, without which Covenant of Grace, and being found in that, there is no soul can have the least hope of eternal life, no joy in the Holy Ghost, no share in the privileges of saints, because they are tied up from them by the limits and bonds of the Covenant of Works. For you must understand that these two covenants have their several bounds and limitations, for the ruling and keeping in subjection, or giving of freedom, to the parties under the said covenants. Now they that are under the law are within the compass and the jurisdiction of that, and are bound to be in subjection to that; and living and dying under that, they must stand and fall to that, as Paul saith, "To his own master he standeth or falleth." The Covenant of Grace doth admit to those that are under it also liberty and freedom, together with commanding of subjection to the things contained in it, which I shall speak to further hereafter.

For What Purpose the Law Was Added and Given

But now, that the former things may be further made to appear—that is, what the sad condition of all them that are under the law is, as I have shown you something of the nature of the law, so also shall I show that the law was added and given for this purpose, that it might be so with those that are out of the Covenant of Grace.

FIRST, God did give the law that sin might abound, not that it should take away sin in any, but to discover the sin which is already begotten, or that may be hereafter begotten, by lust and Satan (Romans 5:20). I say, this is one proper work of the law, to make manifest sin; it is sent to find fault with the sinner, and it doth also watch that it may do so, and it doth take all advantages for the accomplishing of its work in them that give ear thereto, or do not give ear, if it have the rule over them. I say, it is like a man that is sent by his lord to see and pry into the labors and works of other men, taking every advantage to discover their infirmities and failings, and to chide them? yea, to throw them out of the Lord's favor for the same.

SECOND, Another great end why the Lord did add or give the law, it was that no man might have anything to lay to the charge of the Lord for His condemning of them that do transgress against the same. You know that if a man should be had before an officer or judge, and there be condemned, and yet by no law, he that condemns him might be very well reprehended or reproved for passing the judgment; yea, the party himself might have better ground to plead for his liberty than the other to plead for the condemning of him; but this shall not be so in the judgment-day, but contrariwise; for then every man shall be forced to lay his hand on his mouth, and hold his tongue at the judgment of God when it is passed upon them; therefore saith the Apostle, "What things soever the law saith, it saith to them who are under the law"; that is, all the commands, all the cursings and threatenings that are spoken by it, are spoken, saith he, "that every mouth may be stopped"; mark, I beseech you, "it saith," saith he, "that every mouth may be stopped, and all the world may become guilty before God" (Romans 3:19). So that now, in case any in the judgment-day should object against the judgment of God, as those in the 25th of Matthew do, saying, Lord, when saw we Thee thus and thus? and why dost Thou pass such a sad sentence of condemnation upon us? surely this is injustice, and not equity: now for the preventing of this the law was given; ay, and that it might prevent thee to purpose, God gave it betimes, before either thy first father had sinned, or thou wast born. So that again, if there should be these objections offered against the proceedings of the Lord in justice and judgment, saying, Lord, why am I thus condemned, I did not know it was sin? Now against these two was the law given and that betimes, so that both these are answered. If the first come in and say, Why am I judged? why am I damned? then will the law come in, even all the Ten Commandments, with every one of their cries against thy soul; the First saying, He hath sinned against Me, damn him; the Second saying also, He hath transgressed against Me, damn him; the Third also saying the same, together with the Fourth, Fifth, Sixth, Seventh, Eighth, Ninth, Tenth; even all of them will discharge themselves against thy soul if thou die under the first covenant, saying, He or they have transgressed against us, damn them, damn them: and I tell thee also, that these ten great guns, the Ten Commandments, will, with discharging themselves in justice against thy soul, so rattle in thy conscience, that thou wilt in spite of thy teeth be immediately put to silence, and have thy mouth stopped. And let me tell thee further, that if thou shalt appear before God to have the Ten Commandments discharge themselves against thee, thou hadst better be tied to a tree, and have ten, yea, ten thousand of the biggest pieces of ordnance in the world to be shot off against thee; for these could go no further but only to kill the body; but they, both body and soul, to be tormented in Hell with the devil to all eternity.

THIRD, Again; if the second thing should be objected, saying, But Lord, I did not think this had been sin, or the other had been sin, for nobody told me so; then also will the giving of the law take off that, saying, Nay, But I was given to thy father Adam before he had sinned, or before thou wast born, and have ever since been in thy soul to convince thee of thy sins, and to control thee for doing the thing that was not right. Did not I secretly tell thee at such a time, in such a place, when thou wast doing of such a thing, with such an one, or when thou was all alone, that this was a sin, and that God did forbid it, therefore if thou didst commit it, God would be displeased with thee for it: and when thou was thinking to do such a thing at such a time, did not I say, Forbear, do not so? God will smite thee, and punish thee for it if thou dost do it. And besides, God did so order it that you had me in your houses, in your Bibles, and also you could speak and talk of me; thus pleading the truth, thou shalt be forced to confess it is so; nay, it shall be so in some sort with the very Gentiles and barbarous people that fall far short of that light we have in these parts of the world; for, saith the Apostle, "The Gentiles which have not the law, do by nature the things contained in the law, these, having not the law," that is, not written as we have, yet they "are a law unto themselves: which show the works of the law written in their hearts" (Romans 2:14-15). That is, they have the law of works in them by nature, and therefore they shall be left without excuse; for their own consciences shall stand up for the truth of this where he saith, "Their conscience also bearing witness, and their thoughts the meanwhile accusing or else excusing one another." Ay, but when? Why, "in the day when God shall judge the secrets of men by Jesus Christ according to my Gospel" (Romans 2:15-16). So this, I say, is another end for which the Lord did give the law—namely, that God might pass a sentence in righteousness, without being charged with any injustice by those that shall fall under it in the judgment.

Fourth, A fourth end why the Lord did give the law it was, because they that die out of Jesus Christ might not only have their mouths stopped, but also that their persons "might become guilty before God" (Romans 3:19). And indeed this will be the ground of silencing, as I said before, they finding themselves guilty, their consciences backing the truth of the judgment of God passed upon them, "they shall become guilty"—that is, they shall be fit vessels for the wrath of God to be poured out into, being filled with guilt by reason of transgressions against the commandments; thus, therefore, shall the parties under the first covenant be "fitted to destruction" (Romans 9:22) even as wood or straw, being well dried, is fitted for the fire; and the law was added and given, and speaks to this very end, that sins might be shown, mouths might be stopped from quarrelling, and that "all the world," mark, "the world may become guilty before God," and so be in justice for ever and ever overthrown because of their sins.

And this will be so for these reasons:

1.) Because God hath a time to magnify His justice and holiness, as well as to show His forbearance and mercy. We read in Scripture that His eyes are too pure to behold iniquity, and then we shall find it true (Habakkuk 1:13). We read in Scripture that He will magnify the law, and make it honorable, and then He will do it indeed. Now, because the Lord doth not strike so soon as He is provoked by sin, therefore poor souls will not know nor regard the justice of God, neither do they consider the time in which it must be advanced, which will be when men drop under the wrath of God as fast as hail in a mighty storm (2 Peter 3:9; Psalms 50:21:22). Now, therefore, look to it all you that count the long-suffering and forbearance of God slackness; and because for the present He keepeth silence, therefore to think that He is like unto yourselves. No, no; but know that God hath His set time for every purpose of His, and in its time it shall be advanced most marvellously, to the everlasting astonishment and overthrow of that soul that shall be dealt withal by justice and the law. O! how will God advance His justice! O! how will God advance His holiness! First, by showing men that He in justice can not, will not regard them, because they have sinned; and, secondly, in that His holiness will not give way for such unclean wretches to abide in His sight, His eyes are so pure.

2.) Because God will make it appear that He will be as good as His Word to sinners. Sinners must not look to escape always, though they may escape awhile, yet they shall not go far all ado unpunished; no, but they shall have their due to a farthing, when every threatening and curse shall be accomplished and fulfilled on the head of the transgressor. Friend, there is never an idle word that thou speakest but God will account with thee for it; there is never a lie thou tellest, but God will reckon with thee for it; nay, there shall not pass so much as one passage in all thy lifetime but God, the righteous God, will have it in the trial by His law, if thou die under it, in the judgment-day.

WHO THEY ARE THAT ARE UNDER THE COVENANT OF WORKS

III. QUESTION:
"But who are those that are thus under the law?"

ANSWER: Those that are under the law may be branched out into three ranks of men; either, first, such as are grossly profane, or such as are more refined; which may be two ways, some in a lower sort, and some in a more eminent way.

First, Then they are under the law as a Covenant of Works who are open profane, and ungodly wretches, such as delight not only in sin, but also make their boast of the same, and brag at the thoughts of committing of it. Now, as for such as these are, there is a Scripture in the First Epistle of Paul to Timothy Chapter 1, verses 9, 10, which is a notable one to this purpose, "The law," saith he, "is not made for a righteous man," not as it is a Covenant of Works, "but for the" unrighteous or "lawless and disobedient, for the ungodly and for sinners, for unholy and profane, for murderers of fathers and murderers of mothers, for manslayers, for whoremongers, for them that defile themselves with mankind, for men-stealers, for liars," look to it, liars, "for perjured persons, and," in a word, "if there be any other thing that is not according to sound doctrine." These are one sort of people that are under the law, and so under the curse of the same, whose due is to drink up the brimful cup of God's eternal vengeance, and therefore I beseech you not to deceive yourselves; for "know ye not that the unrighteous shall not inherit the kingdom of God? Neither fornicators, nor idolaters, nor adulterers, nor effeminate, nor abusers of themselves with mankind, nor thieves, nor covetous, nor drunkards, nor revilers, nor extortioners, shall inherit the kingdom of God" (1 Corinthians 6:9-10). Poor souls, you think that you may have your sins, your lusts, and pleasures, and yet you shall do pretty well, and be let to go free in the judgment-day; but see what God saith of such in Deuteronomy 29:19-20—which shall "bless himself in his heart, saying, I shall have peace," I shall be saved, I shall do as well as others, in the day when God shall judge the world by Jesus Christ; but, saith God, I will not spare them, no, but My anger and My jealousy shall smoke against them. How far? Even to the executing all the curses that are written in the Law of God upon them. Nay, saith God, I will be even with them, "for I will blot out their names from under Heaven." And indeed it must of necessity be so, because such souls are unbelievers, in their sins, and under the law, which can not, will not, show any mercy on them; for it is not the administration of mercy and life, but the administration of death and destruction, as you have it (2 Corinthians 3:7, 9); and all those, every one of them, that are open profane, and scandalous wretches are under it, and have been so ever since they came into the world to this day; and they will for certain live and die under the same dispensation, and then be damned to all eternity, if they be not converted from under that covenant into and under the Covenant of Grace, of which I shall speak in its place; and yet for all this, how brag and crank[6] are our poor wantons and wicked ones in this day of forbearance! as if God would never have a reckoning with them, as if there was no law to condemn them, as if there was no hellfire to put them into. But O how will they be deceived when they shall see Christ sitting upon the judgment-seat, having laid aside his priestly and prophetic office, and appearing only as a judge to the wicked? when they shall see all the records of Heaven unfolded and laid open; when they shall see each man his name in the Book of Life, and in the book of the law; when they shall see God in His majesty, Christ in His majesty, the saints in their dignity, but themselves in their impurity. What will they say then? whither will they fly then? where will they leave their glory? O sad state! (Isaiah 10:3).

Second. They are under the law also who do not only so break and disobey the law, but follow after the law as hard as ever they can, seeking justification thereby—that is, though a man should abstain from the sins against the law, and labor to fulfil the law, and give up himself to the law, yet if he look no further than the law he is still under the law, and for all his obedience to the law, the righteous Law of God, he shall be destroyed by that law. Friend, you must not understand that none but profane persons are under the law; no, but you must understand that a man may be turned from a vain, loose, open, profane conversation and sinning against the law, to a holy, righteous, religious life, and yet be in the same state, under the same law, and as sure to be damned as the other that are more profane and loose. And though you may say this is very strange, yet I shall both say it and prove it to be true. Read with understanding that Scripture in Romans 9:30-31, where the Apostle, speaking of the very thing, saith, "But Israel, which followed after the law of righteousness"; mark, that followed after the law of righteousness; they notwithstanding their earnest pursuit, or hunting after the law of righteousness, "hath not attained to the law of righteousness." It signifies thus much to us, that let a man be never so earnest, so fervent, so restless, so serious, so ready, so apt and willing to follow the law and the righteousness thereof, if he be under that covenant, he is gone, he is lost, he is deprived of eternal life, because he is not under the ministration of life if he die there. Read also that Scripture, Galatians 3:10, which saith, "For as many as are of the works of the law are under the curse"; mark, they that are of the works of the law. Now, for to be of the works of the law, it is to be of the works of the righteousness thereof—that is, to abstain from sins against the law, and to do the commands thereof as near as ever they can for their lives, or with all the might they have: and therefore I beseech you to consider it, for men's being ignorant of this is the cause why so many go on supposing they have a share in Christ, because they are reformed, and abstain from the sins against the law, who, when all comes to all, will be damned notwithstanding, because they are not brought out from under the Covenant of Works, and put under the Covenant of Grace.

OBJECTION: "But can you in very deed make these things manifestly evident from the Word of God? Methinks to reason thus is very strange, that a man should labor to walk up according to the Law of God as much as ever he can, and yet that man notwithstanding this, should be still under the curse. Pray clear it."

ANSWER: Truly this doth seem very strange, I do know full well, to the natural man, to him that is yet in his unbelief, because he goeth by beguiled reason; but for my part, I do know it is so, and shall labor also to convince thee of the truth of the same.

Part 1.) Then, the law is thus strict and severe, that if a man do sin but once against it, he, I say, is gone for ever by the law, living and dying under that covenant. If you would be satisfied as touching the truth of this, do but read Galatians 3:10, where it saith "Cursed is every one," that is, not a man shall miss by that covenant, "that continueth not in all," mark, in all "things which are written in the book of the law to do them."

a.) Pray mark, here is a curse, in the first place, if all things written in the book of the law be not done, and that, continually too—that is, without any failing or one slip, as I said before. Now there is never a one in the world but before they did begin to yield obedience to the least command, they in their own persons did sin against it by breaking of it. The Apostle, methinks, is very notable for the clearing of this in Romans 3:5. In the one he endeavors for to prove that all had transgressed in the first Adam as he stood a common person, representing both himself and us in his standing and falling. "Wherefore," saith he, "as by one man sin entered into the world, and death by sin; and so death passed upon all men," mark that; but why? "for that all have sinned" (Romans 5:12). That is, forasmuch as all naturally are guilty of original sin, the sin that was committed by us in Adam; so this is one cause why none can be justified by their obedience to the law, because they have in the first place broken it in their first parents. But:

b.) In case this should be opposed and rejected by quarrelsome persons, though there be no ground for it, Paul hath another argument to back his doctrine, saying, For we have proved (already) that both Jews and Gentiles are all under sin. "As it is written, There is none righteous, no, not one." "They are all gone out of the way, they are together," mark, together, "become unprofitable, there is none that doeth good, no, not one." "Their throat is an open sepulchre; with their tongues they have used deceit, the poison of asps is under their lips." Their "mouths are full of cursing and bitterness." "Their feet are swift to shed blood." In a word, "Destruction and misery are in their ways; and the way of peace have they not known." Now then, saith he, having proved these things so clearly, the conclusion of the whole is this, "That what things soever the law saith," in both showing of sin, and cursing for the same, "it saith" all "to them who are under the law that every mouth may be stopped, and all the world may become guilty before God" (Romans 3:10, 19). So that here, I say, lieth the ground of our not being justified by the law, even because, in the first place, we have sinned against it; for know this for certain, that if the law doth take the least advantage of thee by thy sinning against it, all that ever thou shalt afterwards hear from it is nothing but Curse, curse, curse him, "for not continuing in all things which are written in the book of the law to do them."

Part 2.) Thou canst not be saved by the righteous Law of God, the first covenant, because that, together with this thy miserable state, by original and actual sins, before thou didst follow the law, since thy turning to the law thou hast committed several sins against the law—"In many things we offend all." So that now thy righteousness to the law being mixed with sometimes the lust of concupiscence, fornication, covetousness, pride, heart-risings against God, coldness of affection towards Him, backwardness to good duties, speaking idle words, having of strife in your hearts, and such like; I say, these things being thus, the righteousness of the law is become too weak through this our flesh (Romans 8:3), and so, notwithstanding all our obedience to the law, we are yet through our weakness under the curse of the law; for, as I said before, the law is so holy, so just, and so good, that it can not allow that any failing or slip should be done by them that look for life by the same. "Cursed is every one that continuteth not in everything" (Galatians 3:10). And this Paul knew full well, which made him throw away all his righteousness. But you will say, that was his own.

ANSWER: But it was even that which while he calls it his own, he also calls it the righteousness of the law (Philippians 3:7-10) and to account it but dung, but as dirt on his shoes, and that, that he might be found in Christ, and so be saved by Him "without the deeds of the law" (Romans 3:28). But,

Part 3.) Set the case, the righteousness of the law which thou hast was pure and perfect, without the least flaw or fault, without the least mixture of the least sinful thought, yet this would fall far short of presenting of thee blameless in the sight of God. And that I prove by these arguments:

a.) The first argument is, that that which is not Christ can not redeem souls from the curse, it can not completely present them before the Lord; now the law is not Christ; therefore the moral law can not, by all our obedience to it, deliver us from the curse that is due to us (Acts 4:12).

b.) The second argument is, that that righteousness that is not the righteousness of faith, that is, by believing in Jesus Christ, can not please God; now the righteousness of the law as a Covenant of Works is not the righteousness of faith; therefore the righteousness of the law as acted by us, being under that covenant, can not please God. The first is proved in Hebrews 11:6, "But without faith *it is* impossible to please *Him*"; mark, it is impossible. The second thus, "The law is not of faith" (Galatians 3:12; Romans 10:5-6), compared with Galatians 3:11. "But that no man is justified by the law in the sight of God, *it is* evident; for, The just shall live by faith. And the law is not of faith."

But for the better understanding of those that are weak of apprehension, I shall prove it thus—1. The soul that hath eternal life, he must have it by right of purchase or redemption (Hebrews 9:12; Ephesians 1:7). 2. This purchase of redemption must be through the blood of Christ. "We have redemption through His blood." "Without shedding of blood is no remission." Now the law is not in a capacity to die, and so to redeem sinners by the purchase of blood, which satisfaction justice calls for. Read the same Scriptures (Hebrews 9:22). Justice calls for satisfaction, because thou hast transgressed and sinned against it, and that must have satisfaction; therefore all that ever thou canst do can not bring in redemption, though thou follow the law up to the to the nail-head, as I may say, because all this is not shedding of blood; for believe it, and know it for certain, that though thou hadst sinned but one sin before thou didst turn to the law, that one sin will murder thy soul, if it be not washed away by blood, even by the precious blood of Jesus Christ, that was shed when He did hang upon the cross on Mount Calvary.

OBJECTION: But you will say, "Methinks, that giving of ourselves up to live a righteous life should make God like the better of us, and so let us be saved by Christ, because we are so willing to obey His law."

ANSWER: The motive that moveth God to have mercy upon sinners is not because they are willing to follow the law, but because

He is willing to save them. "Not for thy righteousness, or for the uprightness of thine heart dost thou go to possess their land" (Deuteronomy 9:4-6). Now understand this: if thy will to do righteousness was the first moving cause why God had mercy on thee through Christ, then it must not be freely by grace—I say, freely. But the Lord loves thee and saves thee upon free terms, having nothing beforehand to make Him accept of thy soul, but only the blood of Christ; therefore to allow of such a principle it is to allow that grace is to be obtained by the works of the law, which is as gross darkness as lies in the darkest dungeon in Popery, and is also directly opposite to Scripture—For we are "justified freely by His grace, through the redemption that is in Christ"; not through the good that is in ourselves, or done by us, no, "but by faith, without"—mark that—"without the deeds of the law" (Romans 3:24-28). Again, "Not of works, least any man should boast" (Ephesians 2:9). No, no, saith he, "Not according to our works," or righteousness, "but according to His own purpose"; mark "according to His own purpose and grace, which was" a free gift, "given us in Christ Jesus," not lately, but "before the world began" (2 Timothy 1:9).

OBJECTION: But you will say, "Then why did God give the law, if we can not have salvation by following of it?"

ANSWER: I told you before that the law was given for these following reasons—1. That thou mightest be convinced by it of thy sins, and that thy sins might indeed appear very sinful unto thee, which is done by the law these ways—a. By showing of thee what a holy God He is that did give the law; and, b. By showing thee thy vileness and wickedness, in that thou, contrary to this holy God, hast transgressed against and broken this His holy Law; therefore, saith Paul, "the law entered, that the offence might abound," that is, by showing the creature the holiness of God, and also its own vileness (Romans 5:20). 2. That thou mayest know that God will not damn thee for nothing in the judgment-day. 3. Because He would have no quarrelling at His just condemning of them at that day. 4. Because He will make thee to know that He is a holy God and pure.

WHAT MEN MAY ATTAIN TO THAT ARE UNDER THIS COVENANT OF WORKS

IV. QUESTION:

"Would you do so much as to show in some particulars, *both what men have done,* and how far they have gone, and what they *have received, being yet under this covenant,* which you call the ministration of condemnation?"

ANSWER: This is somewhat a difficult question, and had need be not only warily, but also home and soundly answered. The question consists of three particulars—*First*, What men have done; *Second*, How far men have gone; *Third*, What they have received, and yet to be under the law, or Covenant of Works, and so in a state of condemnation.

FIRST. As for the first, I have spoken something in general to that already; but for thy better understanding I shall yet speak more particularly.

1.) A man hath and may be convinced and troubled for his sins, and yet be under this covenant, and that in a very heavy and dreadful manner, insomuch that he find the weight of them to be intolerable and too heavy for him to bear, as it was with Cain, "My punishment," saith he, "*is* greater than I can bear" (Genesis 4:13).

2.) A man living thus under a sense of his sins may repent and be sorry for them, and yet be under this covenant, and yet be in a damned state. And when he, Judas, saw what was done, he "repented" (Matthew 27:3).

3.) Men may not only be convinced, and also repent for their sins, but they may also desire the prayers of the children of God for them too, and yet be under this covenant and curse, "Then Pharaoh called for Moses and Aaron, in haste, and he said, I have sinned; entreat the LORD your God that He may take away from me this death" (Exodus 10:16-17).

4.) A man may also humble himself for his offences and disobedience against his God, and yet be under this covenant (1 Kings 21:24-19).

5.) A man may make restitution unto men for the offence he hath done unto them, and yet be under this covenant.

6.) A man may do much work for God in his generation, and yet be under this first covenant; as Jehu, who did do that which God bid him (2 Kings 9:25-26). And yet God threateneth even Jehu, because though he did do the thing that the Lord commanded him, yet he did it not from a right principle; for had he, the Lord would not have said, "Yet a little while, and I will avenge the blood of Jezreel upon the house of Jehu" (Hosea 1:4).

7.) Men may hear and fear the servants of the Lord, and reverence them very highly; yea, and when they hear, they may not only hear, but hear and do, and that gladly too, not one or two things, but many; mark, many things gladly, and yet be lost, and yet be damned, "For Herod feared John," why? not because he had any civil power over him, but because "he was a just man and an holy, and observed him; and when he heard him, he did many things, and heard him gladly" (Mark 6:20). It may be that thou thinkest that because thou hearest such and such, therefore thou art better than thy neighbors; but know for certain that thou mayest not only hear, but thou mayest hear and do, and that not with a backward will, but gladly—mark, "gladly"—and yet be Herod still, an enemy to the Lord Jesus still. Consider this, I pray you.

SECOND. But to the second thing, which is this, How far may such an one go? To what may such an one attain? Whither may he arrive, and yet be an undone man, under this covenant? Answer:

1.) Such an one may be received into fellowship with the saints, as they are in a visible way of walking one with another; they may walk hand in hand together, "The Kingdom of Heaven," that is, a visible company of professors of Christ, is likened to ten virgins, which took their lamps, and went forth to meet the Bridegroom, "five of them were wise, and five were foolish" (Matthew 25:1-2). These, in the first place, are called virgins—that is, such as are clear from the pollutions of the world; secondly, they are said to go forth—that is, from the rudiments and traditions of men; thirdly, they do agree to take their lamps with them—that is, to profess themselves the servants of Jesus Christ, that wait upon Him, and for Him; and yet when He came, He found half of them, even the virgins, that had lamps, that also went forth from the pollutions of the world and the customs of men, to be such as lost their precious souls (verse 12) which they should not have done, had they been under the Covenant of Grace, and so not under the law.

2.) They may attain to a great deal of honor in the said company of professors, that which may be accounted honor, insomuch that they may be put in trust with church affairs, and bear the bag, as Judas did. I speak not this to shame the saints, but, being beloved, I warn them; yet I speak this on purpose that it might, if the Lord will, knock at the door of the souls of professors. Consider Demas!

3.) They may attain to speak of the Word as ministers, and become preachers of the Gospel of Jesus Christ, insomuch that the people where they dwell may even take up a proverb concerning them, saying, "Is he among the prophets?" his gifts may be so rare, his tongue may be so fluent, and his matter may be so fit, that he may speak with a tongue like an angel, and speak of the hidden mysteries, yea, of them all; mark that, and yet be nothing, and yet be none of the Lord's anointed ones, with the Spirit of grace savingly, but may live and die under the curse of the law (1 Corinthians 13:1-4).

4.) They may go yet further; they may have the gifts of the Spirit of God, which may enable them to cast out devils, to remove the biggest hills or mountains in the world; nay, thou mayest be so gifted as to prophesy of things to come, the most glorious things, even the coming of the Lord Jesus Christ to reign over all His enemies, and yet be but a Balaam, a wicked and a mad prophet (2 Peter 2:16; Numbers 24:16-25).

5.) There may not only stand thus for awhile, for a little season, but they may stand thus till the coming of our Lord Jesus Christ with His holy angels; ay, and not be discovered of the saints till that very day. "Then all those virgins arose"—the wise and the foolish; then! when? why, when this voice was heard, "Behold the Bridegroom cometh, go ye out to meet him" (Matthew 25:1-6). And yet were out of the Lord Jesus Christ, and yet were under the law.

6.) Nay, further, they may not only continue in a profession till then, supposing themselves to be under the grace of the Gospel, when indeed they are under the curse of the law, but even when the Bridegroom is come, they may still be so confident of their state to be good, that they will even reason out the case with Christ why they are not let into the kingdom of glory, saying, "Lord, Lord, we have eaten and drunk in Thy presence; and Thou hast taught in our streets." Nay, further, "Have we not prophesied in Thy name? and in Thy name have cast out devils?" Nay, not only thus, but, "done many," mark, we have "done many wonderful works." Nay, further, they were so confident, that they commanded, in a commanding way, saying, "Lord, open to us." See here, I beseech you, how far these went; they thought they had had intimate acquaintance with Jesus Christ, they thought He could not choose but save them; they had eat and drunk with Him, sat at the table with Him, received power from Him, executed the same power. In Thy name have we done thus and thus; even wrought many wonderful works (Matthew 7:22; Luke 13:25-26). And yet these poor creatures were shut out of the kingdom. O consider this, I beseech you, before it be too late, lest you say, Lord, let us come in, when Christ saith, Thrust him out (Verse 28). Hears you cry, "Lord open to us," when He saith, "Depart, I know you not"; lest though you think of having joy, you have "weeping and gnashing of teeth."

THIRD. But the third thing touched in the question was this—What may such a one receive of God who is under the curse of the law?

1.) They may receive an answer to their prayers from God at some times, for some things as they do stand in need of. I find in Scripture that God did hear these persons that the Apostle saith were cast out (Genesis 21:17). "And God heard the voice of the lad," even of cast-out Ishmael; "and the angel of God called to Hagar" which was the bond-woman, and under the law (Galatians 4:30). "out of heaven, and said unto her, Fear not; for God hath heard the voice of the lad where he *is*." Friends, it may be you may think, because you have your prayers answered in some particular things, therefore you may suppose that as to your eternal state your condition is very good. But you must know that God doth hear the cry of a company of Ishmaelites, the sons of the bondwomen, who are under the law as a Covenant of Works. I do not say He hears them as to their eternal state, but He heareth them as to several straits that they go through in this life, ay, and gives them ease and liberty from their trouble. Here this poor wretch was almost perished for a little water, and he cried, and God heard him, yea, He heard him out of Heaven. Read also Psalm 107:23-29. "He gave them their desire, but He sent leanness into their soul" (Psalms 106:15).[7]

But some may say,—*Methinks this is yet stranger still: that God should hear the prayers,—the cries of those that are under the law, and answer them.*

ANSWER:

Part 1.) I told you before, He doth not hear them as to their eternal state, but as to their temporal state; for God as their Creator hath a care for them, and causeth the sun to shine upon them, and the rain to distil upon their substance (Matthew 5:45). Nay, He doth give the beasts in the field their appointed food, and doth hear the young ravens when they cry, which are far inferior to man (Psalms 147:9). I say, therefore, that God doth hear the cries of His creatures, and doth answer them too, though not as to their eternal state; but may damn them nevertheless when they die for all that.

Part 2.) They may receive promises from the mouth of the Lord. There are many that have promises made to them by the Lord in a most eminent way, and yet, as I said before, are such as are cast out and called the children of the bond-woman, which is the law—"And the angel of God called to Hagar out of Heaven," that was the bond-woman, saying, "Fear not; for God hath heard the voice of the lad where he is. Arise, lift up the lad, and hold him in thine hand; FOR I WILL MAKE HIM"—mark, there is the promise—"for I will make him," of the son of the bond-woman, "a great nation" (Genesis 21:17-18).

Part 3.) Nay, they may go further; for they may receive another heart than they had before, and yet be under the law. There is no man, I think, but those that do not know what they say, that will think or say that Saul was under the Covenant of Grace; yet after he had talked with Samuel, and had turned his back to go from him, saith the Scripture, "God gave him another heart" (1 Samuel 10:9). Another heart, mark that, and yet an out-cast, a rejected person (1 Samuel 15:26, 29). Friends, I beseech you, let not these things offend you, but let them rather beget in your hearts an inquiring into the truth of your condition, and be willing to be searched to the bottom; and also, that everything which hath not been planted by the Lord's right hand may be rejected, and that there may be a reaching after better things, even the things that will not only make thy soul think thy state is good now, but that thou mayest be able to look sin, death, Hell, the curse of the law, together with the Judge, in the face with comfort, having such a real, sound, effectual work of God's grace in thy soul, that when thou hearest the trumpet sound, seest the graves fly open, and the dead come creeping forth out of their holes; when thou shalt see the judgment set, the books opened, and all the world standing before the judgment-seat; I say, that then thou mayest stand, and have that blessed sentence spoken to thy soul, "Come, ye blessed of My Father, inherit the kingdom prepared for you from the foundation of the world" (Matthew 25:34).

Objection to This Head

FIRST PART OF THE OBJECTION

But, you will say, for all this, *We cannot believe that we are under the law*, for these reasons—

First. Because we have found a change in our hearts.

Second. Because we deny that the Covenant of Works will save any.

Third. Because, for our parts, we judge ourselves far from legal principles; for we are got up into as perfect a Gospel order, as to matter of practice and discipline in church affairs, as any this day in England, as we judge.

Answer to the First Part of the Objection

That man's belief that is grounded upon anything done in him, or by him only, that man's belief is not grounded upon the death, burial, resurrection, ascension, and intercession of Jesus Christ; for that man that hath indeed good ground of his eternal salvation, his faith is settled upon that object which God is well pleased or satisfied withal, which is that man that was born of Mary, even her first-born Son—that is, he doth apply by faith to his soul the virtues of His death, blood, righteousness, etc., and doth look for satisfaction of soul nowhere else than from that, neither doth the soul seek to give God any satisfaction as to justification any other ways; but doth willingly and cheerfully accept of and embrace the virtues of Christ's death, together with the rest of His things done by Himself on the cross as a sacrifice, and since also as a priest, advocate, mediator, etc.; and doth so really and effectually receive the glories of the same, that thereby—mark that—thereby he is "changed into the same image, from glory to glory" (2 Corinthians 3:18). Thus in general; but yet more particular:

1.) To think that your condition is good because there is some change in you from a loose profane life, to a more close, honest, and civil life and conversation; I say, to think this testimony sufficient to ground the stress of thy salvation upon is very dangerous. First, because such a soul doth not only lay the stress of its salvation besides the man Christ Jesus that died upon the cross; but secondly, because that his confidence is not grounded upon the Savior of sinners, but upon his turning from gross sins to a more refined life—and it may be to the performance of some good duties—which is no Savior; I say, this is very dangerous; therefore read it, and the Lord help you to understand it; for unless you lay the whole stress of the salvation of your souls upon the merits of another man—namely, Jesus—and that by what He did do and is a-doing without you, for certain, as sure as God is in Heaven, your souls will perish. And this must not be notionally neither, as with an assenting of the understanding only; but it must be by the wonderful, invisible, invincible power of the Almighty God, working in your souls by His Spirit such a real, saving, holy faith, that can, through the operation of the same Spirit by which it is wrought, lay hold on and apply these most heavenly, most excellent, most meritorious benefits of the man Christ Jesus, not only to your heads and fancies, but to your very souls and consciences, so effectually, that you may be able by the same faith to challenge the power, madness, malice, rage, and destroying nature either of sin, the law, death, the devil, together with Hell and all other evils, throwing your souls upon the death, burial, resurrection, and intercession of that man Jesus without (Romans 8:32-39). But,

2.) Do you think that there was no change in the five foolish virgins spoken of (Matthew 25:1-3). Yes; there was such a change in those very people, that the five wise ones could give them admittance of walking with them in the most pure ways and institutions of the Gospel of Christ, and yet but foolish; nay, they walked with them, or shall walk with them, until the Lord Jesus Christ shall break down from Heaven, and yet be but foolish virgins, and yet but under the law, and so under the curse, as I said before.

SECOND PART OF THE OBJECTION

But, you say,—We have disowned the Covenant of Works, and turned from that also.

Answer to Second Part of the Objection

This is sooner said than done. Alas, alas! poor souls think because they say, "Grace, grace, it is freely by grace," therefore they are under the Covenant of Grace. A very wide mistake. You must understand thus much, that though you be such as can speak of the grace of the Gospel, yet if you yourselves be not brought under the very Covenant of Grace, you are yet, notwithstanding your talk and profession, very far wide of a sense and of a share in the Covenant of the Grace of God held forth in the Gospel.

The Jews were of a clearer understanding many of them than to conclude that the law, and only the law, was the way to salvation; for they, even they that received not the Christ of God, did expect a Savior should come (John 7:27, 41-43). But they were men that had not the Gospel Spirit, which alone is able to lead them to the very life, marrow, or substance of the Gospel in right terms; and so being muddy in their understandings, being between the thoughts of a Savior and the thoughts of the works of the law, thinking that they must be accomplished for the obtaining of a Savior, and His mercy towards them; I say, between these they fell short of a Savior. As many poor souls in these days, they think they must be saved alone by the Savior, yet they think there is something to be done on their parts for the obtaining of the good-will of the Savior, as their humiliation for sin, their turning from the same, their promises, and vows, and resolutions to become new men, join in church-fellowship, and what not; and thus they, bringing this along with them as a means to help them, they fall short of eternal salvation if they are not converted; see that Scripture (Romans 9:30-32). The Apostle saith there, that they that sought not did obtain, when they that did seek fell short. "What shall we say then?" saith he. "That the Gentiles which sought not after righteousness, have attained to righteousness," yea, "even the righteousness which is of faith." And what else? Why, "but Israel which followed after the law of righteousness, hath not attained to the law of righteousness." How came that to pass? "Because," saith he, "*they sought it* not by faith, but as it were"—mark, he doth not say, altogether, no, "but as it were"—that is, because as they sought, they did a little by the bye lean upon the works of the law. And let me tell you, that this is such a hard thing to beat men off of, that though Paul himself did take the work in hand, he did find enough to do touching it; how is he fain to labor in the ten first chapters of his Epistle to the Romans, for the establishing of those that did even profess largely in the doctrine of grace, and also in that Epistle to the Galatians; and yet lost many, do what he could. Now, the reason why the doctrine of grace doth so hardly down—even with professors—in truth, effectually, it is because there is a principle naturally in man that doth argue against the same, and that thus: Why, saith the soul,

I am a sinner, and God is righteous, holy, and just; His holy Law, therefore, having been broken by me, I must, by all means, if ever I look to be saved, in the first place, be sorry for my sins; secondly, turn from the same; thirdly, follow after good duties, and practise the good things of the law and ordinances of the Gospel, and so hope that God for Christ's sake may forgive all my sins; which is not the way to God as a Father in Christ, but the way, the very way to come to God by the Covenant of Works, or the law, which things I shall more fully clear when I speak to the second doctrine.

Again, therefore, those that this day profess the Gospel, for the generality of them they are such, that, notwithstanding their profession, they are very ignorant of that glorious influence and lustre of the same; I say, they are ignorant of the virtue and efficacy of the glorious things of Christ held forth by and in the Gospel, which doth argue their not being under the Covenant of Grace, but rather under the law or old covenant (2 Corinthians 4:3). As, for instance, if you do come among some professors of the Gospel, in general you shall have them pretty busy and ripe; also able to hold you in a very large discourse in several points of the same glorious Gospel; but if you come to the same people and ask them concerning heart-work, or what work the Gospel hath wrought on them, and what appearance they have had of the sweet influences and virtues on their souls and consciences, it may be they will give you such an answer as this—I do find by the preaching thereof that I am changed, and turned from my sins in a good measure, and also have learned (but only in tongue), to distinguish between the law and the Gospel, so that for the one—that is, for the Gospel—I can plead, and also can show the weakness and unprofitableness of the other. And thus far, it is like they may go, which is not far enough to prove them under the Covenant of Grace, though they may have their tongues so largely tipped with the profession of the same (2 Peter 2:20) where he saith "For if after they have escaped the pollutions of the world through the knowledge of the Lord and Savior Jesus Christ," which was not a saving knowledge, "they are again entangled therein, and overcome, the latter end" of that man "is worse than the beginning" (Matthew 25:1-4, etc; 7:22).

OBJECTION:

But, you will say, is not this a fair declaring of the work of grace, or doth it not discover that, without all gainsaying, we are under the Covenant of Grace, when we are able, not only to speak of the glorious Gospel of Jesus Christ, but also to tell, and that by experience, that we have been changed from worse to better, from sin to a holy life, by leaving of the same, and that by hearing of the Word preached?

ANSWER:

Part 1.) A man may, in the first place, be able to talk of all the mysteries of the Gospel, and that like an angel of God, and yet be no more in God's account than the sounding of a drum, brass, or the tinkling of a cymbal, which are things that, notwithstanding their sound and great noise, are absolutely void of life and motion, and so are accounted with God as nothing—that is, no Christians, no believers, not under the Covenant of Grace for all that (1 Corinthians 13:1-4).

Part 2.) Men may not only do this, but may also be changed in reality, for a season, from what they formerly were, and yet be nothing at all in the Lord's account as to an eternal blessing. Read 2 Peter 2:20, the Scripture which I mentioned before; for, indeed, that one Scripture is enough to prove all that I desire to say as to this very thing; for, if you observe, there is enfolded therein these following things—a. That reprobates may attain to a knowledge of Christ. b. This knowledge may be of such weight and force, that, for the present, it may make them escape the pollutions of the world, and this by hearing the Gospel. "For if after they have escaped the pollutions of the world through the knowledge of the Lord and Savior Jesus Christ, they are again entangled therein, and overcome, the latter end of that man is worse than the beginning." (Some professors, take them at the best, they are but like dogs, spewing out their filth for a time.) Now that they are reprobates, dogs, or sows, read further; "But," saith he, "it is happened unto them according to the true proverb, The dog is turned to his own vomit again; and the sow that was washed to her wallowing in the mire" (Verse 22).

THIRD PART OF THE OBJECTION

The last part of the Objection. But, say you, our practices in the worship of God shall testify for us that we are not under the law; for we have by God's goodness attained to as exact a way of waking in the ordinances of God, and as near the examples of the Apostles, as ever any churches since the primitive times, as we judge.

Answer to the Third Part of the Objection

What then? Do you think that the walking in the order of the churches of old, as to matter of outward worship, is sufficient to clear you of your sins at the judgment-day? or, do you think that God will be contented with a little bodily subjection to that which shall vanish and fade like a flower, when the Lord shall come from Heaven in flaming fire, with His mighty angels (2 Thessalonians 1:7-8). Alas, alas, how will such professors as these are fall before the judgment-seat of Christ! Then such a question as this, "Friend, how camest thou in hither, not having a wedding garment?" will make them be speechless, and fall down into everlasting burnings, thousands on a heap; for you must know that it is not then your crying, Lord, Lord, that will stand you in stead; not your saying, We have ate and drank in Thy presence, that will keep you from standing on the left hand of Christ. It is the principle as well as the practice that shall be inquired into at that day.

QUESTION: The principle, you will say, what do you mean by that?

ANSWER: My meaning is, the Lord Jesus Christ will then inquire and examine whether the spirit from which you acted was legal or evangelical—that is, whether it was the Spirit of adoption that did draw you out to the thing you took in hand, or a mere moral principle, together with some shallow and common illuminations into the outward way of the worship of God, according to Gospel rule.

QUESTION: But, you will say, it is like, How should this be made manifest and appear?

ANSWER: I shall speak briefly in answer hereunto as followeth—First, then, that man that doth take up any of the ordinances of

God—namely, as prayer, baptism, breaking of bread, reading, hearing, alms-deeds, or the like; I say, he that doth practise any of these, or such like, supposing thereby to procure the love of Christ to his own soul, he doth do what he doth from a legal, and not from an evangelical or Gospel spirit: as thus—for a man to suppose that God will hear him for his prayer's sake, for his alm's sake, for his humiliation's sake, or because he hath promised to make God amends hereafter, whereas there is no such thing as a satisfaction to be made to God by our prayers or whatever we can do; I say, there is no such way to have reconciliation with God in. And so also for men to think, because they are got into such and such an ordinance, and have crowded themselves into such and such a society, that therefore they have got pretty good shelter from the wrath of the Almighty; when, alas, poor souls, there is no such thing. No, but God will so set His face against such professors, that His very looks will make them to tear their very flesh; yea, make them to wish would they had the biggest millstone in the world hanged about their neck, and they cast into the midst of the sea. For, friends, let me tell you, though you can now content yourselves without the holy, harmless, undefiled, perfect righteousness of Christ; yet there is a day a-coming in which there is not one of you shall be saved but those that are and shall be found clothed with that righteousness; God will say to all the rest, "Take them, bind them hand and foot, and cast them into outer darkness; there shall be weeping and gnashing of teeth" (Matthew 22:13). For Christ will not say unto men in that day, Come, which of you made a profession of Me, and walked in church-fellowship with My saints: no; but then it shall be inquired into, who have the reality of the truth of grace wrought in their hearts. And, for certain, he that misseth of that shall surely be cast into the Lake of Fire, there to burn with the devils and damned men and women; there to undergo the wrath of an eternal God, and that not for a day, a month, a year, but for ever, for ever, for ever and ever; there is *that* which cutteth to the quick. Therefore, look to it, and consider now what you do, and whereon you hang your souls; for it is not every pin that will hold in the judgment, not every foundation that will be able to hold up the house against those mighty, terrible, soul-drowning floods and destroying tempests which then will roar against the soul and body of a sinner (Luke 6:47-49). And, if the principle be rotten, all will fall, all will come to nothing. Now, the principle is this—Not to do things because we would be saved, but to do them from this—namely, because we do really believe that we are and shall be saved. But do not mistake me; I do not say we should slight any holy duties; God forbid; but I say, he that doth look for life because he doth do good duties, he is under the Covenant of Works, the law; let his duties be never so eminent, so often, so fervent, so zealous. Ay, and I say, as I said before, that if any man or men, or multitudes of people, do get into never so high, so eminent; and clear practices and Gospel order, as to church discipline, if it be done to this end I have been speaking of, from this principle, they must and shall have these sad things fall to their share which I have made mention of.

OBJECTION: But, you will say, can a man use Gospel ordinances with a legal spirit?

ANSWER: Yes, as easily as the Jews could use and practise circumcision, though not the moral or Ten Commandments. For this I shall be bold to affirm, that it is not the commands of the New Testament administration that can keep a man from using of its self (that administration) in a legal spirit; for know this for certain, that it is the principle, not the command, that makes the subjector to the same either legal or evangelical, and so his obedience from that command to be from legal convictions or evangelical principles.

Now, herein the devil is wondrous subtle and crafty, in suffering people to practise the ordinances and commands of the Gospel, if they do but do them in a legal spirit, (I beseech you, do not think because I say this, therefore I am against the ordinances of the Gospel, for I do honor them in their places, yet would not that any of them should be idolised, or done in a wrong spirit,) from a spirit of works; for he knows then, that if he can but get the soul to go on in such a spirit, though they do never so many duties, he shall hold them sure enough; for he knows full well that thereby they do set up something in the room of, or, at the least, to have some, though but a little, share with the Lord Jesus Christ in their salvation; and if he can but get thee here, he knows that he shall cause thee by thy depending a little upon the one, and so thy whole dependence being not upon the other, that is, Christ, and taking of him upon his own terms, thou wilt fall short of life by Christ, though thou do very much busy thyself in a suitable walking, in an outward conformity to the several commands of the Lord Jesus Christ. And let me tell you plainly, that I do verily believe that as Satan by his instruments did draw many of the Galatians by circumcision (though, I say, it was none of the commands of the moral law) to be debtors to do upon pain of eternal damnation the whole of the moral law, so also Satan, in the time of the Gospel, doth use even the commands laid down in the Gospel, some of them, to bind the soul over to do the same law; the thing being done and walked in, by and in the spirit; for, as I said before, it is not the obedience to the command that makes the subjector thereto evangelical, or of a Gospel spirit; but, contrariwise, the principle that leads out the soul to the doing of the command, that makes the persons that do thus practise any command, together with the command by them practised, either legal or evangelical. As, for instance, prayer—it is a Gospel command; yet if he that prays doth it in a legal spirit, he doth make that which in itself is a Gospel command an occasion of leading him into a Covenant of Works, inasmuch as he doth it by and in that old covenant spirit.

Again; giving of alms is a Gospel command; yet if I do give alms from a legal principle, the command to me is not Gospel, but legal, and it binds me over, as aforesaid, to do the whole law—"For he is not a Jew," nor a Christian, "which is one outwardly"—that is, one only by an outward subjection to the ordinances of prayer, hearing, reading, baptism, breaking of bread, etc.—"But he *is* a Jew," a Christian, "which is one inwardly," who is rightly principled, and practiseth the ordinances of the Lord from the leadings forth of the Spirit of the Lord, from a true and saving faith in the Lord (Romans 2:28-29). Those men spoken of in the 7th of Matthew, for certain, for all their great declaration, did not do what they did from a right Gospel spirit; for had they, no question but the Lord would have said, "Well done, good and faithful servant." But in that the Lord Jesus doth turn them away into Hell, notwithstanding their great profession of the Lord, and of their doing in His name, it is evident that notwithstanding all that they did do, they were still under the law, and not under that covenant as true believers are—to wit, the Covenant of Grace; and if so, then all their duties that they did, of which they boasted before the Lord, was not in and by a right evangelical principle or spirit.

Again, saith the Apostle, "Whatsoever is not of faith is sin," (Romans 14:23); but there are some that do even practise baptism, breaking of bread, together with other ordinances, and yet are unbelievers; therefore unbelievers doing these things, they are not done in faith but sin. Now to do these things in sin, or without faith, it is not to do things in an evangelical or Gospel spirit; also they that do these things in a legal spirit, the very practising of them renders them not under the law of Christ, as Head of His Church, but the works they do are so much contradiction to the Gospel of God, or the Covenant of Grace, that they that do them thus do even set up against the Covenant of Grace; and the very performance of them is of such force that it is sufficient to drown them that are subjects there-unto, even under the Covenant of Works; but this poor souls are not aware of, and there is their misery.

QUESTION: But have you no other way to discover the things of the Gospel, how they are done with a legal principle, but those you have already made mention of?

ANSWER: That thou mightest be indeed satisfied herein, I shall show you the very manner and way that a legal, or old-covenant-converted professor, bear with the terms, doth take both in the beginning, middle, and the end of his doing of any duty or command, or whatsoever it be that he doth do. 1. He thinking this or that to be his duty, and considering of the same, he is also presently persuaded in his own conscience that God will not accept of him if he leave it undone; he seeing that he is short of his duty, as he supposeth, while this is undone by him, and also judging that God is angry with him until the thing be done, he, in the second place, sets to the doing of the duty, to the end he may be able to pacify his conscience by doing of the same, persuading of himself that now the Lord is pleased with him for doing of it. 2. Having done it, he contents himself, sits down at his ease, until some further convictions of his duty to be done, which when he seeth and knoweth, he doth do it as aforesaid, from the same principle as he did the former, and so goeth on in his progress of profession. This is to do things from a legal principle, and from an old-covenant spirit; for thus runs that covenant, "The man that doth these things shall live in them," of "by them" (Leviticus 18:5; Galatians 3:12; Romans 10:5). But more of this in the use of this doctrine.

OBJECTION: But, you will say, by these words of yours you do seem to deny that there are conditional promises in the Gospel, as is clear, in that you strike at such practices as are conditional, and commanded to be done upon the same.

ANSWER: The thing that I strike at is this, that a man in or with a legal spirit should not, nay, can not, do any conditional command of the Gospel acceptably, as to his eternal state, because he doth it in an old-covenant spirit. "No man putteth new wine into old bottles"; but new wine must have new bottles, a Gospel command must have a Gospel spirit, or else the wine will break the bottles, or the principle will break the command.

OBJECTION: Then you do grant that there are conditional promises in the New Testament, as in the moral law, or Ten Commandments?

ANSWER: Though this be true, yet the conditional promises in the New Testament do not call to the same people in the same state of unregeneracy to fulfil them upon the same conditions.

The Law and the Gospel being two distinct covenants, they are made in divers ways, and the nature of the conditions also being not the same, as saith the Apostle, the righteousness of the law saith one thing, and the righteousness of faith saith another (Romans 10:4-6). That is, the great condition in the law is, If you do these things, you shall live by them; but the condition, even the greatest condition laid down for a poor soul to do, as to salvation—for it is that we speak of—is to believe that my sins be forgiven me for Jesus Christ's sake, without the works or righteousness of the law, on my part, to help forward. "To him that worketh not," saith the

Apostle (that is) for salvation, "but believeth on Him that justifieth the ungodly, his faith"—mark, "his faith is counted for righteousness" (Romans 4:5). So that we, saith, he, "conclude that a man is justified by faith without"—mark again, "without the deeds of the law" (Romans 3:28).

But again; there is never a condition in the Gospel that can be fulfilled by an unbeliever; and therefore, whether there be conditions or whether there be none, it makes no matter to thee who art without the faith of Christ; for it is impossible for thee in *that* state to do them, so as to be ever the better as to thy eternal estate; therefore, lest thou shouldst split thy soul upon the conditions laid down in the Gospel, as thou wilt do if thou go about to do them only with a legal spirit; but, I say, to prevent this, see if thou canst fulfil the first condition; that is, to believe that all thy sins are forgiven thee, not for any condition that hath been or can be done by thee, but merely for the Man's sake that did hang on Mount Calvary, between two thieves, some sixteen hundred years ago and odd. And, I say, see if thou canst believe that at that time He did, when He hanged on the Cross, give full satisfaction, for all thy sins, before thou in thy person hadst committed ever a one. I say, see if thou canst believe this; and take heed thou deceive not thyself with an historical, notional, or traditional acknowledgment of the same. And, secondly, see if thou canst so well fulfil this condition, that the very virtue and efficacy that it hath on thy soul will engage thee to fulfil those other conditions, really in love to that Man whom thou shouldst believe hath frankly and freely forgiven thee all, without any condition acted by thee to move Him thereto, according to that saying in 2 Corinthians 5:14-15; and then thy doing will arise from a contrary principle than otherwise it will do—that is, then thou wilt not act and do because thou wouldst be accepted of God, but because thou hast some good hope in thy heart that thou art accepted of Him already, and not on thine, but wholly and alone upon another man's account; for here runs the Gospel spirit of faith: "We believe"—mark, "We believe, and therefore speak." So we believe, and therefore do (2 Corinthians 4:13). Take heed, therefore, that you do not DO, that you may believe, but rather believe so effectually that you may DO, even all that Jesus doth require of you from a right principle, even out of love to your dear Lord Jesus Christ, which thing I shall speak to more fully by and by.

OBJECTION: But what do you mean by those expressions? Do not *do* that you may believe, but *believe* so effectually that you may *do*.

ANSWER: When I say, Do not do that you may believe, I mean, do not think that any of the things that thou canst do will procure or purchase faith from God unto thy soul; for that is still the old-covenant spirit, the spirit of the law, to think to have it for thy doing. They that are saved, they are saved by grace, through faith, and that not of themselves, not for anything that they can do, for they are both the free gift of God, "Not of" doing, or of "works, lest any man should," be proud, and "boast" (Ephesians 2:8-9). Now, some people be so ignorant as to think that God will give them Christ, and so all the merits of His, if they will be but valiant, and do something to please God, that they may obtain Him at His hands; but let me tell them, they may lose a thousand souls quickly, if they had so many, by going this way to work, and yet be never the better; for the Lord doth not give His Christ to any upon such conditions, but He doth give Him freely; that is, without having respect to anything that is in thee (Revelation 22:17; Isaiah 55:1-2). To him that is athirst will I give; He doth not say, I will sell; but, I will give him the water of life freely (Revelation 21:6).

Now, if Christ doth give it, and that freely, then He doth not sell if for anything that is in the creature; but Christ doth give Himself, as also doth His Father, and that freely, not because there is anything in us, or done by us, that moves Him there-unto. If it were by doing, then, saith Paul, "Grace is not grace," seeing it is obtained by works; but grace is grace, and that is the reason it is given to men without their works. And if it be by grace, that is, if it be a free gift from God, without anything foreseen as done, or to be done, by the creature, then it is not of works, which is clear; therefore it is grace, without the works of the law. But if you say, Nay, it is of something in the man done by him that moves God thereunto; then you must conclude that either grace is no grace, or else that works are grace and not works. Do but read with understanding (Romans 11:6).

Now before I go any further, it may be necessary to speak a word or two to some poor souls that are willing to close in with Jesus Christ, and would willingly take Him upon His own terms, only they being muddy in their minds, and have not yet attained the understanding of the terms and conditions of the two covenants, they are kept off from closing with Christ; and all is, because they see they can do nothing (to merit His favor). As, for example, come to some souls, and ask them how they do, they will tell you presently that they are so bad that it is not to be expressed. If you bid them believe in Jesus Christ, they will answer that they can not believe; if you ask them why they can not believe, they will answer, because their hearts are so hard, so dead, so dull, so backward to good duties; and if their hearts were but better, if they were more earnest, if they could pray better, and keep their hearts more from running after sin, then they could believe; but should they believe with such vile hearts, and presume to believe in Christ, and be so filthy? Now all this is because the spirit of the law still ruleth in such souls, and blinds them so that they can not see the terms of the Gospel. To clear this, take the substance or the drift of these poor souls, which is this—"If I were better, then I think I could believe; but being so bad as I am, that is the reason that I can not." This is just to do something that I may believe, to work that I may have Christ, to do the law that I may have the Gospel; or thus, to be righteous that I may come to Christ. O man! thou must go quite back again, thou art out of the way, thou must believe, *because* thou canst not pray, *because* thou canst not do; thou must believe, because there is nothing in thee naturally that is good, or desireth after good, or else thou wilt never come to Christ as a sinner; and if so, then Christ will not receive thee; and if so, then thou mayest see that to keep off from Christ because thou canst not do, is to be kept from Christ by the law, and to stand off from Him because thou canst not buy Him. Thus having spoken something by the way for the direction of those souls that would come to Christ, I shall return to the former discourse, wherein ariseth this objection:

OBJECTION: But you did but even now put souls upon fulfilling the first condition of the Gospel, even to believe in Christ, and so be saved; but now you say it is alone by grace, without condition; and therefore by these words, there is first a contradiction to your former sayings, and also that men may be saved without the condition of faith, which to me seems a very strange thing. I desire, therefore, that you would clear out what you have said, to my satisfaction.

ANSWER: 1.) Though there be a condition commanded in the Gospel, yet He that commands the condition doth not leave His children to their own natural abilities, that in their own strength they should fulfil them, as the law doth; but the same God that doth command that the condition be fulfilled, even He doth help His children by His Holy Spirit to fulfil the same condition; "For it is God which worketh in you"—mark "in you," believers, "both to will and to do of *His* own good pleasure" (Philippians 2:13). "Thou also hast wrought all our works in us, and for us" (Isaiah 26:12). So that, if the condition be fulfilled, it is not done by the ability of the creature. But,

2.) Faith, as it is a gift of God, or an act of ours, take it which way you will, if we speak properly of salvation, it is not the first nor the second cause of our salvation, but the third, and that but instrumentally neither—that is, it only layeth hold of and applieth to us that which saveth us, which is the love of God, through the merits of Christ, which are the two main causes of our salvation, without which all other things are nothing, whether it be faith, hope, love, or whatever can be done by us. And to this the great Apostle of the Gentiles speaks fully, for, saith he, "God, who is rich in mercy, loved us, even when we were dead in sins" (Ephesians 2:4-5). That is, when we were without faith, and that was the cause why we believed for He thereby hath quickened us together, through the meritorious cause, which is Christ, and so hath saved us by grace—that is, of His own voluntary love and good will; the effect of which was this, He gave us faith to believe in Christ. Read soberly Ephesians 2:4-8. Faith, as the gift of God, is not the Savior, as our act doth merit nothing; faith was not the cause that God gave Christ as the first, neither is it the cause why God converts men to Christ; but faith is a gift bestowed upon us by the gracious God, the nature of which is to lay hold on Christ, that God afore did give for a ransom to redeem sinners; this faith hath its nourishment and supplies from the same God that at the first did give it, and is the only instrument, through the Spirit, that doth keep the soul in a comfortable frame, both to do and suffer for Christ; helps the soul to receive comfort from Christ when it can get none from itself, beareth up the soul in its progress heavenwards. But that it is the first cause of salvation, that I deny, or that it is the second, I deny; but it is only the instrument, or hand, that receiveth the benefits, that God hath prepared for thee before thou hadst any faith; so that we do nothing for salvation as we are men. But if we speak properly, it was God's grace that moved Him to give Christ a ransom for sinners; and the same God, with the same grace, that doth give to the soul faith to believe, and so, by believing, to close in with Him whom God out of His love and pity did send into the world to save sinners, so that all the works of the creature are shut out as to justification and life, and men are saved freely by grace. I shall speak no more here; but in my discourse upon the second covenant, I shall answer a Hell-bred objection or two, to forewarn sinners how they turn the grace of God into wantonness.

And thus, you see, I have briefly spoken to you something touching the law. First, what it is, and when given; secondly, how sad those men's conditions are that are under it; thirdly, who they are that be under it; fourthly, how far they may go, and what they may do and receive, and yet be under it; which hath been done by way of answers to several questions, for the better satisfaction of those that may stand in doubt of the truth of what hath been delivered.

Now, in the next place, I shall come to some application of the truth of that which hath been spoken; but I shall in the first place speak something to he second doctrine, and then afterwards I shall speak something by way of use and application to this first doctrine.

THE SECOND DOCTRINE

THE PEOPLE OF GOD ARE NOT UNDER THE LAW BUT UNDER GRACE

The second doctrine now to be spoken to is, TO SHOW THAT THE PEOPLE OF GOD ARE NOT UNDER THE LAW BUT UNDER GRACE—

"For ye are not under the law, but under grace." —Rom. 6:14

You may well remember that from these words I did observe these two great truths of the Lord—FIRST, That there are some in Gospel times that are under the law, or Covenant of Works. SECOND, That there is never a believer under the law, or Covenant of Works, but under grace. I have spoken something to the former of these truths—to wit, that there are some under the law, together with who they are, and what their condition is, that are under it. Now I am to speak to the second, and to show you who they are, and what their condition is, that are under that (Covenant of Grace).

But before I come to that, I shall speak a few words to show you what the word "grace" in this place signifies; (I touched upon this in the first doctrine) for the word "grace" in the Scripture referreth sometimes to favor with men (Genesis 33:10; 39:4; 50:4). Sometimes to holy qualifications of saints (2 Corinthians 8:7). And sometimes to hold forth the condescension of Christ in coming down from the glory which He had with His Father before the world was, to be made of no reputation, and a servant to men (2 Corinthians 8:9; Philippians 2:7). Again: sometimes it is taken for the free, rich, and unchangeable love of God to man, through Jesus Christ, that for our cause and sakes did make Himself poor; and so it is to be understood in these words, "For ye are not under the law," to be cursed, and damned, and sent headlong to Hell, "but" you are "under grace," to be saved, to be pardoned, to be preserved, "and kept by the mighty power of God, through faith," which alone is the gift of grace, "unto eternal glory." This one Scripture alone proves the same—"For by grace are ye saved" (Ephesians 2:8), by free grace, by rich grace, by unchangeable grace. And you are saved from the curse of the law; from the power, guilt, and filth of sin; from the power, malice, madness, and rage of the devil; from the wishes, curses, and desires of wicked men; from the hot, scalding, flaming, fiery furnace of Hell; from being arraigned as malefactors, convinced, judged, condemned, and fettered with the chains of our sins to the devils to all eternity; and all this freely, freely by His grace (Romans 3:24) by rich grace unchangeable grace; for, saith He, "I *am* the LORD, I change not: therefore ye sons of Jacob are not consumed" (Malachi 3:6). This is grace indeed.

The word "grace," therefore, in this Scripture (Romans 6:14) is to be understood of the free love of God in Christ to sinners, by virtue of the new covenant, in delivering them from the power of sin, from the curse and condemning power of the old covenant, from the destroying nature of sin, by its continual workings; as is all evident if you read with understanding the words as they lie—"For," saith he, "sin shall not have dominion over you," or, it shall not domineer, reign, or destroy you, though you have transgressed against the Covenant of Works, the law; and the reason is rendered in these words, "For ye are not under the law"—that is, under that which accuseth, chargeth, condemneth and brings execution on the soul for sin—"but under grace"; that is, under that which frees you, forgives you, keeps you, and justifies you from all your sins, adversaries, or whatever may come in to lay anything to your charge to damn you. For that is truly called grace in this sense that doth set a man free from all his sins, deliver him from all the curses of the law, and what else can be laid to His charge, freely, without any foresight in God to look at what good will be done by the party that hath offended; and also that doth keep the soul by the same power through faith—which also is his own proper gift—unto eternal glory.

Again; that it is a pardon not conditional, but freely given, consider, first, it is set in opposition to works—"Ye are not under the law." Secondly, The promise that is made to them (saying, "Sin shall not have dominion over you") doth not run with any condition as on their part to be done; but merely and alone because they were under, or because they had the grace of God extended to them. "Sin shall not have dominion over you: for," mark the reason, "ye are not under the law, but under grace."

The words being thus opened, and the truth thus laid down,—HOW THERE IS NEVER A BELIEVER UNDER THE COVENANT OF WORKS, BUT UNDER GRACE, the free, rich, unchangeable love of God, it remaineth that, in the first place, we prove the doctrine, and after that proceed.

THE DOCTRINE PROVED

Now in the doctrine there are two things to be considered and proved—FIRST, *That believers are under grace.* SECONDLY, *Not under the law as a Covenant of Works;* for so you must understand me. For these two we need go no further than the very words themselves; the first part of the words proves the first part of the doctrine, "Ye are not under the law"; the second part proves the other, "but" ye are "under grace." But besides these, consider with me a few things for the demonstrating of these truths, as,

FIRST. They are not under the law, because their sins are pardoned, which could not be if they were dealt withal according to the law, and their being under it; for the law alloweth of no repentance, but accuseth, curseth and condemneth every one that is under it—"Cursed is every one that continueth not in all things which are written in the Book of the Law to do them" (Galatians 3:10). But, I say, believers having their sins forgiven them, it is because they are under another, even a new covenant—"Behold, the days come, saith the LORD, when I will make a new covenant with them."—"For I will be merciful to their unrighteousness, and their sins and their iniquities will I remember no more" (Hebrews 8:12).

SECOND. They are not under the law, because their sins and iniquities are not only forgiven, but they are forgiven them freely.

They that stand in the first covenant, and continue there, are to have never a sin forgiven them unless they can give God a complete satisfaction; for the law calls for it at their hands, saying, "Pay me that thou owest." O! but when God deals with His saints by the Covenant of Grace it is not so; for it is said, "And when" He saw "they had nothing to pay, He frankly" and freely "forgave them" all—"I will heal their backsliding; I will love them freely."—I will blot "out thy transgressions for Mine own sake," etc. (Luke 7:42; Hosea 14:4; Isaiah 43:25).

THIRD. The saints are not under the law, because the righteousness that they stand justified before God in is not their own actual righteousness by the law, but by imputation, and is really the righteousness of Another—namely, of God in Christ (2 Corinthians 5:21; Philippians 3:9). "Even the righteousness of God, *which is* by faith of Jesus Christ unto all and upon all," that is, imputed to "them that believe" (Romans 3:22). But if they were under the old covenant, the Covenant of Works, then their righteousness must be their own, (But it is impossible that the righteousness of man by the law should save him.) or no forgiveness of sins—"If thou doest well, shalt thou not be accepted?" but if thou transgress, "sin lieth at the door," saith the law (Genesis 4:7).

FOURTH. In a word, whatsoever they do receive, whether it be conversion to God; whether it be pardon of sin; whether it be faith or hope; whether it be righteousness; whether it be strength" whether it be the Spirit, or the fruits thereof; whether it be victory over sin, death, or Hell; whether it be Heaven, everlasting life, and glory inexpressible; or whatsoever it be, it comes to them freely, God having no first eye to what they would do, or should do, for the obtaining of the same. But to take this in pieces—1.) In a word, are they converted? God finds them first, for, saith He, "I am found of *them that* sought Me not" (Isaiah 65:1). 2.) Have they pardon of sin? They have that also freely—"I will heal their backsliding, I will love them freely" (Hosea 14:4). 3.) Have they faith? It is the gift of God in Christ Jesus, and He is not only the Author, that is, the beginner thereof, but He doth also perfect the same (Hebrews 12:2). 4.) Have they hope? It is God that is the first cause thereof—"Remember the word unto Thy servant, upon which Thou hast caused me to hope" (Psalms 119:49). 5.) Have they righteousness? It is the free gift of God (Romans 5:17). 6.) Have they strength to do the work of God in their generations, or any other thing that God would have them do? That also is a free gift from the Lord, for without Him we neither do nor can do anything (John 15:5). 7.) Have we comfort, or consolation? We have it not for what we have done, but from God through Christ; for He is the God of all comforts and consolation (2 Corinthians 1:3-7). 8.) Have we the Spirit, or the fruits thereof? it is the gift of the Father—"how much more shall *your* heavenly Father give the Holy Spirit to them that ask Him (Luke 11:13)? "Thou has wrought all our works in us" (Isaiah 26:12).

And so, I say, whether it be victory over sin, death, Hell, or the devil, it is given us by the victory of Christ—"But thanks be to God which giveth us the victory through our Lord Jesus Christ" (1 Corinthians 15:57; Romans 7:24-25). Heaven and glory it is also the gift of Him who giveth us richly all things to enjoy (Matthew 25:34).

So that these things, if they be duly and soberly considered, will give satisfaction in this thing. I might have added many more for the clearing of these things; as 1. When God came to man to convert him, He found him a dead man (Ephesians 2:1-2). He found him an enemy to God, Christ, and the salvation of his own soul; He found him wallowing in all manner of wickedness; He found him taking pleasure therein; with all delight and greediness. 2.) He was fain to quicken him by putting His Spirit into him, and to translate him by the mighty operation thereof. He was fain to reveal Christ Jesus unto him, man being altogether senseless and ignorant of this blessed Jesus (Matthew 11:25, 27; 1 Corinthians 2:7-10). 4.) He was fain to break the snare of the devil, and to let poor man, poor bound and fettered man, out of the chains of the enemy.

I. THE NEW COVENANT FREE AND UNCHANGEABLE,
II. WHO ARE BROUGHT UNDER IT,
III. AND THEIR PRIVILEGES

Now we are to proceed, and the things that we are to treat upon in the second place are these—

FIRST. (Besides the reasons already given.) *Why is it a free and unchangeable grace?* SECOND. *Who they are that are actually brought into His free and unchangeable Covenant of Grace, and how they are brought in?* THIRD. *What are the privileges of those that are actually brought into this free and glorious grace of the glorious God of Heaven and glory?*

I. THE NEW COVENANT IS FREE AND UNCHANGEABLE BECAUSE IT WAS MADE WITH CHRIST

1. WHY IT IS A FREE AND UNCHANGEABLE GRACE

And for the opening of this we must consider, first, How and through Whom this grace doth come to be, first, free to us, and, secondly, unchangeable? This grace is free to us through conditions in Another—that is, by way of covenant or bargain; for this grace comes by way of covenant or bargain to us, yet made with Another for us.

FIRST. That it comes by way of covenant, contract, or bargain, though not personally with us, be pleased to consider these Scriptures, where it is said, "I have made a covenant with My Chosen: I have sworn unto David (The word David in this place signifieth Christ, as also in these Scriptures—(Ezekiel 34:23-24; 37:24-25).) My servant" (Psalms 89:3). "And as for Thee also, by the blood of Thy covenant," speaking of Christ, "I have sent forth Thy prisoners out of the pit wherein is no water," (Zechariah 9:9-11).

Again; "Ye have sold yourselves for nought; and ye shall be redeemed without money" (Isaiah 52:3). Blessed be the Lord," therefore, saith Zacharias, "for He hath visited and" also "redeemed His people, and hath raised up an horn of salvation for us in the house of His servant David; as He spake by the mouth of His holy Prophets, which have been since the world began; that we should be saved from our enemies, and from the hands of all that hate us; to perform the mercy promised to our fathers, and to remember His holy covenant," or bargain (Luke 1:68-72). (I might give you more Scriptures; but pray consider the second thing.) And if any should be offended with the plainness of these words, as some poor souls may be through ignorance, let them be pleased to read soberly Isaiah 49:1-12, and there they may see that it runs as plain a bargain as if two would be making of a bargain between themselves, and concluding upon several conditions on both sides. But more of this hereafter. Now,

SECOND. This covenant, I say, was made with One, not with many, and also confirmed in the conditions of it with One, not with several. First, that the covenant was made with One (Galatians 3:16). "Now to Abraham and his Seed were the promises made. He saith not, And to seeds, as of many; but as of one, And to thy Seed, which is Christ" (Verse 17). "And this, I say, *that* the covenant that was confirmed before of God, in Christ," etc. The covenant was made with the Seed of Abraham; not the seeds, but the Seed, which is the Lord Jesus Christ, our Head and Undertaker in the things concerning the covenant.

THIRD. The condition was made with One, and also accomplished by Him alone, and not by several; yet in the nature, and for the everlasting deliverance of many; even by one man Jesus Christ, as it is clear from Romans 5:15-17, etc., and in Zechariah 9:11, the Lord saith to Christ, "And as for Thee"—mark, "As for Thee also, by the blood of Thy covenant," or as for Thee whose covenant was by blood; that is, the condition of the covenant was, that Thou shouldst spill Thy blood; which having been done in the account of God, saith He, I according to My condition have let go the prisoners, or sent them "out of the pit wherein is no water." Those Scriptures in Galatians 3:16-17 that are above cited, are notably to our purpose;

Verse 16 saith it was made with Christ, Verse 17 saith it was also confirmed in or with God in Him. Pray read with understanding. "Now," saith Paul, "the promises were not made unto seeds, as of many; but as of one, And to thy Seed, which is Christ." ... "The law, which was four hundred and thirty years after, can not disannul, that it should make the promise of none effect." Not that the covenant was made with Abraham and Christ together, as two persons that were the undertakers of the same; the promise was made with, or to, Abraham afterwards; but the covenant with Christ before.

Neither Abraham Nor The Fathers Were Able To Undertake The Accomplishment Of This Covenant

Further, that the covenant was not personally made with Abraham, no, nor with any of the fathers, neither so as that they were the persons that should stand engaged to be the accomplishers thereof, either in whole or in part; which is very clear.

FIRST. Because this covenant was not made with God and the creature; not with another poor Adam, that only stood upon the strength of natural abilities; but this covenant was made with the second Person, with the Eternal Word of God; with Him that was every-ways as holy, as pure, as infinite, as powerful, and as everlasting as God (Proverbs 8:22-31; Isaiah 9:6; Zechariah 13:7; Philippians 2:6; Hebrews 1; Revelation 1:11-17; 22:13, 17).

SECOND. This covenant or bargain was made in deed and in truth before man was in being. O! God thought of the salvation of man before there was any transgression of man; for then, I say, and not since then, was the Covenant of Grace made with the Undertaker thereof; for all the other sayings are to show unto us that glorious plot and contrivance that was concluded on before time between the Father and the Son, which may very well be concluded on for a truth from the Word of God, if you consider, 1. That the Scripture doth declare that the price was agreed on by the Son before time; 2. The promise was made to Him by the Father that He should have His bargain before time; 3. The choice, and who they were that should be saved was made before time, even before the world began.

1.) For the first, That the price was agreed upon before the world began. Consider the word which speaketh of the price that was paid for sinners, even the precious blood of Christ; it saith of Him, "Who verily was foreordained before the foundation of the world, but was manifest in these last times for you, who by Him do believe," etc. (1 Peter 1:20-21). Mark, it was foreordained or concluded on between the Father and the Son before the world began.

2.) The promise from God to the Son was also made in the same manner, as it is clear where the Apostle saith with comfort to his soul, that he had "hope of eternal life, which God, that can not lie, promised before the world began," (Titus 1:2) which could be to none but the Mediator of the new covenant, because there was none else to whom it should be made but He.

3.) The choice was also made then, even before man had a being in this world, as it is evident where he saith, "Blessed *be* the God and Father of our Lord Jesus Christ, who hath blessed us with all spiritual blessings in heavenly *places* IN Christ: according as He hath chosen us in Him before the foundation of the world, that we should be holy and without blame before Him in love" (Ephesians 1:3-4). (Did I think this would meet with any opposition, I should be in this more large.) Nay, did I look upon it here to be necessary, I should show you very largely and clearly that God did not only make the covenant with Christ before the world began, and the conditions thereof, but I could also show you that the very saints' qualifications, as part of the covenant, was then concluded on by the Father and the Son according to these Scriptures, which, it may be, I may touch upon further anon (Ephesians 1:3-4; 2:10; Romans 8:28). But,

THIRD. This covenant was not made with any of the fathers, neither in whole nor in part, as the undertakers thereof; for then it must be also concluded that they are co-partners with Christ in our salvation, and so that Christ is not Mediator alone; but this would be blasphemy for any once to surmise. And therefore, by the way, when thou readest of the new covenant in Scripture as though it was made with Adam, Noah, Abraham, or David, thou art to consider thus with thyself—1. That God spake to them in such a way for to show or signify unto us how He did make the covenant that He did make with Christ before the world began, they being types of Him. 2. That He thereby might let them understand that He was the same then as He is now, and now as He was then; and that then it was resolved on between His Son and HIM, that in after ages His Son should in their natures, from their loins, and for their sins, be born of a woman, hanged on the Cross, etc., for them: for all along you may see that when He speaketh to them of the new covenant, He mentions their seed—their seed—still aiming at Christ; Christ, the Seed of the woman, was to break the serpent's head (Genesis 3:15, 17; Psalms 89:36). Now to Abraham and his Seed was the promise made; his Seed shall endure for ever, and His throne as the days of Heaven, etc.; still pointing at Christ. And, 3. To stir up their faith and expectations to be constant unto the end in waiting for that which He and His Son had concluded on before time, and what He had since the conclusion declared unto the world by the Prophets. 4. It appeareth that the heart of God was much delighted therein also, as is evident, in that He was always in every age declaring of that unto them which before He had prepared for them. O this good God of Heaven!

OBJECTION: But you will say, perhaps, the Scriptures say plainly that the new covenant was and is made with believers, saying, "The days come, saith the Lord, that I will make a new covenant with the house of Israel, and with the house of Judah; not according to the covenant that I made with their fathers in the day when I led them out of the land of Egypt," etc. (Hebrews 8:8-10). So that it doth not run with Christ alone, but with believers also—I will make a new covenant with the house of Israel and Judah, etc. (Jeremiah 31:33).

ANSWER #1: It can not be meant that the new covenant was made with Christ, and the house of Israel and Judah as the undertakers thereof; for so it was made with Christ alone, which is clear, in that it was made long before the house of Israel and Judah had a being, as I showed before. But,

ANSWER #2: These words here are spoken, first, to show rather the end of the ceremonies than the beginning or rise of the new covenant. Mind a little; the Apostle is laboring to beat the Jews, to whom he wrote this Epistle, off of the ceremonies of the law, of the priests, altar, offerings, temple, etc., and to bring them to the right understanding of the thing and things that they held forth, which were to come, and to put an end to those. If you do but understand the Epistle to the Hebrews, it is a discourse that showeth that the Son of God being come, there is an end put to the ceremonies; for they were to continue so long and no longer—"It," saith the Apostle, "*stood in meats and drinks, and divers washings, and carnal ordinances imposed on them* until the time of reformation"; that is, until Christ did come. "But Christ being come an high priest of good things to come," etc., puts an end to the things and ordinances of the Levitical priesthood. Read the 7th, 8th, 9th, and 10th Chapters of Hebrews, and you will find this true. So, then, when He saith, "The days come in which I make a new covenant," it is rather to be meant a changing of the administration, taking away the type, the shadow, the ceremonies from the house of Israel and Judah, and relieving by the birth of Christ, and the death of Christ, and the offering of the body of Him whom the shadows and types did point out to be indeed He whom God the Father had given for a ransom by covenant for the souls of the saints; and also to manifest the truth of that covenant which was made between the Father and the Son before the world began; for though the new covenant was made before the world began, and also every one in all ages was saved by the virtue of that covenant, yet that covenant was never so clearly made manifest as at the coming, death, and resurrection of Christ; and therefore, saith the Scripture, "He hath brought life and immortality to light through the Gospel." "Who hath saved us, and called *us* with an holy calling" not according to" the "works" of righteousness which we have done, "but according to His own purpose and grace, which was given us in Christ Jesus before the world began," there is the covenant, but it was "made MANIFEST by the APPEARING of our Savior Jesus Christ, who hath abolished death, and brought life and immortality to LIGHT through the Gospel" (2 Timothy 1:9-10). Therefore, I say, these words are therefore to discover that the time was come to change the dispensation, to take away the type, and bring in the substance, and so manifesting that more clearly which before lay hid in dark sayings and figures. And this is usual with God to speak in this manner.

Again; if at any time you do find in Scripture that the Covenant of Works is spoken of as the first covenant that was manifested, and so before the second covenant, yet you must understand that it was so only as to manifestation—that is, it was first given to man, yet not made before that which was made with Christ; and indeed it was requisite that it should be given or made known first, that thereby there might be a way made for the second, by its discovering of sin, and the sad state that man was in after the Fall by reason of that. And again, that the other might be made the more welcome to the sons of men. Yet the second Adam was before the first, and also the second covenant before the first. This is a riddle). And in this did Christ in time most gloriously answer Adam, who was the figure of Christ, as well as of other things. Romans 5. For, Was the first covenant made with the first Adam? so was the second covenant made with the second; for these are and were the two great public persons, or representers of the whole world, as to the first and second covenants; and therefore you find God speaking on this wise in Scripture concerning the new covenant—"My covenant shall stand fast with HIM." "My mercy will I keep for HIM for evermore," saith God: "My covenant shall stand fast with HIM" (Psalms 89:28, 34-35); this HIM is Christ, if you compare this with Luke 1:32, "My covenant will I not break"—namely, that which was made with HIM—"nor alter the thing that is gone out of My mouth. Once I have sworn by My holiness that I will not lie unto David," (David here is to be understood Christ.) to whom this was spoken figuratively in the Person of Christ; for that was God's usual way to speak of the glorious things of the Gospel in the time of the Law, as I said before.

The Conditions of the New Covenant

The conditions also were concluded on and agreed to be fulfilled by Him: as it is clear, if you understand His saying in the 12th of John, at the 27th verse, where He foretelleth His death, and saith, "Now is My soul troubled; and what shall I say? Father, save Me from this hour: but for this cause came I" into the world "unto this hour"; as if He had said, My business is now not to shrink from My sufferings that are coming upon Me; for these are the things that are a great part of the conditions contracted in the covenant which stands between My Father and Me; therefore I shall not pray that this might be absolutely removed from Me; For, "for this cause came I" into the world; even this was the very terms of the covenant. By this you may see, "we are under grace."

Now in a covenant there are these three things to be considered—1.) What it is that is covenanted for. 2.) The conditions upon which the persons who are concerned in it do agree. 3.) If the conditions on both sides be not according to the agreement fulfilled, then the covenant standeth not, but is made void. And this new covenant in these particulars is very exactly fulfilled and made out in Christ.

FIRST. The thing or things covenanted for was the salvation of man, but made good in Christ—"The Son of Man is come to seek and to save that which was lost. The Son of Man did not come to destroy men's lives, but to save them. I gave My life a ransom for many. And this is the will," or covenant, "of Him that sent Me, that of all which He hath given Me, I should lose nothing, but should raise it up again at the last day" (John 6:39).

SECOND. As touching the conditions agreed on, they ran thus—

1.) On the Mediator's side, that He should come into the world; and then on the Father's side, that He should give Him a body. This was one of the glorious conditions between the Father and Christ; "Wherefore, when He cometh into the world, He saith, Sacrifice and offering Thou wouldest not"—that is, the old covenant must not stand, but give way to another sacrifice which Thou hast prepared, which is the giving up My Manhood to the strokes of Thy justice—"for a body Thou hast prepared Me" (Hebrews 10:5). This doth prove us under grace.

2.) On the Mediator's side, that He should be put to death; and on God the Father's side, that He should raise Him up again; this was concluded on also to be done between God the Father and His Son Jesus Christ. On Christ's side, that He should die to give the justice of His Father satisfaction, and so to take away the curse that was due to us, wretched sinners, by reason of our transgressions; and that God His Father, being every ways fully and completely satisfied, should by His mighty power revive and raise Him up again. He hath "brought again—our Lord Jesus"; that is, from death to life, through the virtue or effectual satisfaction that He received from the blood that was shed according to the terms "of the Everlasting Covenant" (Hebrews 13:20).

3.) On the Mediator's side, that He should be made a curse; and on the Father's side, that through Him sinners should be inheritors of the blessing. What wonderful love doth there appear by this in the heart of our Lord Jesus, in suffering such things for our poor bodies and souls? (Galatians 3:13-14). This is grace.

4.) That on the Mediator's side there should be by Him a victory over Hell, death, and the devil, and the curse of the Law; and on the Father's side, that these should be communicated to sinners, and they set at liberty thereby—"Turn you to the stronghold," saith God, "ye prisoners of hope; even today do I declare *that* I will render double unto thee" (Zechariah 9:12). Why so? It is because of the blood of My Son's covenant (Verse 11); which made Paul, though sensible of a body of death, and of the sting that death did strike into the souls of all those that are found in their sins, bold to say, "O death! where is thy sting? O grave! where is thy victory? The sting of death is sin." That is true, and the terrible Law of God doth aggravate and set it home with insupportable torment and pain. But shall I be daunted at this? No, "I thank my God through Jesus Christ He hath given me this victory." So that now, though I be a sinner in myself, yet I can, by believing in Jesus Christ, the Mediator of this new covenant, triumph over the devil, sin, death, and Hell; and say, Do not fear, my soul, seeing the victory is obtained over all my enemies through my Lord Jesus Christ (1 Corinthians 15:55-57). This is the way to prove ourselves under grace.

5.) That on the Mediator's side He should by thus doing bring in everlasting righteousness for saints (Daniel 9:24); and that the Father for this should give them an everlasting kingdom (1 Peter 1:3-5; Ephesians 1:4; 2 Timothy 4:18; Luke 22:28-29). But:

THIRD. (How the conditions are fulfilled). In the next place, this was not all—that is, the Covenant of Grace, with the conditions thereof, was not only concluded on by both parties to be done, but Jesus Christ (Christ is put into office by the Father, to do all things contained in the new covenant). must be authorised to do what was concluded on touching this covenant by way of office. I shall therefore speak a word or two also touching the offices, at least, some of them, that Christ Jesus did and doth still execute as the Mediator of the new covenant, which also were typed out in the Levitical law; for this is the way to prove that we are not under the law, but under grace. And,

I. Christ is *the Surety* of the New Covenant

His first office, after the covenant was made and concluded upon, was that Jesus should *become bound as a Surety*, (His Surety-ship). and stand engaged upon oath to see that all the conditions of the covenant that were concluded on between Him and His Father should, according to the agreement, be accomplished by Him; and that after that, He should be the Messenger from God to the world to declare the mind of God touching the tenor and nature of both the covenants, especially of the new one. The Scripture saith, that Jesus Christ was not only made a priest by an oath, but also a Surety, or bondsman, as in Hebrews 7:21-22. In the 21st Verse he speaketh of the priesthood of Christ, that it was with an oath; and saith, in the 22nd Verse, "By so much" also "was Jesus made a Surety of a better testament," or covenant.

Now the covenant was not only made on Jesus Christ's side with an oath, but also on God the Father's side, that it might be for the better ground of establishment to all those that are, or are to be, the children of the promise. Methinks it is wonderful to consider that the God and Father of our souls, by Jesus Christ, should be so bent upon the salvation of sinners, that He would covenant with His Son Jesus for the security of them, and also that there should pass an oath on both sides for the confirmation of Their resolution to do good. As if the Lord had said, My Son, Thou and I have here made a covenant, that I on My part should do thus and thus, and that Thou on Thy part shouldst do so and so. Now that We may give these souls the best ground of comfort that may be, there shall pass an oath on both sides, that Our children may see that We do indeed love them. "Wherein God, willing more abundantly to show unto the heirs of promise the immutability of His counsel," in making of the covenant, "confirmed it by an oath: that we might have a strong consolation, who have fled for refuge to lay hold upon the hope set before us" (Hebrews 6:17-18; 7:21). Mark, the 6th Chapter saith, God confirmed His part by an oath; and the 7th saith, Christ was made or set on His office also by an oath. Again, "Once," saith God, "have I sworn by My holiness, that I will not lie unto David," "nor alter the thing that is gone out of My mouth," (Psalms 89:34-35) as was before cited.

Herein you may see that God and Christ were in good earnest about the salvation of sinners; for as soon as ever the covenant was made, the next thing was, who should be bound to see all those things fulfilled which were conditioned on between the Father and the Son: the angels, they could have no hands in it; the world could not do it; the devils had rather see them damned than they would wish them the least good; thus Christ looked, and there was none to help; though the burden lay never so heavy upon His shoulder, He must bear it Himself; for there was none besides Himself to uphold, or so much as to step in to be bound, to see the conditions, before mentioned, fulfilled neither in whole nor in part (Isaiah 63:1-7). So that He must not be only He with whom the covenant was made, but He must also become the bondsman or surety thereof, and so stand bound to see that all and every particular thing conditioned for should be, both in manner, and matter, at the time and place, according to the agreement, duly and orderly fulfilled. Is not this grace?

Now as touching the nature of a surety and his work, in some things it is well known to most men; therefore I shall be very brief upon it.

1.) You know a surety is at the bargain's making; and so was Christ—"Then was I beside Him" (Proverbs 8:30).

2.) A surety must consent to the terms of the agreement, or covenant; and so did Christ Jesus. Now that which He did engage should be done for sinners, according to the terms of the covenant; it was this—1. That there should be a complete satisfaction given to God for the sins of the world; for that was one great thing that was agreed upon when the covenant was made (Hebrews 10:5, 17). 2. That Jesus Christ should, as aforesaid, bring in an everlasting righteousness to clothe the saints (His body) withal (Daniel 9:24-25). Here is grace. 3. That He should take in charge to see all those forthcoming without spot or wrinkle at the day of His glorious appearing from Heaven in judgment, and to quit them before the Judgment-seat. Again,

3.) In the work of a surety there is required by the creditor that the surety should stand to what he is bound; and on the surety's side there is a consenting there-unto. 1. The creditor looks, that in case the debtor proves a bankrupt, that then the surety should engage the payment. Is not this grace? (However it is in other engagements, it is thus in this). 2. The creditor looks that the surety should be an able man. Now our Surety was, and is, in this case, every way suitable; for He is heir of all things. 3. The creditor appoints the day, and also looks that the covenant should be kept, and the debt paid, according to the time appointed; and it is required of sureties, as well as stewards, that they be found faithful—namely, to pay the debt according to the bargain; and therefore it is said, "When the fullness of the time was come, God sent forth His Son—made under the law, to redeem them that were under the law," (Galatians 4:4-5). Thus comes grace to saints. 4. The creditor looks that his money should be brought into his house, to his own habitation. Jesus, our Surety, in this also is faithful; for by His own blood, which was the payment, He is entered into the holy place, even into Heaven itself, which is God's dwelling-place, to render the value and price that was agreed upon for the salvation of sinners. But I shall speak more of this in another head, therefore I pass it. Again,

4.) If the surety stands bound, the debtor is at liberty; and if the law do issue out any process to take any, it will be the surety. (Though the debtor, together with the surety, is liable to pay the debt by the law of man, yet Christ our Surety only by the Covenant of Grace). And, O! how wonderfully true was this accomplished in that, when Christ our Surety came down from Heaven, God's Law did so seize upon the Lord Jesus, and so cruelly handle Him, and so exact upon

Him, that it would never let Him alone until it had accused Him and condemned Him, executed Him, and screwed His very heart's blood out of His precious heart and side; nay, and more than this too, as I shall show hereafter. But,

II. Christ is *the Messenger* of the New Covenant

After that Jesus Christ had stood bound, and was become our Surety in things pertaining to this covenant, His next office was *to be the Messenger* of God touching His mind and the tenor of the covenant unto the poor world; and this did the Prophet foresee long before, when he saith, "Behold, I will send My messenger, and he shall prepare the way before Me"; speaking of John the Baptist. "And he shall prepare the way before Me." And then He speaketh of Christ to the people, saying, "And the Lord whom ye seek shall suddenly come to His temple." Who is He? Even the Messenger of the covenant, whom ye delight in," that is Christ. "Behold, He shall come, saith the LORD of Hosts" (Malachi 3:1).

Now the covenant being made before between the Father and the Son, and Jesus Christ becoming bound to see all the conditions fulfilled, this being done, He could come down from Heaven to earth, to declare to the world what God the Father and HE had concluded on before, and what was the mind of the Father towards the world concerning the salvation of their souls; and indeed, who could better come on such an errand than He that stood by when the covenant was made? than He that shook hands with the Father in making of the covenant? than He that was become a Surety in the behalf of poor sinners, according to the terms of the covenant.

Now, you know, a messenger commonly when he cometh, doth bring some errand to them to whom he is sent, either of what is done for them, or what they would have them whom they send unto do for them, or such like. Now what a glorious message was that which our Lord Jesus Christ came down from Heaven withal to declare unto poor sinners, and that from God His Father? I say, how glorious was it; and how sweet is it to you that have seen yourselves lost by nature? and it will also appear a glorious one to you who are a seeking after

Jesus Christ, if you do but consider these following things about what He was sent:

1.) Jesus Christ was sent from Heaven to declare unto the world from God the Father that He was wonderfully filled with love to poor sinners. First, in that He would forgive their sins. Secondly, in that He would save their souls. Thirdly in that He would make them heirs of His glory. "For God so loved the world, that He gave His only begotten Son—For God sent not His Son into the world to condemn the world, but that the world through Him might be saved" (John 3:16-17).

2.) God sent Jesus Christ to tell the poor world how that He would do this for poor sinners, and yet be just, and yet do His justice no wrong; and that was to be done by Jesus Christ's dying of a cursed death in the room of poor sinners, to satisfy justice, and make way for mercy; to take away the stumbling-blocks, and set open Heaven's gates; to overcome Satan, and break off from sinners his chains (Luke 4:18) to set open the prison doors, and to let the prisoners go free (Isaiah 61:1-3). And this was the message that Christ was to deliver to the world by commandment from His Father; and this did He tell us when He came of His errand, where he saith, "I lay down My life for the sheep—no man taketh it from Me, but I lay it down of Myself. I have power to lay it down, and to take it again. This commandment have I received of My Father" (John 10:15-18). Even this commandment hath My Father given Me, that I should both do this thing and also tell it unto you.

3.) He was not only sent as a Messenger to *declare* this His father's love, but also how dearly He himself loved sinners, what a heart He had to do them good, where He saith, "All that the Father giveth Me shall come to Me"; and let me tell you, MY heart too, saith Christ—"Him that cometh to Me, I will in no wise cast out" (John 6:37). As My Father is willing to give you unto Me, even so am I as willing to receive you. As My Father is willing to give you Heaven, so am I willing to make you fit for it, by washing you with My own blood; I lay down My life that you might have life; and this I was sent to tell you of My Father.

4.) His message was further; He came to tell them how and which way they should come to enjoy these glorious benefits; also by laying down motives to stir them up to accept of the benefits. The way is laid down in John 3:14-15, where Christ saith, "As Moses lifted up the serpent in the wilderness, even so must the Son of Man be lifted up," or caused to be hanged on the Cross, and die the death—"that whosoever believeth in Him should not perish but have everlasting life." The way, therefore, that thou shalt have the benefit and comfort of that which My Father and I have covenanted for, for thee, I am come down from Heaven to earth on purpose to give thee intelligence, and to certify thee of it. Know, therefore, that as I have been born of a woman, and I have taken this Body upon Me, it is on purpose that I might offer it up upon the Cross a sacrifice to God, to give Him satisfaction for thy sins, that His mercy may be extended to thy soul, without any wrong done to justice; and this thou art to believe, and not in the notion but from thy very whole soul. Now the motives are many. 1. If they do not leave their sins, and come to Jesus Christ, that their sins may be washed away by His blood, they are sure to be damned in Hell; for the law hath condemned them already (John 3:18-19). 2. But if they do come, they shall have the bosom of Christ to lie in, the Kingdom of Heaven to dwell in, the angels and saints for their companions, shall shine there like the sun, shall be there for ever, shall sit upon the thrones of judgment, etc. Here is grace.

Methinks if I had but the time to speak fully to all things that I could speak to from these two heavenly truths, and to make application thereof, surely, with the blessing of God, I think it might persuade some vile and abominable wretch to lay down his arms that he hath taken up in defiance against God, and is marching Hell-wards, post-haste with the devil; I say, methinks it should stop them, and make them willing to look back and accept of salvation for their poor condemned souls, before God's eternal vengeance is executed upon them. O, therefore! you that are upon this march, I beseech you consider a little. What! shall Christ become a drudge for you; and will you be drudges for the devil? Shall Christ covenant with God for the salvation of sinners; and shall sinners covenant with Hell, death, and the devil for the damnation of their souls?

Shall Christ come down from Heaven to earth to declare this to sinners; and shall sinners stop their ears against these good tidings? Will you not hear the errand of Christ, although He telleth you tidings of peace and salvation? How, if He had come, having taken a commandment from His Father to damn you, and to send you to the devils in Hell? Sinner, hear His message; He speaketh no harm, His words are Eternal Life; all men that give ear unto them, they have eternal advantage by them; advantage, I say, that never hath an end.

Besides, do but consider these two things, it is like they have some sway upon thy soul—1. When He came on His message, He came with tears in His eyes, and did even weepingly tender the terms of reconciliation to them; I say, with tears in his eyes. And when He came near the city—*i.e.*, with His message of peace—beholding the hardness of their hearts, He wept over it, and took up a lamentation over it; because He saw they rejected His mercy, which was tidings of peace; I say, wilt thou then slight a weeping Jesus, One that so loveth thy soul that, rather than He will lose thee, He will with tears persuade with thee? 2. Not only so, but also when He came, He came all on a gore blood to proffer mercy to thee, to show thee still how dearly He did love thee; as if He had said, Sinner, here is mercy for thee; but behold My bloody sweat, My bloody wounds, My cursed death; behold and see what danger I have gone through to come unto thy soul; I am come indeed unto thee, and do bring thee tidings of salvation, but it cost Me My heart's blood before I could come at thee, to give thee the fruits of My everlasting love. But more of this anon.

Thus have I spoken something concerning Christ's being the Messenger of the new covenant; but because I am not willing to cut too short of what shall come after, I shall pass by these things not half touched, and come to the other which I promised even now; which was to show you, that as there were Levitical ceremonies in or belonging to the first covenant, so these types, or Levitical ceremonies, did represent the glorious things of the new covenant. In those ceremonies you read of *a sacrifice*, of *a priest to offer up the sacrifice*, the *place where*, and the *manner how, he was to offer it*; of which I shall speak something.

III. Christ *the Sacrifice* of the New Covenant

As touching the sacrifice; you find that it was not to be offered up of all kind of beasts, as of lions, bears, wolves, tigers, dragons, serpents, or such like; to signify, that not all kind of creatures that had sinned, as devils, the fallen angels, should be saved; but the sacrifice was to be taken out of some kind of beasts and birds, to signify, that some of God's creatures that had sinned He would be pleased to reconcile them to Himself again; as poor fallen man and woman, those miserable creatures, God, the God of Heaven, had a good look for after their fall; but not for the cruel devils, though more noble creatures by creation than we. Here is grace.

Now though these sacrifices were offered, yet they were not offered to the end they should make the comers to, or offerers thereof, perfect; but the things were to represent to the world what God had in after ages for to do, which was even the salvation of His creatures by that offering of the body of Jesus Christ, of which these were a shadow and a type for the accomplishing of the second covenant. For Christ was by covenant to offer a sacrifice, and that an effectual one too, if He intended the salvation of sinners—"A body hast Thou prepared for Me; I am come to do Thy will" (Hebrews 10:5). I shall therefore show you, *First*. What was expected by God in the sacrifice in the type, and then show you how it was answered in the antitype. *Second*. I shall show you the manner of the offering of the type, and so answerable thereto to show you the fitness of the sacrifice of the body of Christ, by way of answering some questions.

1.) For the first of these, (What was expected by God in the sacrifice in the type, and how answered in the antitype)—1. God did expect that sacrifice which He Himself had appointed, and not another, to signify, that none would serve His turn but the body and soul of His appointed Christ, the Mediator of the new covenant (John 1:29). 2. This sacrifice must not be lame nor deformed; it must have no scar, spot, or blemish; to signify, that Jesus Christ was to be a complete sacrifice by covenant (1 Peter 1:19). 3. This sacrifice was to be taken out of the flock or herd; to signify, that Jesus Christ was to come out of the race of mankind, according to covenant (Hebrews 10:5). But:

2.) As to the manner of it (The offering of the types, and so answerable thereto, to show the fitness of the sacrifice of the body of Christ)—1. The sacrifice, before it was offered, was to have all the sins of the children of Israel confessed over it; to signify, that Jesus Christ must bear the sins of all His children by covenant (Isaiah 53:4-7; 1 Peter 2:24). "As for Thee also, by the blood of Thy covenant," in His own body on the tree (Zechariah 9:11). 2. It must be had to the place appointed—namely, without the camp of Israel; to signify, that Jesus Christ must be led to the Mount Calvary (Luke 23:33). 3. The sacrifice was to be killed there; to signify, that Jesus Christ must and did suffer without the city of Jerusalem for our salvation. 4. The sacrifice must not only have its life taken away, but also some of its flesh burned upon the altar; to signify, that Jesus Christ was not only to die a natural death, but also that He should undergo the pains and torments of the damned in Hell. 5. Sometimes there must be a living offering and a dead offering, as the goat that was killed, and the scape-goat, the dead bird and the living bird, to signify, that Jesus Christ must die, and come to life again (Leviticus 19:4-6). 6. The goat that was to die was to be the sin-offering; that is, to be offered as the rest of the sin-offerings, to make an atonement as a type; and the other goat was to have all the sins of the children of Israel confessed over him, and then let go into the wilderness, never to be caught again (Leviticus 16:7-22). To signify, that Christ's death was to make satisfaction for sin, and His coming to life again was to bring in everlasting justification from the power, curse, and destroying nature of sin (Romans 4:25). 7. The scape-goat was to be carried by a fit man into the wilderness; to signify that Jesus Christ should both be fit and able to carry our sins quite a way from us, so as they should never be laid to our charge again. Here is grace. 8. The sacrifices under the law, commonly part of them must be eaten; to signify, that they that are saved should spiritually feed on the body and blood of Jesus Christ, or else they have no life by Him (Exodus 12:5-11; John 6:51-53). 9. This sacrifice must be eaten with unleavened bread; to signify, that they which love their sins, that devilish leaven of wickedness, they do not feed upon Jesus Christ.[8]

Now of what hath been spoken this is the sum, that there is a sacrifice under the new covenant, as there were sacrifices under the old; and that this sacrifice did every way answer that, or those; indeed, they did but suffer for sin in show, but He in reality; they are the shadow, but He as the substance. O! when Jesus Christ did come to make Himself a sacrifice, or to offer Himself for sin, you may understand that our sins were indeed charged to *purpose* upon Him. O! how they scarred his soul, how they brake His body, insomuch that they made the blood run down His blessed face and from His precious side; therefore thou must understand these following things—First, that Jesus Christ by covenant did die for sin. Secondly, that His death was not a mere natural death, but a "cursed death," even such an one as men do undergo from God for their sins, though He Himself had none, even such a death as to endure the very pains and torments of Hell. O sad pains and inexpressible torments that this our Sacrifice for sin went under! The pains of His body were not all; no, but the pains of His soul; for His soul was made an offering as well as His body, yet all but one sacrifice (Isaiah 53). (As Christ did not suffer in His body without suffering in soul, nor yet in soul without His suffering in body; it was because not the body without the soul, but both the body and soul of the saints should be for ever saved). To signify, that the suffering of Christ was not only a bodily suffering, but a soul suffering; not only to suffer what man could inflict upon Him, but also to suffer soul torments that none but God can inflict, or suffer to be inflicted upon Him. O, the torments of His soul! they were the torments indeed; His soul was that that felt the wrath of God. "My soul," saith He, "is exceeding sorrowful, even unto death" (Matthew 26:38). "Now is My soul troubled, and what shall I say?" (John 12:27). The rock was not so rent as was His precious soul; there was not such a terrible darkness on the face of the earth then as there was on His precious soul. O! the torments of Hell and the eclipsings of the Divine smiles of God were both upon Him at once; the devils assailing of Him, and God forsaking of Him, and all at once! "My God, My God," saith He, "why hast Thou forsaken Me?" (Matthew 27:46). Now in my greatest extremity; now sin is laid upon Me, the curse takes hold of Me, the pains of Hell are clasped about Me, and Thou hast forsaken Me. O sad! Sinners, this was not done in pretence, but in reality; not in show, but in very deed; otherwise Christ had dissembled, and had not spoken the truth; but the truth of it His bloody sweat declares, His mighty cries declare, the things which and for what He suffered declare. Nay, I must say thus much, that all the damned souls in Hell, with all their damnations, did never yet feel that torment and pain that did this blessed Jesus in a little time. Sinner, canst thou read that Jesus Christ was made an offering for sin, and yet go in sin? Canst thou hear that the load of thy sins did break the very heart of Christ, and spill His precious blood? and canst thou find in thy heart to labor to lay more sins upon His back? Canst thou hear that He suffered the pains, the fiery flames of Hell, and canst thou find in thy heart to add to His groans by slighting of His sufferings? O hard-hearted wretch! how canst thou deal so unkindly with such a sweet Lord Jesus?

QUESTION: But why did Christ offer Himself in sacrifice?
ANSWER: That thou shouldst not be thrown to the very devils.

QUESTION: But why did He spill His precious blood? ANSWER: That thou mightest enjoy the joys of Heaven. QUESTION: But why did He suffer the pains of Hell?
ANSWER: That thou mightest not fry with the devil and damned souls.

QUESTION: But could not we have been saved if Christ had not died?
ANSWER: No; for without the shedding of blood there is no remission; and besides, there was no death that could satisfy God's justice but His, which is evident, because there was none in a capacity to die, or that was able to answer an infinite God by His so suffering but He.[9]

QUESTION: But why did God let Him die?
ANSWER: He standing in the room of sinners, and that in their names and natures, God's justice must fall upon Him; for justice takes vengeance for sin wheresoever it finds it, though it be on His dear Son. Nay, God favored His Son no more, finding our sins upon

Him, than He would have favored any of us; for, should we have died? so did He. Should we have been made a curse? so was He. Should we have undergone the pains of Hell? so did He.

QUESTION: But did He indeed suffer the torments of Hell?

ANSWER: Yea, and that in such a horrible way too, that it is unspeakable.

QUESTION: Could He not have suffered without His so suffering? Would not His dying only of a natural death have served the turn?

ANSWER: No, in nowise. 1. The sins for which He suffered called for the torments of Hell; the conditions upon which He died did call for the torments of Hell; for Christ did not die the death of a saint, but the death of a sinner, of a cursed and damned sinner; because He stood in their room, the law to which He was subjected called for the torments of Hell; the nature of God's justice could not bate Him anything; the death which He was to suffer had not lost its sting; all these being put together do irresistibly declare unto us that He, as a sacrifice, did suffer the torments of Hell (Galatians 3:13).

But, 2. Had He not died and suffered the cursed death, the covenant had been made void, and His Surety-ship would have been forfeited, and, besides this, the world damned in the flames of Hell-fire; therefore, His being a sacrifice was one part of the covenant; for the terms of the covenant were that He should spill His blood. O blessed Jesus! O blessed grace! (Zechariah 9:10-11)

QUESTION: But why, then, is His death so slighted by some?

ANSWER: Because they are enemies to Him, either through ignorance or presumption; either for want of knowledge or out of malice; for surely did they love or believe Him, they could not choose but break and bleed at heart to consider and to think of Him. (Zechariah 12:10-11)

IV. Christ the High Priest of the New Covenant

Thus, passing this, I shall now speak something to Christ's priestly office. But, by the way, if any should think that I do spin my thread too long in distinguishing His priestly office from His being a sacrifice, the supposing that for Christ to be a priest and a sacrifice is all one and the same thing; and it may be it is, because they have not thought on this so well as they should—namely, that as He was a sacrifice He was passive, that is, led or had away as a lamb to His sufferings (Isaiah 53); but as a priest He was active—that is, He did willingly and freely give up His Body to be a sacrifice. "He hath given His life a ransom for many." This consideration being with some weight and clearness on my spirit, I was and am caused to lay them down in two particular heads.

And therefore I would speak something to is this, that as there were priests under the first covenant, so there is a Priest under this, belonging to this new covenant, a High Priest, the Chief Priest; as it is clear where it is said, We "having a high priest over the house of God" (Hebrews 3:1; 5:5, 10; 7:24-26; 8:1, 4; 10:21).

Now the things that I shall treat upon are these—*First*, I shall show you the qualifications required of a priest under the Law; *Second*, his office; and, *Third*, how Jesus Christ did according to what was signified by those under the law; I say, how He did answer the types, and where He went beyond them.

FIRST, For *His Qualifications*:

1.) They must be called thereto of God—"No man taketh this honor unto himself, but he that is called of God, as Aaron" (Hebrews 5:4). Now Aaron's being called of God to be a priest signifies that Jesus Christ is a Priest of God's appointment, such an one that God hath chosen, likes of, and hath set on work—"Called of God an High Priest," etc. (Hebrews 5:10).

2.) The priests under the law they must be men, complete, not deformed—"Speak unto Aaron," saith God to Moses, "saying, Whosoever *he be* of thy seed in their generations that hath *any* blemish, let him not approach to offer the bread of his God. For whatsoever man *he be* that hath a blemish, he shall not approach; a blind man, or a lame, or he that hath a flat nose, or any thing superfluous, or a man that is broken-footed, broken-handed, or having a crooked back, or a dwarf, or that hath a blemish in his eye, or be scurvy, or scabbed, or hath his stones broken; no man that hath a blemish of the seed of Aaron the priest shall come nigh to offer the offerings of the Lord made by fire; he that hath a blemish; he shall not come nigh to offer the bread of his God" (Leviticus 21:17-21). What doth all this signify but that, a.) He must not be lame, to signify he must not go haltingly about the work of our salvation. b.) He must not be blind, to signify that he must not go ignorantly to work, but he must be quick of understanding in the things of God. c.) He must not be scabbed, to signify that the priest must not be corrupt of filthy in his office. d.) In a word, he must be every way complete, to signify to us that Jesus Christ was to be, and is, most complete and most perfect in things pertaining to God in reference to His second covenant.

3.) The priests under the law were not to be hard-hearted, but pitiful and compassionate, willing and ready, with abundance of bowels, to offer for the people, and to make an atonement for them (Hebrews 5:1-2). To signify, that Jesus Christ should be a tender-hearted High Priest, able and willing to sympathise and be affected with the infirmities of others, to pray for them, to offer up for them His precious blood; He must be such an One who can have compassion on a company of poor ignorant souls, and on them that are out of the way, to recover them, and to set them in safety (Hebrews 4:15). And that He might thus do, He must be a man that had experience of the disadvantages that infirmity and sin did bring unto those poor creatures (Hebrews 2:17).

4.) The high priests under the law were not to be shy or squeamish in case there were any that had the plague or leprosy, scab or blotches; but must look on them, go to them, and offer for them (Leviticus 13), all which is to signify, that Jesus Christ should not refuse to take notice of the several infirmities of the poorest people, but to teach them, and to see that none of them be lost by reason of their infirmity, for want of looking to or tending of. [10]

This privilege also have we under this second covenant. This is the way to make grace shine.

5.) The high priests under the law they were to be anointed with very excellent oil, compounded by art (Exodus 29:7; 30:30). To signify, that Jesus, the Great High Priest of this new covenant, would be in a most eminent way anointed to His priestly office by the Holy Spirit of the Lord.

6.) The priest's food and livelihood in the time of his ministry was to be the consecrated and holy things (Exodus 29:33). To signify, that it is the very meat and drink of Jesus Christ to do His priestly office, and to save and preserve His poor, tempted, and afflicted saints. O what a new-covenant High Priest have we!

7.) The priests under the law were to be washed with water (Exodus 29:4). To signify, that Jesus Christ should not go about the work of His priestly office with the filth of sin upon Him, but was without sin to appear as our High Priest in the presence of His Father, to execute His priestly office there for our advantage—"For such a high priest became us, *who is* holy, harmless, undefiled, separate from sinners, and made higher than the heavens" (Hebrews 7:26).

8.) The high priest under the law, before they went into the holy place, there were to be clothed—with a curious garment, a breastplate, and an ephod, and a robe, and a broidered coat, a mitre, and a girdle, and they were to be made of gold, and blue, and purple, and scarlet, and fine linen; and in his garment and glorious ornaments there must be precious stones, and on those stones there must be written the names of the children of Israel (read Exodus 28), and all this was to signify what a glorious High Priest Jesus Christ should be, and how in the righteousness of God He should appear before God as our High Priest, to offer up the sacrifice that was to be offered for our salvation to God His Father. But I pass that.

SECOND, Now I Shall Consider *His Office*:

The office of the high priest in general was twofold. 1. To offer the sacrifice without the camp. 2. To bring it within the veil—that is, into the holiest of all, which did type out Heaven.

1.) [First part of the high priest's office]. a.) It was the office of the priest to offer the sacrifice; and so did Jesus Christ; He did offer His own Body and Soul in sacrifice. I say, HE did OFFER it, and not another, as it is written, "No man taketh away My life, but I lay it down of Myself; I have power to lay it down, and I have power to take it again" (John 10:17-18). And again it is said, "When He,"

Jesus, "had offered up one sacrifice for sin, for ever sat down on the right hand of God" (Hebrews 10:12). b.) The priests under the law must offer up the sacrifice that God had appointed, and none else, a complete one without any blemish; and so did our High Priest, where He saith, "Sacrifice and offering Thou wouldest not, but a body has Thou prepared Me," and that I will offer (Hebrews 10:5). c.) The priest was to take of the ashes of the sacrifice, and lay them in a clean place; and this signifies, that the Body of Jesus, after it had been offered, should be laid into Joseph's sepulchre, as in a clean place, where never any man before was laid (Leviticus 6:11, compared with John 19:41-42).

2.) [Second part of the high priest's office]. This being one part of his office, and when this was done, then in the next place he was, a.) To put on the glorious garment, when he was to go into the holiest, and take of the blood, and carry it thither, etc., he was to put on the holy garment which signifieth the righteousness of Jesus Christ. b.) He was in this holy garment, which hath in it the stones, and in the stones the names of the twelve tribes of the children of Israel, to appear in the holy place. "And thou shalt take two onyx stones, and grave on them the names of the children of Israel: six of their names on one stone, and *the other* six names of the rest on the other stone, according to their birth (Exodus 28:9-10). And this was to signify, that Jesus Christ was to enter into the holiest, then He was there to bear the names of His elect in the tables of His heart before the Throne of God and the Mercy-seat (Hebrews 12:23). c.) With this he was to take of the blood of the sacrifices, and carry it into the holiest of all, which was a type of Heaven, and there was he to sprinkle the mercy-seat; and this was to be done by the high priest only; to signify, that none but Jesus Christ must have this office and privilege, to be the people's High Priest to offer for them. "But into the second *went* the high priest alone once every year, not without blood, which he offered for himself, and *for* the errors of the people" (Hebrews 9:7). d.) He was there to make an atonement for the people with the blood, sprinkling of it upon the mercy-seat; but this must be done with much incense. "And Aaron shall bring the bullock of the sin-offering which *is* for himself, and for his house, and shall kill the bullock of the sin-offering which *is* for himself: and he shall take a censor full of burning coals of fire from off the altar before the Lord, and his hands full of sweet incense beaten small, and bring it within the veil: and he shall put the incense upon the fire before the Lord, that he cloud of the incense may cover the mercy-seat that *is* upon the testimony, that he die not: and he shall take of the blood of the bullock, and sprinkle *it* with his finger upon the mercy-seat eastward, and before the mercy-seat shall he sprinkle of the blood with his finger seven times. Then shall he kill the goat of the sin-offering, that is for the people, and bring his blood within the veil, and do with that blood as he did with the blood of the bullock, and sprinkle it upon the mercy-seat and before the mercy-seat." (Leviticus 16:11-15). Now this was for the priest and the people; all which doth signify that Jesus Christ was after His death to go into Heaven itself, of which this holy place was a figure, and there to carry the sacrifice that He offered upon the Cross into the presence of God, to obtain mercy for the people in a way of justice (Hebrews 9). And in that he is said to take his hands full of sweet incense, it signifies that Jesus Christ was to offer up His sacrifice in the presence of His Father in a way of intercession and prayers.

I might have branched these things out into several particulars, but I would be brief. I say, therefore, the office of the priest was to carry the blood into the holy place, and there to present it before the mercy-seat, with his heart full of intercessions for the people for whom he was a priest (Luke 1:8-11). This is Jesus Christ's work now in the Kingdom of Glory, to plead His own blood, the nature and virtue of it, with a perpetual intercession to the God of Mercy on behalf of us poor miserable sinners (Hebrews 7:25).

Comforting Considerations from Christ's intercession

Now, in the intercession of this Jesus, which is part of His priestly office, there are these things to be considered for our comfort:

1.) There is a pleading of the virtue of His Blood for them that are already come in, that they may be kept from the evils of heresies, delusions, temptations, pleasures, profits, or anything of this world which may be too hard for them. "Father, I pray not that Thou shouldest take them out of the world," saith Christ, "but that Thou shouldest keep them from the evil" (John 17:15).

2.) In case the devil should aspire up into the presence of God, to accuse any of the poor saints, and to plead their backslidings against them, as he will do if he can, then there is Jesus, our Lord Jesus, ready in the Court of Heaven, at the right hand of God, to plead the virtue of His Blood, not only for the great and general satisfaction that He did give when He was on the Cross, but also the virtue that is in it now for the cleansing and fresh purging of His poor saints under their several temptations and infirmities; as saith the Apostle, "For if when we were enemies we were reconciled to God by the death of His Son, much more being reconciled, we shall be saved by His life"—that is, by His intercession (Romans 5:10).

3.) The maintaining of grace, also, is by Jesus Christ's intercession, being the second part of His priestly office. O, had we not a Jesus at the right hand of God making intercession for us, and to convey fresh supplies of grace unto us through the virtue of His Blood being pleaded at God's right hand, how soon would it be with us as it is with those for whom He prays not at all (John 17:9)? But the reason why thou standest while others fall, the reason why thou goest through the many temptations of the world, and shakest them off from thee, while others are ensnared and entangled therein, it is because thou hast an interceding Jesus. "I have prayed," saith He, "that thy faith fail not" (Luke 22:32).

4.) It is partly by the virtue of Christ's intercession that the elect are brought in. There are many that are to come to Christ which are not yet brought in to Christ: and it is one part of His work to pray for their salvation too—"Neither pray I for these alone, but for them also which shall believe," though as yet they do not believe "on Me," but that they may believe "through their word" (John 17:20). And let me tell thee, soul, for thy comfort, who art a-coming to Christ, panting and sighing, as if thy heart would break, I tell thee, soul, thou wouldst never have come to Christ, if He had not first, by the virtue of His blood and intercession, sent into thy heart an earnest desire after Christ; and let me tell thee also, that it is His *business* to make intercession for thee, not only that thou mightest come in, but that thou mightest be preserved when thou art come in. (Compare Hebrews 7:25; Romans 8:33-39)

5.) It is by the intercession of Christ that the infirmities of the saints in their holy duties are forgiven. Alas, if it were not for the priestly office of Christ Jesus, the prayers, alms, and other duties of the saints might be rejected, because of the sin that is in them; but Jesus being our High Priest, He is ready to take away the iniquities of our holy things, perfuming our prayers with the glory of His own perfections; and therefore it is that there is an answer given to the saints' prayers, and also acceptance of their holy duties (Revelation 8:3-4). "But Christ being come an high priest of good things to come, by a greater and more perfect tabernacle, not made with hands, that is to say, not of this building; neither by the blood of goats and calves, but by His own blood He entered in once into the holy place, having obtained eternal redemption *for us*. For if the blood of bulls and of goats, and the ashes of an heifer sprinkling the unclean, sanctifieth to the purifying of the flesh: how much more shall the blood of Christ, who through the eternal Spirit offered Himself without spot to God, purge your conscience from dead works to serve the living God? And for this cause He is the mediator of the New Testament," or covenant, "that by means of death, for the redemption of the transgressions *that were* under the first testament, they which are called," notwithstanding all their sins, "might receive the promise of eternal inheritance" (Hebrews 9:11-15).

THIRD. *Where and how Jesus Christ excels these priests*, **in every qualifications and office, being a comfort to poor saints.**

1.) They that were called to the priesthood under the law were but men; but He is both God and man (Hebrews 7:3, 28).

2.) Their qualifications were in them in a very scanty way; but Jesus was every way qualified in an infinite and full way.

3.) They were consecrated but for a time, but He for evermore (Hebrews 7:23-24).

4.) They were made without an oath, but He with an oath (vv. 20-21).

5.) They as servants; but He as a Son (Hebrews 3:6).

6.) Their garments were but such as could be made with hands, but His the very righteousness of God (Exodus 28; Romans 3:22; Philippians 3:8-9).

7.) Their offerings were but the body and blood of beasts, and such like, but His offering was His own body and soul (Hebrews 9:12-13; 10:4-5; Isaiah 53:10).

8.) Those were at best but a shadow or type, but He the very substance and end of all those ceremonies (Hebrews 9:1, 10-11).

9.) Their holy place was but made by men, but His, or that which Jesus is entered, is into Heaven itself (Hebrews 9:2-3, 24).

10.) When they went to offer their sacrifice, they were forced to offer for themselves, as men compassed about with infirmity, but He holy, harmless, who did never commit the least transgression (Hebrews 7:26; 10:11).

11.) They when they went to offer they were fain to do it standing, to signify that God had no satisfaction therein; but He, when "He had offered one sacrifice for sins for ever, sat down on the right hand of God," to signify that God was very well pleased with His offering (Hebrews 10:12).

12.) They were fain to offer "oftentimes the same sacrifices, which can never take away sins"; but He, "by one offering hath perfected for ever them that are sanctified" (Hebrews 10:11, 14).

13.) Their sacrifices at the best could but serve for the cleansing of the flesh, but His for cleansing both body and soul—the blood of Jesus Christ doth purge the conscience from dead works, to live a holy life (Hebrews 9:13-14).

14.) Those high priests could not offer but once a year in the holiest of all, but our High Priest He ever liveth to make intercession for us (Hebrews 9:7; 12:24-25).

15.) Those high priests, notwithstanding they were priests, they were not always to wear their holy garments; but Jesus never puts them off of Him, but is in them always.

16.) Those high priests, death would be too hard for them, but our High Priest hath vanquished and overcome that cruel enemy of ours, and brought life and immortality to light through the glorious Gospel (Hebrews 7:21, 23; 2:15; 2 Timothy 1:10).

17.) Those high priests were not able to save themselves; but this is able to save Himself, and all that come to God, by Him (Hebrews 7:25).

18.) Those high priests" blood could not do away sin; but the blood of Jesus Christ, who is our High Priest, "cleanseth us from all sin" (1 John 1:7).

19.) Those high priests sometimes by sin caused God to reject their sacrifices; but this High Priest doth always the things that please Him.

20.) Those high priests could never convey the Spirit by virtue of their sacrifices or office; but this High Priest, our Lord Jesus, He can and doth give all the gifts and graces that are given to the sons of men.

21.) Those high priests could never by their sacrifices bring the soul of any sinner to glory by virtue of itself; but Jesus hath by one offering, as I said before, perfected for ever those that He did die for. Thus in brief I have showed in some particulars how and wherein Jesus our High Priest doth go beyond those high priests; and many more without question might be mentioned, but I forbear.

V. Christ the Forerunner of the Saints

The fifth office of Christ in reference to the second covenant was, that He should be the forerunner to Heaven before His saints that were to follow after. First, He strikes hands in the covenant, (and then) He stands bound as a Surety to see everything in the covenant accomplished that was to be done on His part; (next) He brings the message from Heaven to the world; and before He goeth back, He offereth Himself for the same sins that He agreed to suffer for; and so soon as this was done, He goeth post-haste to Heaven again, not only to exercise the second part of His priestly office, but as our forerunner, to take possession for us, even into Heaven itself, as you may see, where it is said, "Whither the Forerunner is for us entered" (Hebrews 6:20).

First. He is run before to open Heaven's gates—Be ye open, ye everlasting doors, that the King of Glory may enter in.

Second. He is run before us to take possession of glory in our natures for us.

Third. He is run before to prepare us our places against we come after—"I go to prepare a place for you" (John 14:1-3).

Fourth. He is run thither to make the way easy, in that He hath first trodden the path Himself.

Fifth. He is run thither to receive gifts for us. All spiritual and heavenly gifts had been kept from us had not Christ, so soon as the time appointed was come, run back to the Kingdom of Glory to receive them for us. But I can not stand to enlarge upon these glorious things, the Lord enlarge them upon your hearts by meditation. (These things have I spoken to show you that saints are under grace.

Christ Completely Fulfilled the Conditions of the New Covenant

Here now I might begin to speak of His prophetic and kingly office, and the privileges that do and shall come thereby, but that I fear I shall be too tedious, therefore at this time I shall pass them by. Thus you may see how the Covenant of Grace doth run, and with Whom it was made, and also what were the conditions thereof.

Now, then, this grace, this everlasting grace of God, comes to be free to us through the satisfaction, according to the conditions, given by Another for us; for though it be free, and freely given to us, yet the obtaining of it did cost our Head, our public Man, a very dear price. "For ye are bought with a price," even with the precious blood of Christ. So it is by Another, I say, not by us; yet it is as surely made over to us, even to so many of us as do or shall believe, as if we had done it, and obtained the grace of God ourselves (1 Corinthians 6:20; 1 Peter 1:9). Nay, surer; for consider, I say, this grace is free to us, and comes upon a clear score, by virtue of the labor and purchase of Another for us; mark, that which is obtained by Another for us is not obtained for us by ourselves—No, but Christ hath, not by the blood of goats and calves, "obtained eternal redemption *for us*," which were things offered by men under the law, "but by His own blood," meaning Christ's, "He entered in once into the holy place, having obtained eternal redemption *for us*" (Hebrews 9:12).

It comes to be unchangeable through the perfection of that satisfaction that was given to God through the Son of Mary for us; for whatever the Divine, infinite, and eternal justice of God did call for at the hands of man, if ever he intended to be a partaker of the grace of God, this Jesus, this one Man, this public Person, did, did completely give a satisfaction to it, even so effectually; which caused God not only to say, I am pleased, but "I am well pleased"; completely and sufficiently satisfied with Thee on their behalf; for so you must understand it (Matthew 3:17). Mark therefore these following words—"And, having made peace," or completely made up the difference, "through the blood of His cross, by Him to reconcile all things unto Himself; by Him, *I say*, whether *they be* things in earth, or things in heaven. And you, that were sometime alienated and enemies in *your* mind by wicked works, yet now hath He reconciled," how? "in the body of His flesh through death, to present you holy," mark, "holy and unblamable and unreprovable in His sight" (Colossians 1:20-22). And thus it is grace, unchangeable grace to us; because it was obtained, yea, completely obtained, for us, by Jesus Christ, God-man.

OBJECTION: But some may say, How was it possible that one man Jesus, by one offering, should so completely obtain and bring in unchangeable grace for such an innumerable company of sinners as are to be saved?

ANSWER: 1.) In that He was every way fitted for such a work. And, 2.) In that, as I said before, He did every way completely satisfy that which was offended by our disobedience to the former covenant.

FIRST. He was every way fitted for such a work.

And, for the clearing of this:

1.) Consider, was it man that had offended? He was Man that gave the satisfaction—"For since *by man* came death, by *man* came also the resurrection of the dead" (1 Corinthians 15:21).

2.) Was it God that was offended? He was God that did give a satisfaction—"Unto us a child is born, unto us a son is given.—and His name shall be called The mighty God" (Isaiah 9:6). "He thought it not robbery to be equal with God: but," for our sakes, He "made Himself of no reputation," etc. (Philippians 2:6-7).

3. For the further clearing of this, to show you that in everything He was rightly qualified for this great work, see what God Himself saith of Him; He calls Him, in the first place, Man; and, secondly, He owns Him to be His Fellow, saying, "Awake, O sword, against My Shepherd, and against the Man"—mark, "the *Man* that is My Fellow, saith the LORD of hosts" (Zechariah 13:7).

So that now, let Divine and infinite justice turn itself which way it will, it finds one that can tell how to match it; for if it say, I will require the satisfaction of man, here is a Man to satisfy its cry; and if it say, But I am an infinite God, and must and will have an infinite satisfaction; here is One also that is infinite, even fellow with God, fellow in His essence and being; fellow in His power and strength; fellow in His wisdom; fellow in His mercy and grace; together with the rest of the attributes of God; so that, I say, let justice turn itself which way it will, here is a complete Person to give a complete satisfaction (Proverbs 8:23; 1 Corinthians 1:24; Titus 2:10; compared with verse 11). Thus much of the fitness of the Person.

Second. For the completeness of the satisfaction given by Him for us. And that is discovered in these particulars:

1.) Doth justice call for the blood of that nature that sinned? here is the heart-blood of Jesus Christ—"We have redemption through His blood," (Ephesians 1:7, 14; 1 Peter 1:18-19; Zechariah 9:10-11).

2.) Doth justice say that this blood, if it be not the blood of One that is really and naturally God, it will not give satisfaction to infinite justice? then here is God, purchasing His Church "with His own blood" (Acts 20:28).

3.) Doth justice say, that it must not only have satisfaction for sinners, but they that are saved must be also washed and sanctified with this blood? then here is He that so loved us, that He "washed us from our sins in His own blood" (Revelation 1:5).

4.) Is there to be a righteousness to clothe them with that is to be presented before Divine justice? there here is the righteousness of Christ, which is "even the righteousness of God by faith" (Romans 3:22; Philippians 3:8-10).

5.) Are there any sins now that will fly upon this Savior like so many lions, or raging devils, if He take in hand to redeem man? He will be content to bear them all Himself alone, even in His own body upon the tree (1 Peter 2:24).

6.) Is there any law now that will curse and condemn this Savior for standing in our persons to give satisfaction to God for the transgression of man? He will be willing to be cursed, yea, to be made a curse for sinners, rather than they shall be cursed and damned themselves (Galatians 3:13).

7.) Must the great and glorious God, whose eyes are so pure that He can not behold iniquity; I say, must He not only have the blood, but the very life of Him that will take in hand to be the Deliverer and Savior of us poor miserable sinners? He is willing to lay down His life for His sheep (John 10:11).

8.) Must He not only die a natural death, but must His soul descend into hell, though it should not be left there, He will suffer that also Psalms 16:10; and Acts 2:31.[11]

9.) Must He not only be buried, but rise again from the dead, and overcome death, that He might be the first-fruits to God of them that sleep, which shall be saved? He will be buried, and also through the strength of His Godhead, He will raise Himself out of the grave, though death hold Him never so fast, and the Jews lay never such a great stone upon the mouth of the sepulchre, and seal it never so fast (1 Corinthians 15:4; Luke 24:34).

10.) Must He carry that body into the presence of His Father, to take possession of Heaven, and must He appear there as a priest, as a forerunner, as an advocate, as prophet, as a treasure-house, as an interceder and pleader of the causes of His people? He will be all these, and much more, to the end the grace of God by faith in Jesus Christ might be made sure to all the seed. "Who then can condemn?

It is God that justifieth; because Christ hath died, yea rather, that is risen again." Who, now seeing all this is so effectually done, shall lay anything, the least thing? who can find the least flaw, the least wrinkle, the least defect or imperfection, in this glorious satisfaction (Romans 8:33-34; Hebrews 6:20; 9:24; John 14:2-3; 1 John 2:1)?

OBJECTION: But is it possible that He should so *soon* give infinite justice a satisfaction, a complete satisfaction? for the eternal God doth require an eternal lying under the curse, to the end He may be eternally satisfied.

ANSWER: Indeed, that which is infinite must have an eternity to satisfy God in—that is, they that fall into the prison and pit of utter darkness must be there to all eternity, to the end the justice of God may have its full blow at them. But now He that I am speaking of is God, and so is infinite (Isaiah 9:6; Titus 1:16-17; Hebrews 1:8-9; Philippians 2:4-6). Now, He which is true God is able to give in as little a time an infinite satisfaction as Adam was in giving the dissatisfaction. Adam himself might have given satisfaction for himself as soon as Christ had he been very God, as Jesus Christ was. For the reason why the posterity of Adam, even so many of them as fall short of life, must lie broiling in Hell to all eternity is this—they are not able to give the justice of God satisfaction, they being not infinite, as aforesaid. "But Christ," that is, God-man, "being come an High Priest," that is, to offer and give satisfaction, "of good things to come, by a greater and more perfect tabernacle, not made with hands, that is to say, not of this building; neither by the blood of goats and calves, but by His own"—mark you that, "but by His own blood He entered in once into the holy place, having obtained eternal redemption *for us*." But how? "For if the blood of bulls and of goats, and the ashes of an heifer sprinkling the unclean, sanctifieth to the purifying of the flesh: how much more shall the blood of Christ, who through the eternal Spirit," who through the power and virtue of His infinite Godhead, "offered Himself without spot to God, purge your conscience from dead works to serve the living God? And for this cause," that is, for that He is God as well as man, and so able to give justice an infinite satisfaction, therefore, "He is the mediator of the new testament, that by means of death, for the redemption of the transgressions *that were* under the first testament, they which are called might receive the promise of eternal inheritance" (Hebrews 9:11-15). As I said before.

OBJECTION: This is much; but is God connected with this? Is He satisfied now in the behalf of sinners by this Man's thus suffering? If He is, then how doth it appear?

ANSWER: It is evident, yea, wonderful evident, that this hath pleased Him to the full, as appeareth by these following demonstrations:

First. In that God did admit Him into His presence; yea, receive Him with joy and music, even with the sound of the trumpet, at His ascension into Heaven (Psalms 47:5). And Christ makes it an argument to His children that His righteousness was sufficient, in that He went to His Father, and they saw Him no more, "of righteousness," saith He, "because I go to My Father, and ye see Me no more" (John 16:10). As if He had said, My Spirit shall show to the world that I have brought in a sufficient righteousness to justify sinners withal, in that when I go to appear in the presence of My Father on their behalf, He shall give Me entertainment, and not throw Me down from Heaven, because I did not do it sufficiently.

Again; if you consider the high esteem that God the Father doth set on the death of His Son, you will find that He hath received good content thereby. When the Lord Jesus, by way of complaint, told His Father that He and His merits were not valued to the worth, His Father answered, It is a light thing that I should give Thee, O My Servant, to bring Jacob again; "I will also give Thee for a light to the Gentiles, that Thou mayest be My salvation unto the end of the earth" (Isaiah 49:6). As if the Lord had said, "My Son, I do value Thy death at a higher rate than that Thou shouldst save the tribes of Israel only; behold the Gentiles, the barbarous heathens, they also shall be brought in as the price of Thy blood. It is a light thing that Thou shouldest be My Servant only to bring, or redeem, the tribes of Jacob, and to restore the preserved of Israel: I will also give Thee for a light to the Gentiles, that Thou mayest be My salvation unto the end of the earth." [12]

Again; you may see it also by the carriage of God the Father to all the great sinners to whom mercy was proffered. We do not find that God maketh any objection against them to come to Him for the pardon of their sins; because He did want a satisfaction suitable to the greatness of their sins. There was Manasseh, who was one that burned his children in the fire to the devil, that used witchcraft, that used to worship the host of heaven, that turned his back on the Word that God sent unto him; nay, that did worse than the very heathen that God cast out before the children of Israel (2 Chronicles 33:1-13). Also those that are spoken of in the Nineteenth of Acts, that did spend so much time in conjuration, and the like, for such I judge they were, that when they came to burn their books, they counted the price thereof to be fifty thousand pieces of silver (Acts 19:19). Simon Magus also, that was a sorcerer, and bewitched the whole city, yet he had mercy proffered to him once and again (Acts 8). I say, it was not the greatness of the sins of these sinners; no, nor of an innumerable company of others, that made God at all to object against the salvation of their souls, which justice would have constrained Him to had He not had satisfaction sufficient by the blood of the Lord Jesus. Nay, further, I do find that because God the Father would not have the merits of His Son to be undervalued, I say, He doth therefore freely by His consent let mercy be proffered to the greatest sinners—in the first place, for the Jews, that were the worst of men in that day for blasphemy against the Gospel; yet the Apostle proffered mercy to them in the first place—"It was necessary," saith he, "that the Word of God should first have been spoken to you" (Acts 3:26; 13:46). And Christ gave them commission so to do; for, saith He, Let repentance and remission of sins be preached in My name among all nations, and begin—mark that, "beginning at Jerusalem" (Luke 24:47), Let them that but the other day had their hands up to the elbows in My heart's blood have the first proffer of My mercy. And, saith Paul, "For this cause I obtained mercy, that in me first Jesus Christ might show forth all longsuffering, for a pattern to them which should hereafter believe on Him to life everlasting" (1 Timothy 1:16). As the Apostle saith, those sinners that were dead, possessed with the devil, and the children of wrath, He hath quickened, delivered, and saved. That He might, even in the very "ages to come He might show the exceeding riches of His grace in *His* kindness toward us," and that "through Christ Jesus" (Ephesians 2:7).

Second. It is evident that that which this Man did as a common person He did it completely and satisfactorily, as appears by the openness, as I may so call it, which was in the heart of God to Him at His resurrection and ascension—"Ask of Me," saith He, "and I shall give *Thee* the" very "heathen for Thine inheritance, and the uttermost parts of the earth for Thy possession" (Psalms 2:8). And this was at His resurrection (Acts 13:33). Whereas, though He had asked, yet if He had not given a full and complete satisfaction, justice would not have given Him any thing; for justice, the justice of God, is so pure, that if it be not completely satisfied in every particular, it giveth nothing but curses (Galatians 3:10).

Third. It is yet far more evident that He hath indeed pleased God in the behalf of sinners, in that God hath given Him gifts to distribute to sinners, yea, the worst of sinners, as a fruit of His satisfaction, and that at His ascension (Psalms 68:18). Christ hath so satisfied God, that He hath given Him all the treasures both of Heaven and earth to dispose of as He seeth good; He hath so pleased God, that He hath given Him a name above every name, a sceptre above every sceptre, a crown above every crown, a kingdom above every kingdom; He hath given Him the highest place in Heaven, even His own right hand; He hath given Him all the power of Heaven and earth, and under the earth, in His own hand, to bind whom He pleaseth, and to set free whom He thinks meet; He hath, in a word, such a high esteem in the eyes of His Father, that He hath put into His hands all things that are for the profit of His people, both in this world and that which is to come; and all this as the fruit of His faithfulness in doing of His work, as the Mediator of the new covenant (Philippians 2:9; Revelation 19:6). Thou hast ascended on high, Thou hast led captivity captive, Thou hast received gifts—mark, Thou hast received them—for men, even for the worst of men, for the rebellious also; and hath sent forth some, being furnished with these gifts; some, I say, for the work of the ministry, to the edifying of them that are already called, and also for the calling in of all those for whom He covenanted with His Father, till all come in the unity of faith, etc. (Ephesians 4:8-13).

Fourth. It doth still appear yet far more evident; for will you hear what the Father Himself saith for the showing of His well-pleasedness in these two particulars—First, in that He bids poor souls to hear and to do as Christ would have them (Matthew 3:17; Luke 9:35). Secondly, in that He resolves to make them that turn their backs upon Him, that dishonor Him, which is done in a very great measure by those that lay aside His merits done by Himself for justification; I say, He that resolved to make this His footstool, where He saith, "Sit Thou at My right hand, until I make Thine enemies Thy footstool" (Psalms 110:1). Are they enemies to Thee? saith God. I will be even with them. Do they slight Thy merits? Do they slight Thy groans, Thy tears, Thy blood, Thy death, Thy resurrection and intercession, Thy second coming again in heavenly glory? I will tear them and rend them; I will make them as mire in the streets; I will make Thy enemies Thy footstool (Matthew 22:44; Hebrews 1:13; 10:13). Ay, saith He, and "Thou shalt dash them in pieces like a potter's vessel" (Psalms 2:9). Look to it you that slight the merits of the blood of Christ.

Fifth. Again further; yet God will make all the world to know that He hath been and is well pleased in His Son, in that God hath given, and will make it appear He hath given, the world to come into His hand; and that He shall raise the dead, bring them before His judgment-seat, execute judgment upon them, which He pleaseth to execute judgment on to their damnation; and to receive them to eternal life whom He doth favor, even so many as shall be found to believe in His name and merits (Hebrews 2). "For as the Father hath life in Himself; so hath He given to the Son to have life in Himself; and hath given Him authority to execute judgment also, because He is the Son of man. For the hour is coming, in the which all that are in the graves shall hear His voice, and shall come forth; they that have done good, unto the resurrection of life; and they that have done evil, unto the resurrection of damnation" (John 5:26-29). Ay, and the worst enemy that Christ hath now shall come at that day with a pale face, with a quaking heart, and bended knees, trembling before Him, confessing the glory of His merits, and the virtue there was in them to save, "to the glory of God the Father" (Romans 14:11; Philippians 2:11).

Much more might be added to discover the glorious perfection of this Man's satisfaction; but for you that desire to be further satisfied concerning this, search the Scriptures, and beg of God to give you faith and understanding therein; and as for you that slight these things, and continue so doing, God hath another way to take with you, even to dash you in pieces like a potter's vessel; for this hath Christ received of His Father to do unto you (Revelation 2:27).

Thus I have showed you in particular, that the Covenant of Grace of God is free and unchangeable to men—that is, in that it hath been obtained for men, and that perfectly, to the satisfying of justice, and taking all things out of the way that were any ways a hindrance to our salvation (Colossians 2:14).

The Covenant of Grace Unchangeable; the Opposers Answered

The second thing for the discovering of this freeness and constancy of the Covenant of Grace of God is manifested thus:

FIRST. Whatsoever any man hath of the grace of God, he hath it as a free gift of God through Christ Jesus the Mediator of this covenant, even when they are in a state of enmity to Him, whether it be Christ as the foundation-stone, or faith to lay hold of Him, mark that (Romans 5:8-9; Colossians 1:21-22). "For by grace are ye saved through faith; and that not of yourselves," not for anything in you, or done by you for the purchasing of it, but "*it is the gift of God*," (Ephesians 2:8) and that bestowed on you, even when ye "were dead in trespasses and sins" (Ephesians 2:1, 9). Nay, if thou hast so much as one desire that is right, it is the gift of God; for of ourselves, saith the Apostle, we are not able to speak a good word, or think a good thought (2 Corinthians 3:5).

Was it not grace, absolute grace, that God made promise to Adam after transgression? (Genesis 3:15). Was it not free grace in God to save such a wretch as Manasseh was, who used enchantments, witchcraft, burnt his children in the fire, and wrought much evil? (2 Chronicles 33). Was it not free grace to save such as those were that are spoken of in the 16th of Ezekiel, which no eye pitied? Was it not free grace for Christ to give Peter a loving look after he had cursed, and swore, and denied Him? Was it not free grace that met Paul when he was a-going to Damascus to persecute, which converted him, and made him a vessel of mercy?

And what shall I say of such that are spoken of in 1 Corinthians 6:9-10, speaking there of fornicators, idolaters, adulterers, effeminate, abusers of themselves with mankind, thieves, covetous, drunkards, revilers, extortioners, the basest of sinners in the world, and yet were washed, and yet were justified; was it not freely by grace? O saints, you that are in heaven cry out, "We came hither by grace; and you that are on the earth, I am sure you cry, If ever we do go thither, it must be freely by grace!"

SECOND. In the next place, it appears to be unchangeable in this—1. Because justice being once satisfied doth not use to call for the debt again. No; let never such a sinner come to Jesus Christ, and so to God by Him, and justice, instead of speaking against the salvation of that sinner, it will say, I am just as well as faithful to forgive him his sins (1 John 1:9). When justice itself is pleased with a man, and speaks on his side, instead of speaking against him, we may well cry out, Who shall condemn? 2. Because there is no law to come in against the sinner that believes in Jesus Christ; for he is not under that, and that by right comes in against none but those that are under it. But believers are not under that—that is, not their Lord, therefore that hath nothing to do with them; and besides, Christ's blood hath not only taken away the curse thereof, but also He hath in His own Person completely fulfilled it as a public Person in our stead. (Romans 7:1-4). 3. The devil that accused them is destroyed (Hebrews 2:14-15). 4. Death, and the grave, and Hell are overcome (1 Corinthians 15:55; Hosea 13:14). 5. Sin, that great enemy of man's salvation, that is washed away (Revelation 1:5). 6. The righteousness of God is put upon them that believe, and given to them, and they are found in it (Philippians 3:8-10; Romans 3:22). 7. Christ is always in Heaven to plead for them, and to prepare a place for them

(Hebrews 7:24; John 14:1-4). 8. He hath not only promised that He will not leave us, nor forsake us, but He hath also sworn to fulfil His promises. O rich grace! O free grace! Lord, who desired Thee to promise? who compelled Thee to swear? We use to take honest men upon their bare word, but God, "willing more abundantly to show unto the heirs of promise the immutability of His counsel," hath "confirmed *it* by an oath: that by two immutable things," His promise and His oath, "in which it *was* impossible for God to lie," or break either of them, "we might have a strong consolation, who have fled for refuge to lay hold upon the hope set before us" (Hebrews 6:17-18). I will warrant you, God will never break His oath; therefore we may well have good ground to hope from such a good foundation as this, that God will never leave us indeed. Amen.

THIRD. Not only thus, but, 1. God hath begotten believers again to Himself, to be His adopted and accepted children, in and through the Lord Jesus (1 Peter 1:3). 2. God hath prepared a kingdom for them before the foundation of the world, through Jesus Christ (Matthew 25:34). 3. He hath given them an earnest of their happiness while they live here in this world. "After that ye believed, ye were sealed with that holy Spirit of promise, which is the earnest of our inheritance until the redemption of the purchased possession, unto the praise of His glory," and that through this Jesus (Ephesians 1:13-14). (These things are more fully laid down in that part of the book which containeth the discourse of the privileges of the new covenant). 4. If His children sin through weakness, or by sudden temptation, they confessing of it, He willingly forgives, and heals all their wounds, reneweth His love towards them, waits to do them good, casteth their sins into the depths of the sea, and all this freely, without any work done by men as men—Not for your own sakes do I do this, O house of Israel, be it known unto you, saith the Lord, but wholly and alone by the blood of Jesus (Ezekiel 36:23). 5. In a word, if you would see it altogether, God's love was the cause why Jesus Christ was sent to bleed for sinners. Jesus Christ's bleeding stops the cries of Divine justice; God looks upon them as complete in Him, gives them to Him as His by right of purchase. Jesus ever lives to pray for them that are thus given unto Him. God sends His Holy Spirit into them to reveal this to them, sends His angels to minister for them; and all this by virtue of an Everlasting Covenant between the Father and the Son. Thrice happy are the people that are in such a case!

Nay, further, He hath made them brethren with Jesus Christ, members of His flesh and of His bones, the spouse of this Lord Jesus; and all to show you how dearly, how really, how constantly He loveth us, who, by faith of His operation, have laid hold upon Him. (These things I might have treated upon more largely).

Further Arguments and Objections Answered

I shall now lay down a few arguments for the super-abundant clearing of it, and afterwards answer two or three objections that may be made against it, and so I shall fall upon the next thing.

FIRST. God loves the saints as He loves Jesus Christ; and God loves Jesus Christ with an eternal love; therefore the saints also with the same. "Thou hast loved them as Thou has loved Me" (John 17:23).

SECOND. That love which is God Himself, must needs be everlasting love; and that is the love wherewith God hath loved His saints in Christ Jesus; therefore His love towards His children in Christ must needs be an everlasting love. There is none dare say that the love of God is mixed with a created mixture; if not, then it must needs be Himself (1 John 4:16). (You must not understand that love in God is a passion as it is in us; but the love of God is the very essence or nature of God).

THIRD. That love which is always pitched upon us, in an object as holy as God, must needs be an everlasting love. Now the love of God was and is pitched upon us, through an object as holy as God Himself, even our Lord Jesus; therefore it must needs be unchangeable.

FOURTH. If He with whom the Covenant of Grace was made, did in every thing and condition do even what the Lord could desire or require of Him, that His love might be extended to us, and that for ever, then His love must needs be an everlasting love, seeing everything required of us was completely accomplished for us by Him; and all this hath our Lord Jesus done, and that most gloriously, even on our behalf; therefore it must needs be a love that lasts for ever and ever.

FIFTH. If God hath declared Himself to be the God that changeth not, and hath sworn to be immutable in His promise, then surely He will be unchangeable; and He hath done so; therefore it is impossible for God to lie, and so for His eternal love to be changeable (Hebrews 6:13-18). Here is an argument of the Spirit's own making! Who can contradict it? If any object, and say, But still it is upon the condition of believing—I answer, The condition also is His own free gift, and not a qualification arising from the stock of nature (Ephesians 2:8; Philippians 1:28-29). So that here is the love unchangeable; here is also the condition given by Him whose love is unchangeable, which may serve yet further for a strong argument that God will have His love unchangeable. Sinner, this is better felt and enjoyed than talked of.

OBJECTION #1. But if this love of God be unchangeable in itself, yet it is not unchangeably set upon the saints unless they behave themselves the better. (The first objection).

ANSWER: As God's love at the first was bestowed upon the saints without anything foreseen by the Lord in them, as done by them, Deuteronomy 9:4-6, so He goeth on with the same, Saying, "I will never leave thee nor forsake thee" (Hebrews 13:5).

OBJECTION #2. But how cometh it to pass then, that many fall off again from the grace of the Gospel, after a profession of it for some time; some to delusions, and some to their own sins again? (The second objection).

ANSWER: They are all fallen away, not from the everlasting love of God to them, but from the profession of the love of God to them. Men may profess that God loves them when there is no such matter, and that they are the children of God, when the devil is their father; as it is in John 8:40-44. Therefore they that do finally fall away from a profession of the grace of the Gospel, it is, first, because they are bastards and not sons. Secondly, because as they are not sons, so God suffereth them to fall, to make it appear that they are not sons, not of the household of God—"They went out from us, but they were not of us; for if they had been of us, they would *no doubt*," mark that, "no doubt," saith he, "they would have continued with us: but *they went out*," from us, "that they might be made manifest that they were not all of us" (1 John 2:19). And though Hymeneus and Philetus do throw themselves headlong to Hell, "nevertheless the foundation of God standeth sure, having this seal, The Lord knoweth them that are His" (2 Timothy 2:17-19).

OBJECTION #3. But the Scripture saith that there are some that had faith, yet lost it, and have made shipwreck of it. (The third objection). Now God loves no longer than they believe, as is evident; for "he that believeth not shall be damned." So then, if some may have faith, and yet lose it, and so lose the love of God because they have lost their faith, it is evident that God's love is not so immutable as you say it is to every one that believeth.

ANSWER: There are more sorts of faith than one that are spoken of in Scripture:

1.) There is a faith that man may have, and yet be nothing, none of the saints of God, and yet may do great things therewith (1 Corinthians 13:1-4).

2.) There is a faith that was wrought merely by the operation of the miracles that were done in those days by Christ and his followers—"And many of the people believed in Him." How came they by their faith? Why, by the operation of the miracles that He did among them; for said they, "When Christ cometh, will He do more miracles than these which this man hath done?" (John 7:31).

The great thing that wrought their faith in them, was only by seeing the miracles that He did, John 2:23, which is not that saving faith which is called the faith of God's elect, as is evident; for there must not be only miracles wrought upon outward objects to beget that—that being too weak a thing—but it must be by the same power that was stretched out in raising Christ from the dead; yea, the exceeding greatness of that power (Ephesians 1:18-19). So there is a believing, being taken with some marvellous work, visibly appearing to the outward sense of seeing; and there is a believing that is wrought in the heart by an invisible operation of the Spirit, revealing the certainty of the satisfaction of the merits of Christ to the soul in a more glorious way, both for certainty and for durableness, both as to the promise and the constancy of it (Matthew 16:17-18).

3.) There is a faith of a man's own, of a man's self also; but the faith of the operation of God, in Scripture, is set in opposition to that, for, saith He, you are saved by grace, "through faith, and that not of yourselves," of your own making, but that which is the free gift of God (Ephesians 2:8).

4.) We say there is an historical faith—that is, such as is begotten by the cooperation of the Spirit with the Word.

5.) We say there is a traditional faith—that is, to believe things by tradition, because others say they believe them; this is received by tradition, not by revelation, and shall never be able to stand, neither at the day of death, nor at the day of judgment; though possibly men, while they live here, may esteem themselves and states to be very good, because their heads are filled full of it.

6.) There is a faith that is called in Scripture a dead faith, the faith of devils, or of the devil; they also that have only this, they are like the devil, and as sure to be damned as he, notwithstanding their faith, if they get no better into their hearts; for it is far off from enabling of them to lay hold of Jesus Christ, and so to put Him on for eternal life and sanctification, which they must do if ever they be saved (James 2:19, 26).

But all these are short of the saving faith of God's elect, as is manifest; I say, first, Because these may be wrought, and not by that power so exceedingly stretched forth. Secondly, Because these are wrought, partly, a.) By the sense of seeing—namely, the miracles—not by hearing; and, b.) The rest is wrought by a traditional or historical influence of the words in their heads, not by a heavenly, invisible, almighty, and saving operation of the Spirit of God in their hearts.

7.) I do suppose also that there is a faith that is wrought upon men through the influence of those gifts and abilities that God gives sometimes to those that are not His own by election, though by creation; my meaning is, some men, finding that God hath given them very great gifts and abilities—as to the gifts of preaching, praying, working miracles, or the like—I say, therefore do conclude that God is their Father, and they are His children; the ground of which confidence is still begotten, not by the glorious operation of the Spirit, but by a considering of the great gifts that God hath bestowed upon them as to the things before-mentioned. As thus, a. the poor soul considers how ignorant it was, and now how knowing it is. b. Considering how vain it formerly was, and also now how civil it is, presently makes this conclusion—Surely God loves me, surely He hath made me one of His, and will save me. This is now a wrong faith, as is evident, in that it is placed upon a wrong object; for mark, this faith is not placed assuredly on God's grace alone, through the blood and merits of Christ being discovered effectually to the soul, but upon God through those things that God hath given it, as of gifts, either to preach, or pray, or do great works, or the like, which will assuredly come to nought as sure as God is in Heaven, if no better faith and ground of faith be found out for thy soul savingly to rest upon.

As to the second clause of the objection,—that God loves men upon *the account of* their believing, I answer, that God loves men before they believe; He loves them, He calls them, and gives them faith to believe—"But God, who is rich in mercy, for His great love wherewith He loved us," when? when we believed, or before? "even when we were dead in sins," and so, far off from believers, "hath quickened us together with" Christ, "by grace ye are saved" (Ephesians 2:4-5).

Now, also, I suppose that thou wilt say in thy heart, I would you would show us then what is saving faith; which thing it may be I may touch upon a while hence, in the next thing that I am to speak unto. O they that have that are safe indeed!

II. WHO AND HOW MEN ARE ACTUALLY BROUGHT INTO THE NEW COVENANT

The SECOND thing that I am to speak unto is this—WHO they are that are actually brought into this free and unchangeable grace; and also HOW they are brought in.

ANSWER: Indeed, now we come to the pinch of the whole discourse; and if God do but help me to run rightly through this, as I do verily believe He will, I may do thee, reader, good, and bring glory to my God.

The question containeth these two branches—FIRST. Who are brought in; SECOND. How they are brought in.

1. Who Are Brought In?

The first is quickly answered—"Christ Jesus came into the world to save sinners," Jewish sinners, Gentile sinners, old sinners, young sinners, great sinners, the chiefest of sinners. Publicans and harlots—that is, whores, cheaters, and exactors—shall enter into the Kingdom of Heaven (1 Timothy 1:15; Romans 5:7-11; 1 Corinthians 6:9, 11; Matthew 21:31). "For I come not," saith Christ, "to call the righteous, but sinners to repentance" (Mark 2:17).

A sinner in the Scripture is described in *general* to be a transgressor of the law—"Whosoever commiteth sin, transgresseth the law; for sin is the transgression of the law" (1 John 3:4). But *particularly*, they are described in a more particular way, as, 1. Such as in whom dwelleth the devil (Ephesians 2:2-3). 2. Such as will do the service of him (John 8:44). 3. Such as are enemies to God (Colossians 1:21) 4. Such as are drunkards, whoremasters, liars, perjured persons, covetous, revilers, extortionists, fornicators, swearers, possessed with devils, thieves, idolaters, witches, sorcerers, conjurors, murderers, and the like (1 Corinthians 6:9-10; 2 Chronicles 33:1-13; Acts 2:36-37; 9:1-6; 19:9; 1 Timothy 1:14-16). These are sinners, and such sinners that God hath prepared Heaven, happiness, pardon of sin, and an inheritance of God, with Christ, with saints, with angels, if they do come in and accept of grace, as I might prove at large; for God's grace is so great, that if they do come to Him by Christ, presently all is forgiven them; therefore never object that thy sins are too great to be pardoned; but come, taste and see how good the Lord is to any whosoever come unto Him.

2. How Are These Brought into this Everlasting Covenant of Grace?

ANSWER: When God doth in deed and in truth bring in a sinner into this most blessed covenant, (Come to the Touchstone, sinner). for so it is, He usually goeth this way:

FIRST. He slays or kills the party to all things besides Himself, and His Son Jesus Christ, and the comforts of the Spirit. For the clearing of this I shall show you, 1. With what God kills; 2. How God kills; 3. To what God kills those whom He makes alive in Jesus Christ.

1.) When God brings sinners into the Covenant of Grace, He doth first kill them with the Covenant of Works, which is the moral law, or Ten Commandments. This is Paul's doctrine, and also Paul's experience. It is his doctrine where he saith, "The ministration of death, written and engraven in stones—the ministration of condemnation," which is the law, in that place called the letter, "killeth" (2 Corinthians 3:6-9). The letter, saith he, killeth; or the law, or the ministration of death, which in another place is called "the voice of words" (Hebrews 12:19), because they have no life in them, but rather death and damnation, through our inability to fulfil them, doth kill (Romans 8:3; 2 Corinthians 6). It is his experience where he saith, "I was alive" that is, to my own things, "without the law once," that is, before God did strike him dead by it, "but when the commandment came," that is, to do and exercise its right office on me, which was to kill me, then "sin revived, and I died," and I was killed. "And the commandment," or the law, "which *was ordained* to" be unto "life, I found to be unto death. For sin, taking occasion by the commandment, deceived me, and by it *slew me*" (Romans 7:9-11).

2.) But *how* doth God kill with this law, or covenant?

1. By opening to the soul the spirituality of it—"The law is spiritual," saith he, "but I am carnal, sold under sin" (Romans 7:14). Now the spirituality of the law is discovered this way:

> a. By showing to the soul that every sinful thought is a sin against it. Ay, sinner, when the law doth come home indeed upon thy soul in the spirituality of it, it will discover such things to thee to be sins that now thou lookest over and regardest not;

that is a remarkable saying of Paul when he saith, "Sin revived, and I died." Sin revived, saith he; as if he had said, Those things that before I did not value nor regard, but looked upon them to be trifles, to be dead, and forgotten; but when the law was fastened on my soul, it did so raise them from the dead, call them into mind, so muster them before my face, and put such strength into them, that I was overmastered by them, by the guilt of them. Sin revived by the commandment, or my sins had mighty strength, life, and abundance of force upon me because of that, insomuch that they killed me (Matthew 5:28).

b. It showeth that every such sin deserveth eternal damnation. Friends, I doubt there be but few of you that have seen the spirituality of the law of works. But this is one thing in which it discovereth its spirituality, and this is the proper work of the Law.

c. God, with a discovery of this, doth also discover His own Divine and infinite justice, of which the law is a description, which backs what is discovered by the law, and that by discovering of its purity and holiness to be so Divine, so pure, so upright, and so far of from winking at the least sin, that He doth by that law, without any favor, condemn the sinner for that sin (Galatians 3:10). Now, when He hath brought the soul into this praemunire,[13] into this puzzle, then,

2. He showeth to the soul the nature and condition of the law as to its dealings with, or forbearing of, the sinner that hath sinned against it; which is to pass an eternal curse upon both soul and body of the party so offending, saying to him, Cursed be the man that continueth not in everything that is written in the Book of the Law to do it; for, saith the law, this is my proper work; first, to show thee thy sins; and when I have done that, then, in the next place, to condemn thee for them, and that without all remedy, as from ME, or anything within my bounds, for I am not to save any, to pardon any—nay, not to favor any in the least thing that have sinned against me; for God did not send me to make alive, but to discover sin, and to condemn for the same. Now, so soon as this is presented to thy conscience, in the next place, the Lord also by this law doth show that now there

is no righteous act according to the tenor of that covenant that can reprieve him, or take him off from all this horror and curse that lies upon him; because that is not an administration of pardon, as I said before, to forgive the sin, but an administration of damnation, because of transgression. O, the very discovery of this striketh the soul into a deadly swoon, even above half dead! But when God doth do the work indeed, He doth, in the next place, show the soul that he is the man that is eternally under this covenant by nature, and that it is he that hath sinned against this law, and doth by right deserve the curse and displeasure of the same, and that all that ever he can do will not give satisfaction to that glorious justice that did give this law; holy actions, tears of blood, selling all, and giving it to the poor, or whatever else can be done by thee, it comes all short and is all to no purpose (Philippians 3). I will warrant him, he that seeth this, it will kill him to that which he was alive unto before, though he had a thousand lives. Ah, sinners, sinners, were you but sensible indeed of the severity and truth of this, it would make you look about you to purpose! O, how would it make you strive to stop at that that now you drink down with delight! How many oaths would it make you bite asunder! Nay, it would make you bite your tongues to think that they should be used as instruments of the devil to bring your souls into such an unspeakable misery; then also we should not have you hang the salvation of your souls upon such slender pins as now you do; no, no; but you would be in another mind then. O, then we should have you cry out, I must have Christ; what shall I do for Christ? how shall I come at Christ? Would I was sure, truly sure of Christ. My soul is gone, damned, cast away, and must for ever burn with the devils, if I do not get precious Jesus Christ!

3. In the next place, when God hath done this, then He further shows the soul that that covenant which it is under by nature is distinct from the Covenant of Grace; and also they that are under it are by nature without any of the graces which they have that are under the Covenant of Grace; as,

a. That it hath no faith (John 16:9).

b. No hope (Ephesians 2:12). Nor none of the Spirit to work these things in it by nature.

c. Neither will that covenant give to them any peace with God.

d. No promise of safeguard from His revenging law by that covenant.

e. But lieth by nature liable to all the curses, and condemnings, and thunderclaps of this most fiery covenant.

f. That it will accept of no sorrow, no repentance, no satisfaction, as from thee.

g. That it calls for no less than the shedding of thy blood.

h. The damnation of thy soul and body.

i. And if there be anything proffered to it by thee, as to the making of it amends, it throws it back again as dirt in thy face, slighting all that thou canst bring.

Now, when the soul is brought into this condition, then it is indeed dead, killed to that to which it was once alive. And therefore,

3.) In the next place, to show you to what it is killed: and that is:

1. To sin. O, it dares not sin! it sees Hell-fire is prepared for them that sin, God's justice will not spare it if it live in sin; the Law will damn it if it live in sin; the devil will have it if it follows its sins. (Here I am speaking of one that is effectually brought in). O, I say, it trembles at the very thoughts of sin! Ay, if sin do but offer to tempt the soul, to draw away the soul from God, it cries, it sighs, it shunneth the very appearance of sin, it is odious unto it. If God would but serve you thus that love your pleasures, you would not make such a trifle of sin as you do.

2. It is killed to the Law of God as it is the Covenant of Works. O, saith the soul, the law hath killed me to itself, "I through the law am dead to the law" (Galatians 2:19). The law is another thing than I did think it was. I thought it would not have been so soul-destroying, so damning a law! I thought it would not have been so severe against me for my little sins, for my playing, for my jesting, for my dissembling, quarrelling, and the like. I had some thoughts, indeed, that it would hew great sinners, but let me pass! and though it condemned great sinners, yet it would pass me by! But now, would I were free from this covenant, would I were free

from this law! I will tell thee that a soul thus worked upon is more afraid of the Covenant of Works than he is of the devil; for he sees it is the law that doth give him up into his hands for sin; and if he was but clear from that, he should not greatly need to fear the devil. O, now every particular command tears the caul of his heart; now every command is a great gun well charged against his soul; now he sees he had as good run into a fire to keep himself from burning, as to run to the law to keep himself from damning; and this he sees really, ay, and feels it too, to his own sorrow and perplexity. [14]

3. The soul also now is killed to his own righteousness, and counts that but dung, but dross, not worth the dirt hanging on his shoes. O! then, says he, thou filthy righteousness! how hast thou deceived me! How hast thou beguiled my poor soul! (Isaiah 64:6). How did I deceive myself with giving of a little alms; with abstaining from some gross pollutions; with walking in some ordinances, as to the outside of them! How hath my good words, good thinkings, good meanings, as the world calls them, deceived my ignorant soul! I want the righteousness of faith, the righteousness of God; for I see now there is no less will do me any good.

4. It is also killed to its own faith, its notion of the Gospel, its own hope, its own repentings, its own promises and resolutions, to its own strength, its own virtue, or whatsoever it had before. Now, saith the soul, that faith I thought I had, it is but fancy; that hope I thought I had, I see it is by hypocritical, but vain and groundless hope. (These things would be too tedious to enlarge upon). Now the soul sees it hath by nature no saving faith, no saving hope, no grace at all by nature, by the first covenant. Now it crieth out, How many promises have I broken! and how many times have I resolved in vain, when I was sick at such a time, and in such a strait at such a place! Indeed, I thought myself a wise man once, but I see myself a very fool now. O, how ignorant am I of the Gospel now, and of the blessed experience of the work of God on a Christian heart! In a word, it sees itself beset by nature with all evil, and destitute of all good, which is enough to kill the stoutest, hardest-hearted sinner that ever lived on the earth. O,

friends, should you be plainly dealt withal by this discovery of the dealing of God with a sinner when He makes him a saint, and would seriously try your selves thereby, as God will try you one day, how few would there be found of you to be so much as acquainted with the work of God in the notion, much less in the experimental knowledge of the same! And indeed, God is fain to take this way with sinners, thus to kill them with the old covenant to all things below a crucified Christ.

SIX REASONS FOR THIS DISCOURSE

1.) Because otherwise there would be none in the world that would look after this sweet Jesus Christ. There are but a few that go to Heaven in all, comparatively; and those few God is fain to deal with them in this manner, or else His Heaven, His Christ, His glory, and everlasting happiness must abide by themselves, for all sinners. Do you think that Manasseh would have regarded the Lord, had He not suffered his enemies to have prevailed against him? (2 Chronicles 33:1-16). Do you think that Ephraim would have looked after salvation, had not God first confounded him with the guilt of the sins of his youth? (Jeremiah 31:18). What do you think of Paul? (Acts 9:4-6). What do you think of the jailer? (Acts 16:30-32). What do you think of the three thousand? (Acts 2:36-37). Was not this the way that the Lord was fain to take to make them close in with Jesus Christ? Was He not fain to kill them to everything below a Christ, that were driven to their wits" ends, insomuch that they were forced to cry out, "What shall we do to be saved?" I say, God might have kept Heaven and happiness to Himself, if He should not go this way to work with sinners. O stout-hearted rebels! O tender-hearted God!

2.) Because then, and not till then, will sinners accept of Jesus Christ on God's terms. So long as sinners can make a life out of anything below Christ, so long they will not close with Christ without indenting;[15]

But when the God of Heaven hath killed them to everything below Himself and His Son, then Christ will down on any terms in the world. And, indeed, this is the very reason why sinners, when they hear of Christ, yet will not close in with Him; there is something that they can take content in besides Him. The prodigal, so long as he could content himself with the husks that the swine did eat, so long he did keep him away from his father's house; but when he could get no nourishment anywhere on this side of his father's house, then saith he, and not till then, "I will arise, and go to my father," etc.

I say, this is the reason, therefore, why men come no faster, and close no more readily, with the Son of God, but stand halting and indenting[16] about the terms they must have Christ upon; for, saith the drunkard, I look on Christ to be worth the having; but yet I am not willing to lose ALL for him; all but my pot, saith the drunkard; and all but the world, saith the covetous. I will part with anything but lust and pride, saith the wanton. But if Christ will not be had without I forsake all, cast away all, then it must be with me as it was with the young man in the Gospel, such news will make me sorry at the very heart.

But now, when a man is soundly killed to all his sins, to all his righteousness, to all his comforts whatsoever, and sees that there is no way but the devil must leave him, but he must be damned in Hell if he be not clothed with Jesus Christ; O, then, saith he, give me Christ on any terms, whatsoever He cost; though He cost me friends, though He cost me comforts, though He cost me all that ever I have; yet, like the wise merchant in the Gospel, they will sell all to get that pearl. I tell you, when a soul is brought to see its want of Christ aright, it will not be kept back; father, mother, husband, wife, lands, livings, nay, life and all, shall go rather than the soul will miss of Christ. Ay, and the soul counteth Christ a cheap Savior if he can get him upon any terms; now the soul indents[17] no longer. Now, Lord, give me Christ upon any terms, whatsoever He cost; for I am a dead man, a damned man, a castaway, if I have not Christ. What say you, O you wounded sinners? Is not this true as I have said? Would you not give ten thousand worlds, if you had so many, so be you might be well assured that your sins shall be pardoned, and your souls and bodies justified and glorified at the coming of the Lord Jesus Christ?

3.) The Lord goeth this way for this reason also, that it might make the soul sensible what it cost Christ to redeem it from death and Hell. When a man cometh to feel the sting and guilt of sin, death and Hell upon his conscience, then, and not till then, can he tell what it cost Christ to redeem sinners. O! saith the soul, if a few sins are so terrible, and lay the soul under such wrath and torment, what did Christ undergo, who bare the sins of thousands and thousands, and all at once?

This also is one means to make souls tender of sin (it is the burned child that feareth the fire), to make them humble in a sense of their own vileness, to make them count everything that God giveth them a mercy, to make much of the least glimpse of the love of God, and to prize it above the whole world. O sinners, were you killed indeed (to sin), then Heaven would be Heaven, and Hell would be Hell indeed; but because you are not wrought upon in this manner, therefore you count the ways of God as bad as a good man counteth the ways of the devil, and the ways of the devil and Hell as good as a saint doth count the ways of God.

4.) Again, God is fain to go this way, and all to make sinners make sure of Heaven. So long as souls are senseless of sin, and what a damnable state they are in by nature, so long they will even dally with the Kingdom of Heaven and the salvation of their own poor souls; but when God cometh and showeth them where they are, and what it is like to become of them if they miss of the crucified Savior, O, then, saith the soul, would I were sure of Jesus; what shall I do to get assurance of Jesus? And thus is God forced, as I may say, to whip souls to Jesus Christ, they being so secure, so senseless, and so much their own enemies, as not to look out after their own eternal advantage.

5.) A fifth reason why God doth deal thus with sinners it is, because He would bring Christ and the soul together in a right way. Christ and sinners would never come together in a beloved posture, they would not so suitably suit each other, if they were not brought together this way, the sinner being killed. O, when the sinner is killed, and indeed struck dead to everything below a naked Jesus, how suitably then doth the soul and Christ suit one with another. Then here is a naked sinner for a righteousness Jesus, a poor sinner to a rich Jesus, a weak sinner to a strong Jesus, a blind sinner to a seeing Jesus, an ignorant, careless sinner to a wise and careful Jesus. O, how wise is God in dealing thus with the sinner! He strips him of his own knowledge, that He may fill him with Christ's; He killeth him for taking pleasure in sin, that he may take pleasure in Jesus Christ, etc.

6.) *First,* God goeth this way with sinners, because He would have the glory of their salvation. Should not men and women be killed to their own things, they would do sacrifice unto them, and instead of saying to the Lamb, "THOU ART WORTHY," they would say their own arm, their own right hand hath saved them; but God will cut off boasting from ever entering within the borders of eternal glory; for He is resolved to have the glory of the beginning, the middle, and the end; of the contriving, and saving, and giving salvation to them that enter in to the joys of everlasting glory (Romans 3:27; Ephesians 2:8-9; Titus 3:5; Revelation 5:9). "That they might be called trees of righteousness, the planting of the LORD, that He might be glorified" (Isaiah 61:3). I might have run through many things as to this; but I shall pass them, and proceed.

Second. Now, the soul being this killed to itself, (The soul that hath the right work of God upon its heart, is not only killed to itself, but also made alive to Christ). its sins, its righteousness, faith, hope, wisdom, promises, resolutions, and the rest of its things which it trusted in by nature; in the next place, it hath also given unto it a most glorious, perfect, and never-fading life, which is:

1. A life imputed to it, yet so really, that the very thought of it in the soul hath so much operation and authority, especially when the mediation of it is mixed with faith, as to make it, though condemned by the law, to triumph, and to look its enemies in the face with comfort, notwithstanding the greatness of the multitude, the fierceness of their anger, and the continuation of their malice, be never so hot against it.

This imputed life—for so it is—is the obedience of the Son of God as His righteousness, in His suffering, rising, ascending, interceding, and so consequently triumphing over all the enemies of the soul, and given to me, as being wrought on purpose for me. So that, is there righteousness in Christ? that is mine. Is there perfection in that righteousness? that is mine. Did He bleed for sin? it was for mine. Hath He overcome the law, the devil, and Hell? the victory is mine, and I am counted the conqueror, nay, more than a conqueror, through Him that hath loved me. And I do count this a most glorious life; for by this means it is that I am, in the first place, proclaimed both in Heaven and earth guiltless, and such an one who, as I am in Christ, am not sinner, and so not under the law, to be condemned, but as holy and righteous as the Son of God Himself, because He Himself is my holiness and righteousness, and so likewise having by this all things taken out of the way that would condemn me.

Sometimes I bless the Lord my soul hath had the life that now I am speaking of, not only imputed to me, but the very glory of it upon my soul; for, upon a time, when I was under many condemnings of heart, and feared, because of my sins, my soul would miss of eternal glory, methought I felt in my soul such a secret motion of this—Thy righteousness is in Heaven, together with the splendour and shining of the Spirit of Grace in my soul, which gave me to see clearly that my righteousness by which I should be justified from all that could condemn, was the Son of God Himself in His own Person, now at the right hand of His Father representing me complete before the Mercy-seat in His Own-self; so that I saw clearly that night and day, wherever I was, or whatever I was a doing, still there was my righteousness just before the eyes of Divine glory; so that the Father could never find fault with me for any insufficiency that was in my righteousness, seeing it was complete; neither could He say, Where is it? because it was continually at His right hand.[18]

Also, at another time, having contracted guilt upon my soul, and having some distemper of body upon me, I supposed that death might now so seize upon as to take me away from among men; then, thought I, what shall I do now? is all right with my soul? Have I the right work of God on my soul? Answering myself, "No, surely"; and that because there were so many weaknesses in me; yes, so many weaknesses in my best duties. For, thought I, how can such an one as I find mercy, whose heart is so ready to evil, and so backward to that which is good, so far as it is natural. Thus musing, being filled with fear to die, these words come in upon my soul, "Being justified freely by His grace through the redemption that is in Christ Jesus" (Romans 3:24). As if God had said, Sinner, thou thinkest because that thou hast had so many infirmities and weaknesses in thy soul while thou hast been professing of Me, therefore now there can be no hopes of mercy; but be it known unto thee, that it was not anything done by thee at the first that moved Me to have mercy upon thee: neither is it anything that is done by thee now that shall make me either accept or reject thee. Behold My Son, who standeth by Me, He is righteous, He hath fulfilled My Law, and given me good satisfaction; on Him, therefore, do I look, and on thee only as thou art in Him; and according to what He hath done, so will I deal with thee. This having stayed my heart, and taken off the guilt through the strength of its coming on my soul, anon after came in that word as a second testimony—"Who hath saved us, and called *us* with an holy calling, not according to our works," of righteousness which we have done, "but according to His own purpose and grace, which was given us in Christ Jesus before the world began" (2 Timothy 1:9). And thus is the sinner made alive from the dead, being justified by grace through the righteousness of Christ, which is unto all and upon all them that believe, according to the Scriptures—"And the life which I now live—it is "by the faith of the Son of God, who loved me, and gave Himself for me" (Galatians 2:20). "I lay down my life for the sheep." "I am come that they might have life, and that they might have *it* more abundantly" (John 10:10, 15). "For if, when we were enemies, we were reconciled to God by the death of His Son, much more, being reconciled, we shall be saved by His life. That as sin hath reigned unto death, even so might grace reign through righteousness unto eternal life by Jesus Christ our Lord" (Romans 5:10, 21).

 2. This life is not only imputed to him that is wrought on by the Spirit of Grace—that is, not only counted his, but also there is put into the soul an understanding, enlightened on purpose to know

the things of God, which is Christ and His imputed righteousness (1 John 5:20) which it never thought of nor understood before (1 Corinthians 2:9-11). Which understanding being enlightened and made to see such things that the soul can not be contented without it lay hold of and apply Christ unto itself so effectually; I say, that the soul shall be exceedingly revived in a very heavenly measure with the application of this imputed righteousness; for thereby it knoweth it shall find God speaking peace to itself, with a fatherly affection, saying, "Be of good cheer, thy sins are forgiven thee"; the righteousness of My Son I bestow upon thee; "For what the law could not do, in that it was weak through thee," thy "flesh," "I have sent forth My only Son, and have condemned" thy sins in His flesh (Romans 8:3). And though thou hast gone astray like a lost sheep, yet on Him I have laid thine iniquities; and though thou thereby didst undo and break thyself for ever, yet by His stripes I have healed thee. Thus, I say, the Lord causeth the soul by faith to apply that which He doth by grace impute unto it, for thus every soul more or less is dealt withal; the soul being thus enlightened, thus quickened, thus made alive from that dead state it was in before, or at least having the beginnings of this life, it hath these several virtuous advantages, which they have not that are dead in their sins and trespasses, and under the law:

Advantages Possessed By The Quickened

FIRST. It seeth what a sad condition all men by nature are in, they being in that state which itself was in but a while since; but now by grace it is a beginning to scrabble[19] out of it; now it seeth "the whole world lieth in wickedness," and so liable to eternal vengeance, because of their wickedness (1 John 5:19). Ah, friends, let me tell you, though you may be ignorant of your state and condition, yet the poor, groaning, hungering saints of God do see what a sad, woeful, miserable state you are in, which sometimes makes them tremble to think of your most lamentable latter end, your dying so, and also to fly the faster to their Lord Jesus, for very fear that they also should be partakers of that most doleful doom. (Like as the children of Israel, who fled for fear when the ground opened its mouth to swallow up Korah and his company). And this it hath by virtue of its own experience, knowing itself was but awhile ago in the same condition, under the same condemnation. O! there is now a hearth blessing of God that ever He should show to it its sad condition, and that He should incline its heart to seek after a better condition. O blessed be the Lord! saith the soul, that ever He should awaken me, stir up me, and bring me out of that sad condition that I once with them was in (Psalms 103:1-3). It makes also the soul to wonder to see how foolishly and vainly the rest of its neighbors do spend their precious time, that they should be so void of understanding, so forgetful of their latter end, so senseless of the damning nature of their sins. O that their eyes were but enlightened to see whereabouts they are! surely they would be of another mind than they are now in. Now, the soul wonders to see what slender pins those poor creatures do hang the stress of the eternal salvation of their souls upon. O! methinks, saith the soul, it makes me mourn to see that some should think that they were born Christians; and others, that their baptism makes them so;[20] others depend barely upon a traditional, historical faith, which will leave their souls in the midst of perplexity. That they should trust to such fables, fancies, and wicked sleights of the devil, as their good doings, their good thinkings, their civil walking and living with the world. O miserable profession, and the end thereof will be a miserable end!

But now, when the souls is thus wrought upon, it must be sure to look for the very gates of Hell to be set open against it with all their force and might to destroy it. Now Hell rageth, the devil roareth, and all the world resolveth to do the best they can to bring the soul again into bondage and ruin. Also, the soul shall not want enemies, even in its own heart's lust, (But this is but for the exercise of his faith.) as covetousness, adultery, blasphemy, unbelief, hardness of heart, coldness, half-heartedness, ignorance, with an innumerable company of attendants, hanging, like so many blocks, at its heels, ready to sink it into the fire of Hell every moment, together with strange apprehensions of God and Christ, as if now they were absolutely turned to be its enemies, which maketh it doubt of the certainty of its salvation; for you must understand, that though a soul may in reality have the righteousness of the Son of God imputed to it, and also some faith in a very strong manner to lay hold upon it, yet at another time, through temptation, they may fear and doubt again, insomuch that the soul may be put into a very great fear lest it should return again into the condition it once was in (Jeremiah 32:40). O, saith the soul, when I think of my former state, how miserable it was, it makes me tremble; and when I think that I may fall into that condition again, how sad are the thoughts of it to me! I would not be in that condition again for all the world. And this fear riseth still higher and higher, as the soul is sensible of Satan's temptations, or of the working of its own corruptions. Ah! these filthy lusts, these filthy corruptions. O that I were rid of them, that they were consumed in a moment, that I could be quite rid of them, they do so disturb my soul, dishonor my God, so defile my conscience, and sometimes so weaken my hands in the way of God, and my comforts in the Lord; O how glad should I be if I might be stripped of them (Romans 7:24). Which fear puts the soul upon flying to the Lord by prayer for the covering of His imputed righteousness, and for strength against the devil's temptations and its own corruptions; that God would give down His Holy Spirit to strengthen it against the things that do so annoy its soul, and so discourage it in its way, with a resolution, through grace, never to be contented while (until) it doth find in itself a triumphing over it, by faith in the blood of a crucified Jesus.

SECOND. The soul that hath been thus killed by the Law to the things it formerly delighted in, now, O now, it can not be contented with that slender, groundless faith and hope that once it contented itself withal. No, no; but now it must be brought into the right saving knowledge of Jesus Christ, now it must have Him discovered to the soul by the Spirit, now it can not be satisfied because such and such do tell it is so. No; but now it will cry out, Lord, show me continually, in the light of Thy Spirit, through Thy Word, that Jesus that was born in the days of Caesar Augustus, when Mary, a daughter of Judah, went with Joseph to be taxed at Bethlehem, that He is the very Christ. Lord, let me see it in the light of Thy Spirit, and in the operation thereof; and let me not be contented without such a faith that is so wrought even by the discovery of His birth, crucifying, death, blood, resurrection, ascension, intercession, and second—which is His personal—coming again, that the very faith of it may fill my soul with comfort and holiness. And O, how afraid the soul is lest it should fall short of this faith, and of the hope that is begotten by such discoveries as these are! For the soul knoweth that if it hath not this, it will not be able to stand either in death or judgment; and therefore, saith the soul, Lord, whatever other poor souls content themselves withal, let me have that which will stand me in stead, and carry me through a dangerous world; that may help me to resist a cunning devil; that may help me to suck true soul-satisfying consolation from Jesus Christ through Thy promises, by the might and power of Thy Spirit. And now, when the poor soul at any time hath any discovery of the love of God through a bleeding, dying, risen, interceding Jesus, because it is not willing to be deceived, O, how wary (But this may be its temptation, taking place through the timorousness of the soul). is it of closing with it, for fear it should not be right, for fear it should not come from God! Saith the soul, Can not the devil give one such comfort I trow? Can not he transform himself thus into an angel of light? So that the soul, because that it would be upon a sure ground, cries out, Lord, show me Thy salvation, and that not once or twice, but, Lord, let me have Thy presence continually upon my heart, today, and tomorrow, and every day. For the soul, when it is rightly brought from under the Covenant of Works, and planted into the Covenant of Grace, then it can not be, unless it be under some desperate temptation, contented without the presence of God, teaching, comforting, establishing, and helping of the soul to grow in the things of the Lord Jesus Christ; because it knoweth that if God hath but withdrawn His presence in any way from it, as He doth do sometimes for a while, that then the devil will be sure to be near at hand, working with his temptations, trying all ways to get the soul into slavery and sin again; also the corrupt principle, that will be joining and combining with the Wicked One, and will be willing to be a co-partner with him to bring the soul into mischief; which puts a soul upon an earnest, continual panting after more of the strengthening, preserving, comforting, and teaching presence of God, and for strong supplies of faith, that it may effectually lay hold on him.

THIRD. The soul is quickened so that it is not satisfied now without it do in deed and in truth partake of the peace of God's elect; now it is upon the examination of the reality of its joy and peace. Time was indeed that anything would serve its turn, any false conceits of its state to be good; but now all kind of peace will not serve its turn, all kind of joy will not be accepted with it; now it must joy in God through Jesus Christ; now its peace must come through the virtues of the blood of Christ speaking peace to the conscience by taking away both the guilt and filth of sin by that blood; also by showing the soul its free acceptance with God through Christ, He hath completely fulfilled all the conditions of the first covenant, and freely placed it into the safety of what He hath done, and so presents the soul complete and spotless in the sight of God through His obedience. Now, I say, he hath "peace through the blood of His Cross," and sees himself reconciled to God by the death of His Son, or else his comfort will be questioned by him (Colossians 1:20-21). It is not every promise as cometh now upon his heart that will serve his turn, no, but he must see whether the babe Jesus be presented to the soul in and through that promise. Now if the babe leap in his womb, as I may so say, it is because the Lord's promise sounds aloud in his heart, coming to him big with the love and pardoning grace of God in Jesus Christ; I say, this is the first and principal joy that the soul hath that is quickened and brought into the Covenant of Grace.

FOURTH. Now the man finds heavenly sanctification wrought in his soul through the most precious blood of the Man whose name is Jesus Christ—"Jesus, that He might sanctify the people with His own blood, suffered without the gate." Now the souls finds a change in the understanding, in the will, in the mind, in the affections, in the judgment, and also in the conscience; through the inward man a change, and through the outward man a change, from head to foot, as we use to say, "for he that is in Christ," and so in this Covenant of Grace, "*is* a new creature," or hath been twice made—made, and made again (2 Corinthians 5:17). O, now the soul is resolved for Heaven and Glory; now it crieth out, Lord, if there be a right eye that is offensive to Thee, pluck it out; or a right foot, cut it off; or a right hand, take it from me. Now the soul doth begin to study how it may honor God, and bring praise to Him. Now the soul is for a preparation for the second coming of Christ, endeavoring to lay aside everything that may hinder; and for the closing in with those things that may make it in a beloved posture against that day.

FIFTH. And all this is from a Gospel spirit, and not from a legal, natural principle, for the soul hath these things as the fruits and effects of its being separated unto the Covenant of Grace, and so now possessed with that Spirit that doth attend, yea, and dwell in them that are brought into the Covenant of Grace from under the old covenant; I say, these things do spring forth in the soul from another root and stock than any of the actings of other men do; for the soul that is thus wrought upon is as well dead to the law and the righteousness thereof—as the first covenant—as well as to its sins.

SIXTH. Now the soul begins to have some blessed experience of the things of God, even of the glorious mysteries of the Gospel.

1.) Now it knoweth the meaning of those words, "My flesh is meat indeed, and My blood is drink, indeed," and that by experience; for the soul hath received peace of conscience through that blood, by the effectual application of it to the soul (John 6:55). First, by feeling the guilt of sin die off from the conscience by the operation thereof. Secondly, By feeling the power thereof to take away the curse of the law. Thirdly, By finding the very strength of Hell to fail when once the blood of that Man Jesus Christ is received in reality upon the soul.

2.) Now the soul also knoweth by experience the meaning of that Scripture that saith, "Our old man is crucified with *Him*, that the body of sin might be destroyed" (Romans 6:6). Now it sees that when the Man Jesus did hang on the tree on Mount Calvary, that then the body of its sins was there hanged up, dead and buried with Him, though it was then unborn, so as never to be laid to its charge, either here or hereafter; and also, so as never to carry it captive into perpetual bondage, being itself overcome by Him, even Christ, the Head of that poor creature. And indeed this is the way for a soul both to live comfortably as touching the guilt of sin, and also as touching the power of the filth of sin; for the soul that doth or hath received this in deed and in truth, finds strength against them both by and through that Man that did for him and the rest of his fellow-sinners so gloriously overcome it, and hath given the victory unto them, so that now they are said to be overcomers, nay, "more than conquerors through Him," the one Man Jesus Christ (Romans 7:33-37).

3.) Now the soul hath received a faith indeed, and a lively hope indeed, such an one as now it can fetch strength from the fullness of Christ, and from the merits of Christ.

4.) Yea, now the soul can look on itself with one eye, and look upon Christ with another, and say, Indeed, it is true; I am an empty soul, but Christ is a full Christ; I am a poor sinner, but Christ is a rich Christ; I am a foolish sinner, but Christ is a wise Christ; I am an unholy, ungodly, unsanctified creature in myself, but Christ is made of God "unto me, wisdom, and righteousness, and sanctification, and redemption" (1 Corinthians 1:30).

5.) Now also that fiery law, that it could not once endure, nor could not once delight in, I say, now it can delight in it after the inward man; now this law is its delight, it would always be walking in it, and always be delighting in it, being offended with any sin or any corruption that would be anyways an hindrance to it (Romans 7:24-25). And yet it will not abide, it will not endure that that, even that that law should offer to take the work of its salvation out of Christ's hand; no, if it once comes to do that, then out of doors it shall go, if it were as good again. For that soul that hath the right work of God indeed upon it, cries, Not my prayers, not my tears, not my works, not my things, do they come from the work of the Spirit of Christ itself within me, yet these shall not have the glory of my salvation; no, it is none but the blood of Christ, the death of Christ, of the Man Christ Jesus of Nazareth, the carpenter's son, as they called Him, that must have the crown and glory of my salvation. None but Christ, none but Christ. And thus the soul labors to give Christ the pre-eminence (Colossians 1:18).

A Word of Experience

Now, before I go any further, I must needs speak a word from my own experience of the things of Christ; and the rather, because we have a company of silly ones in this day of ignorance that do either comfort themselves with a notion without the power, or else do both reject the notion and the power of this most glorious Gospel; therefore, for the further conviction of the reader, I shall tell him, with David, something of what the Lord hath done for my soul; and indeed a little of the experience of the things of Christ is far more worth than all the world. It would be too tedious for me to tell thee here all from the first to the last; but something I shall tell thee, that thou mayest not think these things are fables. (This conviction seized on my soul one Sabbath day, when I was at play, being one of the first that I had, which when it came, though it scared me with its terror, yet through the temptation of the devil, immediately striking in therewith, I did rub it off again, and became as vile for some time as I was before, like a wretch that I was). [21]

Reader, when it pleased the Lord to begin to instruct my soul, He found me one of the black sinners of the world; He found me making a sport of oaths, and also of lies; and many a soul-poisoning meal did I make out of divers lusts, as drinking, dancing, playing, pleasure with the wicked ones of the world. The Lord finding of me in this condition, did open the glass of His Law unto me, wherein He showed me so clearly my sins, both the greatness of them, and also how abominable they were in His sight, that I thought the very clouds were charged with the wrath of God, and ready to let fall the very fire of His jealousy upon me; yet for all this I was so wedded to my sin, that, thought I with myself, I will have them though I lose my soul, (O wicked wretch that I was!) but God, the great, the rich, the infinite merciful God, did not take this advantage of my soul to cast me away, and say, Then take him, Devil, seeing he cares for Me no more; no, but He followed me still, and won upon my heart, by giving me some understanding, not only into my miserable state, which I was very sensible of, but also that there might be hopes of mercy; also taking away that love to lust, and placing in the room thereof a love to religion; and thus the Lord won over my heart to some desire after the means, to hear the Word, and to grow a stranger to my old companions, and to accompany the people of God, together with giving of me many sweet encouragements from several promises in the Scriptures. But after this, the Lord did wonderfully set my sins upon my conscience, those sins especially that I had committed since the first convictions; temptations also followed me very hard, and especially such temptations as did tend to the making me question of the very way of salvation—viz., whether Jesus Christ was the Savior or no; and whether I had best to venture my soul upon His blood for salvation, or take some other course. But being through grace kept close with God, in some measure, in prayer and the rest of the ordinances, but went about a year and upwards without any sound evidence as from God to my soul touching the salvation that comes by Jesus Christ. But, at the last, as I may say, when the set time was come, the Lord, just before the men called Quakers came into the country, did set me down so blessedly in the truth of the doctrine of Jesus Christ, that it made me marvel to see, first, how Jesus Christ was born of a virgin, walked in the world awhile with His disciples, afterwards hanged on the Cross, spilt His blood, was buried, rose again, ascended above the clouds and heavens, there lives to make intercession, and that He also will come again at the last day to judge the world, and take His saints unto Himself.

These things, I say, I did see so evidently, even as if I had stood when He was in the world, and also when He was caught up. I having such a change as this upon my soul, it made me wonder; and musing with myself at the great alteration that was in my spirit—for the Lord did also very gloriously give me in His precious Word to back the discovery of the Son of God unto me, so that I can say, through grace, it was according to the Scriptures (1 Corinthians 15:1-4). And as I was musing with myself what these things should mean, methought I heard such a word in my heart as this—I have set thee down on purpose, for I have something more than ordinary for thee to do; which made me the more marvel, saying, What, my Lord, such a poor wretch as I? Yet still this continued, I have set thee down on purpose, and so forth, with more fresh incomes of the Lord Jesus, and the power of the blood of His Cross upon my soul, even so evidently that I saw, through grace, that it was the blood shed on Mount Calvary that did save and redeem sinners, as clearly and as really with the eyes of my soul as ever, me thought, I had seen a penny loaf bought with a penny; which things then discovered had such operation upon my soul, that I do hope they did sweetly season every faculty thereof. Reader, I speak in the presence of God, and He knows I lie not; much of this, and such like dealings of His, could I tell thee of; but my business at this time is not so to do, but only to tell what operation the blood of Christ hath had over and upon my conscience, and that at several times, and also when I have been in several frames of spirit.

As, first, sometimes, I have been so loaded with my sins, that I could not tell where to rest, nor what to do; yea, at such times I thought it would have taken away my senses; yet at that time God through grace hath all of a sudden so effectually applied the blood that was spilt at Mount Calvary out of the side of Jesus, unto my poor, wounded, guilty conscience, that presently I have found such a sweet, solid, sober, heart-comforting peace, that it hath made me as if it (my terror) had not been, and withal the same, I may say, and I ought to say, the power of it, hath had such a powerful operation upon my soul, that I have for a time been in a strait and trouble to think that I should love and honor Him no more, the virtue of His blood hath so constrained me.

Again; sometimes methinks my sins have appeared so big to me that I thought one of my sins have been as big as all the sins of all the men in the nation; ay, and of other nations too, reader; these things be not fancies, for I have smarted for this experience, but yet the least stream of the heart blood of this Man[22] Jesus hath vanished all away, and hath made it to fly, to the astonishment of such a poor sinner; and as I said before, hath delivered me up into sweet and heavenly peace and joy in the Holy Spirit.

Again; sometimes when my heart hath been hard, dead, slothful, blind, and senseless, which indeed are sad frames for a poor Christian to be in, yet at such a time, when I have been is such a case, then hath the blood of Christ, the precious blood of Christ, the admirable blood of the God of Heaven, that run out of His body when it did hang on the Cross, so softened, livened, quickened, and enlightened my soul, that truly, reader, I can say, O it makes me wonder!

Again; when I have been loaded with sin, and (I cannot stand here to tell thee of particular temptations). pestered with several temptations, and in a very sad manner, then have I had the trial of the virtue of Christ's blood with the trial of the virtue of other things; and I have found that when tears would not do, prayers would not do, repentings and all other things could not reach my heart; O then, one touch, one drop, one shining of the virtue of the blood, of that blood that was let out with the spear, it hath in a very blessed manner delivered me, that it hath made me to marvel. O! methinks it hath come with such life, such power, with such irresistible and marvellous glory, that it wipes off all the slurs, silences all the outcries, and quenches all the fiery darts, and all the flames of Hell-fire, that are begotten by the charges of the Law, Satan, and doubtful remembrances of my sinful life.

Friends, as Peter saith to the church, so I say to you, I have not preached to you cunningly devised fables in telling you of the blood of Christ, and what authority it hath had upon my conscience; O no, but as Peter saith touching the coming of the Lord Jesus into the world, so in some measure I can say of the blood of the Lord Jesus Christ that was shed when He did come into the world. There is not only my single testimony touching this; no, but there are all the Prophets do agree in advancing this in writing, and also all the saints do now declare the same, in speaking forth the amiableness and many powerful virtues thereof. "As for Thee also, by the blood of Thy covenant," saith God to Christ, "I have sent forth Thy prisoners out of the pit wherein is no water" (Zechariah 9:11). "We have redemption through His blood" (Ephesians 1:7). Again, "We have redemption through His blood" (Colossians 1:14). Our robes are washed and made "white in the blood of the Lamb" (Revelation 7:14). The devil is overcome through "the blood of the Lamb" (Revelation 12:11). Yea, and conscience is purged, too, and that through the blood of the Lamb (Hebrews 9:14). We have free recourse to the Throne of Grace through the blood of Jesus (Hebrews 10:19). I could bring thee a cloud of witnesses out of all the types and shadows, and out of the sundry Prophets, and much more out of the New Testament, but I forebear, because I would not be too tedious to the reader in making too large a digression, though I have committed here in this discourse no transgression, for the blood of Christ is precious blood (1 Peter 1:18-19).

III. THE PRIVILEGES OF THE NEW COVENANT

In the next place, I shall show you the several privileges and advantages that the man or woman hath that is under this Covenant of Grace, over what they have that are under the Covenant of the Law and Works. As,

FIRST. The Covenant of Grace is not grounded upon our obedience, but upon God's love, even His pardoning love to us through Christ Jesus. The first covenant is stood to be broken or kept by us, and God's love or anger to be lost or enjoyed thereafter as we, as creatures, behaved ourselves; but now, the very ground of the Covenant of Grace is God's love, His mere love through Jesus Christ—"The LORD did not set His love upon you, nor choose you, because ye were more in number than any people; for ye were the fewest of all people: but because the LORD loved you, and because He would keep the oath which He had sworn unto your fathers" (Deuteronomy 7:7-8). Again, "In His love and in His pity He redeemed them," "and the angel of His presence saved them," that is, Jesus Christ (Isaiah 63:9). And again, "Who hath saved us—not according to our works" of righteousness which we have done, "but according to His own purpose and grace, which was given us in Christ Jesus before the world began" (2 Timothy 1:9).

SECOND. This love is not conveyed to us through what we have done, as is before proved, but through what He hath done with Whom the covenant was made, which was given us in Christ—According as He hath chosen us in Christ. "Who hath blessed us with all spiritual blessings in heavenly places in Christ." "God for Christ's sake hath forgiven you," that is, through Christ's doings, through Christ's sufferings (2 Timothy 1:9; Ephesians 1:3-4; 4:32). Now if this be but rightly understood, it doth discover abundance of comfort to them, that are within the bounds of the Covenant of Grace. For,

1.) Here a believer seeth he shall stand, if Christ's doings and sufferings stand; which is sure foundation, for God dealeth with him through Christ. And so, secondly, he shall not fall, unless the suffering and merits of Christ be thrown over the bar, being found guilty, which will never be, before the eyes of Divine justice; for with

Him the covenant was made, and He was the Surety of it; that is, as the covenant was made with Him, so He stood bound to fulfil the same (Zechariah 9:11; Hebrews 7:22). For you must understand that the covenant was made between the Father and the Son long before it was accomplished, or manifestly sealed with Christ's blood; it was made before the world began (Titus 1:2; Ephesians 1:4; 1 Peter 1:18-20). But the conditions thereof were not fulfilled until less than two thousand years ago; and all that while did Jesus stand bound as a surety, as I said before, is used to do, till the time in which the payment should be made. And it was by virtue of His Surety-ship, having bound Himself by covenant to do all things agreed on by the Father and Him, that all those of the election that were born before He came, that they might be saved, and did enter into rest. For the forgiveness of sins that were past, though it was through the blood of Christ, yet it was also through the forbearance of God (Romans 3:25). That is, Christ becoming Surety for those that died before His coming, that He should in deed and in truth, at the fullness of time, or at the time appointed, give a complete and full satisfaction for them according to the tenor or condition of the covenant. (Galatians 4:4). Again,

2.) The second covenant, which believers are under, as the ground and foundation, if it is safe, so the promises thereof are *better, surer, freer,* and *fuller,* etc.

a. They are better, if you compare the excellency of the one with the excellency of the other. The first hath promised nothing but an early paradise—Do this, and thou shalt live; namely, here in an earthly paradise. But the other doth bring the promise of a heavenly paradise.

b. As the Covenant of Works doth promise an earthly paradise, yet it is a paradise or blessing, though once obtained, yet might be lost again; for no longer than thou doest well, no longer art thou blessed by that. O, but the promises in the new covenant do bring unto us the benefit of an eternal inheritance—That "they which are called might receive the promise of eternal inheritance." O rare! it is an "eternal inheritance" (Hebrews 9:15).

c. The other, as it is not so good as this, so neither is it so sure as this; and therefore he calls the one such an one as might be, and was, shaken, but this is said to be such an one that can not be shaken. "And this *Word*," saith he, treating of the two covenants from verse the 8th to the 24th—"And this *Word*, yet once more, signifieth the removing of those things that are," or may be, "shaken, as of things that are made, that those things which can not be shaken," which is the second covenant, "may remain," (Hebrews 12:27); for, saith he (verse 28) "which can not be moved." Therefore, ye blessed saints, seeing you have received a kingdom "which can not be moved," therefore, "let us have grace, whereby we may serve" our "God acceptably with reverence and godly fear."

Thus in general, but more particularly.

d. They are *surer*, in that they are founded upon God's love also, and they come to us without calling for those things at our hands that may be a means of putting of a stop to our certain enjoying of them. The promises under, or for the law, they might easily be stopped by our disobedience; but the promises under the Gospel say, "If Heaven above can be measured, and the foundations of the earth searched," then, and not till then, "I will also cast off all the seed of Israel for all that they have done" (Jeremiah 31:37). Again, "I, *even* I, *am* He that blotteth out thy transgressions for Mine own" name's "sake, and will not remember thy sins" (Isaiah 43:25). I will make thee a partaker of My promise; and that I may so do, I will take away that which would hinder; "I will cast all their sins into the depths of the sea," that My promise may be sure to all the seed; and therefore, saith the Apostle, when he would show us that the new-covenant promises were more sure than the old, he tells us plainly that the law and works are set aside and they are merely made ours through the righteousness of faith, which is the righteousness of Christ—"For the promise, that he (Abraham) should be the heir of the world," saith he, "was not to Abraham, or to his seed, through the law," or works, "but through the righteousness of faith. For if they which are of the law," or of works, "*be* heirs," then "faith is made void, and the promise made of none effect. Therefore it is of faith—to the end the promise might be sure to all the seed" (Romans 4:13-14, 16).

e. *Surer*, because that as that is taken away that should hinder, so they are committed to a faithful Friend of ours in keeping. For all the promises of God are in Christ, not yea and nay, but yea and amen; certain and sure; sure, because they are in the hand of our Head, our Friend, our Brother, our Husband, our flesh and bones, even in the heart and hand of our precious Jesus.

f. Because all the conditions of them are already fulfilled for us by Jesus Christ, as aforesaid; every promise that is a new-covenant promise, if there be any condition in it, our Undertaker hath accomplished that for us, and also giveth us such grace as to receive the sweetness as doth spring from them through His obedience to every thing required in them.

g. *Surer*, because that as they are grounded upon the love of God, everything is taken out of the way, in the hand of a sure Friend. And has Christ has fulfilled every condition as to justification that is contained therein, so the Lord hath solemnly sworn with an oath for our better confidence in this particular—"For when God made promise to Abraham," and so to all the saints, "because He could swear by no greater, He sware by Himself, saying, Surely, blessing I will bless thee, and multiplying I will multiply thee. And so, after he had patiently endured, he obtained the promise. For men verily swear by the greater: and an oath for confirmation *is* to them an end of all strife," that there might be no more doubt or scruple concerning the certain fulfilling of the promise. "Wherein God, willing more abundantly to show unto the heirs of promise the immutability of His counsel," or certain, constant, unchangeable decree of God in making of the promise, for the comfort of his children, "confirmed *it* by an oath: that by two immutable things," His promise backed with an oath, "in which *it was* impossible for God to lie, we might have a strong consolation, who have fled for refuge to lay hold upon the hope set before us" (Hebrews 6:13-18).

h. That they are better it appears also in that they are *freer* and fuller. That they are freer, it is evident, in that one saith, No works, no life—Do this, and then thou shalt live; if not, thou shalt be damned. But the other saith, We are saved by believing in what Another hath done, without the works of the Law—"Now to him that worketh not, but believeth on Him that justifieth the ungodly, his faith is counted for righteousness" (Romans 4:4-5). The one saith, Pay me that thou owest; the other say, I do frankly and freely forgive thee all. The one saith, Because thou hast sinned, thou shalt die; the other saith, Because Christ lives, thou shalt live also (John 15).

i. And as they are freer, so they are *fuller*; fuller of encouragement, fuller of comfort; the one, to wit, the law, looks like Pharaoh's seven ill-favored kine, more ready to eat one up than to afford us any food; the other is like the full grape in the cluster, which for certain hath a glorious blessing in it. The one saith, If thou hast sinned, turn again; the other saith, If thou hast sinned, thou shalt be damned, for all I have a promise in me.

3.) They that are of the second are better than they that are of the first; and it also appeareth in this—The promises of the Law, through them we have neither faith, nor hope, nor the Spirit conveyed; but through the promises of the Gospel there are all these—"Whereby are given unto us exceeding great and precious promises, that by these we might be partakers of the Divine nature" (2 Peter 1:4). O therefore "let us hold fast the profession of *our* faith without wavering; for He is faithful that promised" (Hebrews 10:23). "In hope of eternal life," how so? because "God, that can not lie, promised it before the world began" (Titus 1:2).

4.) They that are in this covenant are in a very happy state; for though there be several conditions in the Gospel to be done, yet Christ Jesus doth not look that they should be done by man, as man, but by His own Spirit in them, as it is written, "Thou hast wrought all our works in us." Is there that condition, they must believe? Why, then, He will be both the "author and finisher of *their* faith" (Hebrews 12:2-3). Is there also hope to be in His children? He also doth and hath given them "good hope through His grace" (2 Thessalonians 2:16). Again, are the people of God to behave themselves to the glory of God the Father? then He will work in them "both to will and to do of *His* own good pleasure" (Philippians 2:13).

5.) Again, as He works all our works in us and for us, so also by virtue of this covenant we have another nature given unto us, whereby, or by which we are made willing to be glorifying of God, both in our bodies and in our spirits, which are His—"Thy people *shall* be willing in the day of Thy power" (1 Corinthians 6:20; Psalms 110:3).

6.) In the next place, all those that are under this second covenant are in a wonderful safe condition; for in case they should slip or fall after their conversion into some sin or sins (for who lives and sins not? (Proverbs 24:16), yet through the merits and intercession of Christ Jesus, who is their Undertaker in this covenant, they shall have their sins pardoned, their wounds healed, and they raised up again; which privilege the children of the first covenant have not; for if they sin, they are never afterwards regarded by that covenant— They brake My covenant and I regarded them not, saith the Lord (Hebrews 8:9). But when He comes to speak of the Covenant of Grace, speaking first of the public person under the name of David, He saith thus, "He shall cry unto Me, Thou *art* My Father, My God, and the rock of My salvation. Also I will make Him My firstborn, higher than the kings of the earth. My mercy will I keep for Him for evermore, and My covenant shall stand fast with Him. His seed also will I make to *endure* for ever, and His throne as the days of heaven. If His children forsake My law, and walk not in My judgments; If they break my statutes, and keep not My commandments; Then will I visit their transgression with the rod, and their iniquity with stripes. Nevertheless My loving-kindness will I not utterly take from Him, nor suffer My faithfulness to fail. My covenant will I not break, nor alter the thing that is gone out of My lips. Once have I sworn by My holiness that I will not lie unto David. His seed shall endure for ever, and His throne as the sun before Me. It shall be established for ever as the moon, and as a faithful witness in heaven" (Psalms 89:26-37). "My covenant shall stand fast with him"—mark that. As if God had said, I did not make this covenant with man, but with My Son, and with Him I will perform it; and seeing He hath given Me complete satisfaction, though His children do, through infirmity, transgress, yet My covenant is not therefore broken, seeing He with whom it was made standeth firm, according to the desire of my heart; so that My justice that is satisfied, and My Law, hath nothing to say, for there is no want of perfection in the sacrifice of Christ.

If you love your souls, and would have them live in the peace of God, to the which you are called in one body, even all believers, then I beseech you seriously to ponder, and labor to settle in your souls this one thing, that the new covenant is not broken by our transgressions, and that because it was not made with us. The reason why the very saints of God have so many ups and downs in this their travel towards Heaven, it is because they are so weak in the faith of this one thing; for they think that if they fail of this or that particular performance, if their hearts be dead and cold, and their lusts mighty and strong, therefore now God is angry, and now He will shut them out of His favor, now the new covenant is broken, and now Christ Jesus will stand their Friend no longer; now also the devil hath power again, and now they must have their part in the resurrection of damnation; when, alas! the covenant is not for all this never the more broken, and so the grace of God no more straitened than it was before. Therefore, I say, when thou findest that thou art weak here, and failing there, backward to this good, and thy heart forward to that evil; then be sure thou keep a steadfast eye on the Mediator of this new covenant, and be persuaded that it is not only made with Him, and His part also fulfilled, but that He doth look upon His fulfilling of it, so as not to lay thy sins to thy charge, though He may as a Father chastise thee for the same—"If His children forsake My law, and walk not in My judgments; if they break My statutes, and keep not My commandments; then will I visit their transgression with the rod, and their iniquity with stripes. Nevertheless," mark "nevertheless My loving-kindness will I not utterly take from HIM, nor suffer My faithfulness to fail. My covenant will I not break, nor alter the thing that is gone out of My lips." And what was that? Why, that "His seed shall endure for ever, and His throne as the sun before Me" (Psalms 89:30-34, 36).

7.) Another privilege that the saints have by virtue of the new covenant is, that they have part of the possession or hold of Heaven and Glory already, and that two manner of ways:

a. The Divine nature is conveyed from Heaven into them; and, secondly, the human nature, *i.e.*, the nature of man, is received up, and entertained in, and hath got possession of Heaven. We have the first-fruits of the Spirit, saith the man of God; we have the earnest of the Spirit, which is instead of the whole, for it is the earnest of the whole—"Which is the earnest of our inheritance until the redemption of the purchased possession, unto the praise of His glory" (Ephesians 1:13-14; Romans 8:8-11).

    b. The nature of man, *our* nature is got into glory as the first-fruits of mankind, as a forerunner to take possession till we all come thither (1 Corinthians 15:20). For the Man born at Bethlehem is ascended, which is part of the lump of mankind, into glory as a public Person, as the first-fruits, representing the whole of the children of God; so that in some sense it may be said that the saints have already taken possession of the kingdom of Heaven by their Jesus, their public Person, He being in their room entered to prepare a place for them (John 14:1-4). I beseech you consider, when Jesus Christ came down from Glory, it was that He might bring us to Glory; and that He might be sure not to fail, He clothed Himself with our nature, as if one should take a piece out of the whole lump instead of the whole, until the other comes, and investeth it in that glory which He was in before He came down from Heaven (Hebrews 2:14-15). And thus is that saying to be understood, speaking of Christ and His saints, which saith, "And" He "hath raised *us* up together, and made *us* sit together in heavenly *places* in Christ Jesus" (Ephesians 2:6).

    8.) Again, not only thus, but all the power of God, together with the rest of His glorious attributes, are on our side, in that they dwell in our nature, which is the *Man* Jesus, and doth engage for us poor, simple, empty, nothing creatures as to our eternal happiness (1 Peter 1:5). "For in Him," that is, in the Man Christ, who is our nature, our Head, our root, our flesh, our bone, "dwelleth all the fullness of the Godhead bodily" (Colossians 2:9-10). Mark how they are joined together, "In whom dwelleth the fullness of the Godhead. And ye are complete in Him." God dwelleth completely in Him, and you also are completely implanted in Him, which is the Head of all principality and power; and all this by the consent of the Father—"For it pleased *the Father* that in Him should all fullness dwell" (Colossians 1:19). Now mark, the Godhead doth not dwell in Christ Jesus for Himself only, but that it may be in a way of righteousness conveyed to us, for our comfort and help in all our wants—"All power is given unto Me in heaven and in earth," saith He (Matthew 28:18). And then followeth, "And lo, I am with you alway, *even* unto the end of the world" (Verse 20). "He hath received gifts for men, yea for the rebellious" (Psalms 68:18). "Of His fullness have all we received, and grace for grace" (John 1:16). And this the saints can not be deprived of, because the covenant made with Christ, in every tittle of it, was so completely fulfilled as to righteousness, both active and passive, that justice can not object anything; holiness now can find fault with nothing; nay, all the power of God can not shake anything that hath been done for us by the Mediator of the new covenant; so that now there is no Covenant of Works to a believer; none of the commands, accusations, condemnations, or the least tittle of the old covenant to be charged on any of those that are the children of the second covenant; no sin to be charged, because there is no law to be pleaded, but all is made up by our middle man, Jesus Christ. O blessed covenant! O blessed privilege! Be wise, therefore, O ye poor drooping souls that are the sons of this second covenant, and "stand fast in the liberty wherewith Christ hath made you free, and be not entangled AGAIN," nor terrified in your consciences, "with the yoke of bondage"; neither the commands, accusations, or condemnations of the Law of the old covenant (Galatians 5:1).

Two Hell-Bred Objections Answered

OBJECTION: If it be so, then one need not care what they do; they may sin and sin again, seeing Christ hath made satisfaction. (The first objection).

ANSWER: If I were to point out one that was under the power of the devil, and going post-haste to Hell, for my life I would look no farther for such a man than to him that would make such a use as this of the grace of God. What, because Christ is a Savior, thou wilt be a sinner! because His grace abounds, therefore thou wilt abound in sin! O wicked wretch! rake Hell all over, and surely I think thy fellow will scarce be found! And let me tell thee this before I leave thee—as God's covenant with Christ for His children, which are of faith, stands sure, immutable, unrevocable, and unchangeable, so also hath God taken such a course with thee, that unless thou canst make God forswear Himself, it is impossible that thou shouldst go to Heaven, dying in that condition—"They tempted Me, proved Me," and turned the grace of God into lasciviousness, "so I sware," mark that, "so I sware," and that in My wrath, too, that they should never enter into My rest. Compare Hebrews 3:9-11, with 1 Corinthians 10:5-10. No, saith God; if Christ will not serve their turns, but they must have their sins too, take them, Devil; if Heaven will not satisfy them, take them, Hell; devour them, Hell; scald them, fry them, burn them, Hell! God hath more places than one to put sinners into. If they do not like Heaven, He will fit them with Hell; if they do not like Christ, they shall be forced to have the devil. Therefore we must and will tell of the truth of the nature of the Covenant of Grace of God to His poor saints for their encouragement and for their comfort, who would be glad to leap at Christ upon any terms; yet therewith, we can tell how, through grace, to tell the hogs and sons of this world what a hog-sty there is prepared for them, even such an one that God hath prepared to put the devil and his angels into, is fitly prepared for them (Matthew 25:41).

OBJECTION: But if Christ hath given God a full and complete satisfaction, then though I do go on in sin, I need not fear, seeing God hath already been satisfied. (The second objection). It will be injustice in God to punish for those sins for which He is already satisfied for by Christ.

ANSWER: Rebel, rebel, there are some in Christ and some out of Him.

1.) They that are in Him have their sins forgiven, and they themselves made new creatures, and have the Spirit of the Son, which is a holy, living, self-denying Spirit. And they that are thus in Jesus Christ are so far off from delighting in sin, that sin is the greatest thing that troubleth them; and O how willing would they be rid of the very thoughts of it (Psalms 119:113). It is the grief of their souls, when they are in a right frame of spirit, that they can live no more to the honor and glory of God than they do; and in all their prayers to God, the breathings of their souls are as much sanctifying grace as pardoning grace, that they might live a holy life. They would as willing live holy here as they would be happy in the world to come; they would as willingly be cleansed from the filth of sin as to have the guilt of it taken away; they would as willingly glorify God here as they would be glorified by Him hereafter (Philippians 3:6-22).

2.) But there are some that are out of Christ, being under the Law; and as for all those, let them be civil or profane, they are such as God accounts wicked; and I say, as for those, if all the angels in Heaven can drag them before the judgment-seat of Christ, they shall be brought before it to answer for all their ungodly deeds; and being condemned for them, if all the fire in Hell will burn them, they shall be burned there, if they die in that condition (Jude 15). And, therefore, if you love your souls, do not give way to such a wicked spirit. "Let no man deceive you with" such "vain words," as to think, because Christ hath made satisfaction to God for sin, therefore you may live in your sins. O no, God forbid that any should think so, "for because of these things cometh the wrath of God upon the children of disobedience" (Ephesians 5:6).

Thus have I, reader, given thee a brief discourse touching the Covenant of Works and the Covenant of Grace, also of the nature of the one, together with the nature of the other. I have also in this discourse endeavored to show you the condition of them that are under the Law, how sad it is, both from the nature of the covenant they are under, and also by the carriage of God unto them by that covenant. And now, because I would bring all into as little a compass as I can, I shall begin with the use and application of the whole in as brief a way as I can, desiring the Lord to bless it to thee.

USE AND APPLICATION

A Use of Examination About the Old Covenant

FIRST. And, first of all, let us here begin to examine a little touching the covenant you stand before God in, whether it be the Covenant of Works or the Covenant of Grace; (The first use is a use of examination), and for the right doing of this, I shall lay down this proposition—namely, that all men naturally come into the world under the first of these, which is called the old covenant, or the

Covenant of Works, which is the Law; "And were all by nature the children of wrath, even as others"; which they could not be, had they not been under the law; for there are none that are under the other covenant that are still the children of wrath, but the children of faith, the children of the promise, the accepted children, the children not of the bond-woman, but of the free (Galatians 4:28-31).

QUESTION: Now here lieth the question: Which of these two covenants art thou under, soul?

ANSWER: I hope I am under the Covenant of Grace.

QUESTION: But what ground hast thou to think that thou art under that blessed covenant, and not rather under the Covenant of Works, that strict, that soul-damning covenant?

ANSWER: What ground? Why, I hope I am.

QUESTION: But what ground hast thou for this thy hope? for a hope without a ground is like a castle built in the air, that will never be able to do thee any good, but will prove like unto that spoken of in Job 8, "Whose hope shall be cut off, and whose trust shall be" like "a spider's web. He shall lean upon his house, but it shall not stand; he shall hold it fast," as thou wouldst thy hope, it is like, "but it shall not endure" (Job 8:13-15).

ANSWER: My hope is grounded upon the promises; what else should it be grounded upon?

REPLY: Indeed, to build my hope upon Christ Jesus, upon God in Christ, through the promise, and to have this hope rightly, by the shedding abroad of the love of God in the heart, it is a right-grounded hope (Romans 5:1-7).

QUESTION: But what promises in the Scripture do you find your hope built upon? and how do you know whether you do build your hope upon the promises in the Gospel, the promises of the new covenant, and not rather on the promises of the old covenant, for there are promises in that as well as in the other?

ANSWER: I hope that if I do well I shall be accepted; because God hath said I shall (Genesis 4:7).

REPLY: O soul, if thy hope be grounded there, thy hope is not grounded upon the Gospel promises, or the new covenant, but verily upon the old; for these words were spoken to Cain, a son of the old covenant; and they themselves are the tenor and scope of that; for that runs thus: "Do this, and thou shalt live. The man that doth these things shall live by them. If thou do well, thou shalt be accepted" (Leviticus 18:5; Ezekiel 20:11; Romans 10:5; Galatians 3:12; Genesis 4:7).

REPLY: Why, truly, if a man's doing well, and living well, and his striving to serve God as well as he can, will not help him to Christ, I do not know what will; I am sure sinning against God will not.

QUESTION: Did you never read that Scripture which saith, "Israel, which followed after the law of righteousness, hath not attained to the law of righteousness"? (Romans 9:30-32).

OBJECTION: But doth not the Scripture say, "Blessed are they that do His commandments, that they may have right to the tree of life"? (Revelation 22:14).

ANSWER: There is first, therefore, to be inquired into, whether to keep His commandments be to strive to keep the Law as it is a Covenant of Works, or whether it be meant of the great commandments of the New Testament which are cited in 1 John 3:22-23—"And whatsoever we ask we receive of Him, because we keep His commandments, and do those things that are pleasing in His sight." But what do you mean, John? Do you mean the covenant of the Law, or the covenant to the Gospel? Why, "this is His commandment," saith he, "That we should believe on the name of His Son Jesus Christ, and love one another," as the fruits of this faith, "as He gave us commandment." If it be of the old covenant, as a Covenant of Works, then the Gospel is but a lost thing. If it were of works, then no more of grace; therefore it is not the old covenant, as the old covenant.

QUESTION: But what do you mean by these words—the old covenant as the old covenant? Explain your meaning.

ANSWER: My meaning is, that the Law is not to be looked upon for life, so as it was handed out from Mount Sinai, if ever thou wouldst indeed be saved; though after thou hast faith in Christ, thou mayest and must solace thyself in it, and take pleasure therein, to express thy love to Him who hath already saved thee by His own blood, without thy obedience to the law, either from Sinai or elsewhere.

QUESTION: Do you think that I do mean that my righteousness will save me without Christ? If so, you mistake me, for I think not so; but this I say, I will labor to do what I can; and what I can not do, Christ will do for me.

ANSWER: Ah, poor soul, this is the wrong way too; for this is to make Christ but a piece of a Savior; thou wilt do something, and Christ shall do the rest; thou wilt set thy own things in the first place, and if thou wantest at last, then thou wilt borrow of Christ; thou art such an one that dost Christ the greatest injury of all. First, in that thou dost undervalue His merits by preferring of thy own works before His; and, secondly, by mingling of thy works thy dirty, ragged righteousness with His.

QUESTION: Why, would you have us do nothing? Would you have us make Christ such a drudge as to do all, while we sit idling still?

ANSWER: Poor soul, thou mistakest Jesus Christ in saying thou makest Him a drudge in letting Him do all; I tell thee, He counts it a great glory to do all for thee, and it is a great dishonor unto Him for thee so much as to think otherwise. And this the saints of God that have experienced the work of grace upon their souls do count it also the same—"Saying, Thou art worthy to take the book, and to open the seals thereof" (Revelation 5:9). "Worthy is the Lamb, that was slain, to receive power, and riches, and wisdom, and strength, and honor, and glory, and blessing" (Verse 12). And why so? read again in the 9th verse, "For Thou wast slain, and hast redeemed us to God by Thy" own "blood" (See also Ephesians 1:6-7). "To the praise of the glory of His grace—in whom we have redemption through His blood."

REPLY: All this we confess, that Jesus Christ died for us; but he that thinks to be saved by Christ, and liveth in his sins, shall never be saved.

ANSWER: I grant that. But this I say again, a man must not make his good doings the lowest round of the ladder by which he goeth to Heaven—that is, he that will and shall go to Heaven, must, wholly and alone, without any of his own things, venture his precious soul upon Jesus Christ and His merits.

QUESTION: What, and come to Christ as a sinner?

ANSWER: Yea, with all thy sins upon thee, even as filthy as ever thou canst.

QUESTION: But is not this the way to make Christ to loath us? You know when children fall down in the dirt, they do usually before they go home make their clothes as clean as they can, for fear their parents should chide them; and so I think should we.

ANSWER: This comparison is wrongly applied, if you bring it to show us how we must do when we come to Christ. He that can make himself clean hath no need of Christ; for the whole, the clean, and righteous have no need of Christ, but those that are foul and sick. Physicians, you know, if they love to be honored, they will not bid the patients first make themselves whole, and then come to them; no, but bid them come with their sores all running on them, as the woman with her bloody issue (Mark 5). And as Mary Magdalene with her belly full of devils, and the lepers all scabbed; and that is the right coming to Jesus Christ.

REPLY: Well, I hope that Christ will save me, for His promises and mercy are very large; and as long as He hath promised to give us life, I fear my state the less.

ANSWER: It is very true, Christ's promises are very large, blessed be the Lord for ever; and also so is His mercy; but notwithstanding all that, there are many go in at the broad gate; and therefore I say, your business is seriously to inquire whether you are under the first or second covenant; for unless you are under the second, you will never be regarded of the Lord, forasmuch as you are a sinner (Hebrews 8:9). And the rather, because if God should be so good to you as to give you a share in the second, you shall have all your sins pardoned, and for certain have eternal life, though you have been a great sinner. But do not expect that thou shalt have any part or share in the large promises and mercy of God, for the benefit and comfort of thy poor soul, whilst thou art under the old covenant; because so long thou art out of Christ, through whom God conveyeth His mercy, grace, and love to sinners. "For all the promises of God in Him *are* yea, and in Him amen." Indeed, His mercy, grace, and love are very great, but they are treasured up in Him, "given forth in Him, through Him." "But God, who is rich in mercy, for His great love wherewith He loved us—that He might show the exceeding riches of His grace"—but which way?—"in *His* kindness towards us through Jesus Christ."

But out of Christ thou shalt find God a just God, a sin-avenging God, a God that will by no means spare the guilty; and be sure that every one that is found out of Jesus Christ will be found guilty in the judgment-day, upon whom the wrath of God shall smoke to their eternal ruin. Now, therefore, consider of it, and take the counsel of the Apostle, in 2 Corinthians 13:5, which is, to examine thyself whether thou art "in the faith," and to prove thy ownself whether thou hast received the Spirit of Christ into thy soul, whether thou hast been converted, whether thou hast been born again, and made a new creature, whether thou hast had thy sins washed away in the blood of Christ, whether thou hast been brought from under the old covenant into the new; and do not make a slight examination, for thou hast a precious soul either to be saved or damned.

And that thou mayest not be deceived, consider that it is one thing to be convinced, and another to be converted; one thing to be wounded, and another to be killed, and so to be made alive again by the faith of Jesus Christ. When men are killed, they are killed to all things they lived to before, both sin and righteousness, as all their old faith and supposed grace that they thought they had. Indeed, the old covenant will show thee that thou art a sinner, and that a great one too; but the old covenant, the Law, will not show thee, without the help of the Spirit, that thou are without all grace by nature; no; but in the midst of thy troubles thou wilt keep thyself from coming to Christ by persuading thy soul that thou art come already, and hast some grace already. O, therefore, be earnest in begging the Spirit, that thy soul may be enlightened, and the wickedness of thy heart discovered, that thou mayest see the miserable state that thou art in by reason of sin and unbelief, which is the great condemning sin; and so in a sight and sense of thy sad condition, if God should deal with thee in severity according to thy deservings. Do thou (now) cry to God for faith in a crucified Christ, that thou mayest have all thy sins washed away in His blood, and such a right work of grace wrought in thy soul that may stand in the judgment-day. Again,

SECOND. In the next place, you know I told you that a man might go a great way in a profession, and have many excellent gifts, (Second use). so as to do many wondrous works, and yet be but under the Law; from hence you may learn not to judge yourselves to be the children of God, because you may have some gifts of knowledge or understanding more than others: no, for thou mayest be the knowingest man in all the country as to head-knowledge, and yet be but under the law, and so consequently under the curse, notwithstanding that, 1 Corinthians 13. Now, seeing it is so, that men may have all this and yet perish, then what will become of those that do no good at all, and have no understanding, neither of their own sadness, nor of Christ's mercy? O, sad! Read with understanding, Isaiah 27:11, "Therefore He that made them will not have mercy on them, and He that formed them will show them no favor" (See also 2 Thessalonians 1:8-9).

Now there is one thing which, for want of, most people do miscarry in a very sad manner, and that is, because they are not able to distinguish between the nature of the Law and the Gospel. O, people, people, your being blinded here as to the knowledge of this is one great cause of the ruining of many. As Paul saith, "While Moses is read," or while the law is discovered, "the veil is upon their heart" (2 Corinthians 3:15) that is, the veil of ignorance is still upon their hearts, so that they can not discern either the nature of the law or the nature of the Gospel, they being so dark and blind in their minds, as you may see, if you compare it with Chronicles 4:3-4. And truly I am confident, that were you but well examined, I doubt many of you would be found so ignorant that you would not be able to give a word of right answer concerning either the Law or the Gospel. Nay, my friends, set the case, one should ask you what time you spend, what pains you take, to the end you may understand the nature and difference of these two covenants, would you not say, if you should speak the truth, that you did not so much as regard whether there were two or more? Would you not say, I did not think of covenants, or study the nature of them? I thought that if I had lived honestly, and did as well as I could, that God would accept of me, and have mercy upon me, as He had on others. Ah, friends, this is the cause of the ruin of thousands; for if they are blinded to this, both the right use of the law, and also of the Gospel, is hid from their eyes, and so for certain they will be in danger of perishing most miserably, poor souls that they are, unless God, of His mere mercy and love, doth rend the veil from off their hearts, the veil of ignorance, for that is it which doth keep these poor souls in this besotted and blindfolded condition, in which if they die they may be lamented for, but not helped; they may be pitied, but not preserved from the stoke of God's everlasting vengeance.

A Legal Spirit

In the next place, if you would indeed be delivered from the first into the second covenant, I do admonish you to the observing of these following particulars. First. Have a care that you do not content yourselves, though you do good works—that is, which in themselves are good. Secondly. In and with a legal spirit, which are done these ways as followeth.

FIRST. If you do anything commanded in Scripture, and your doing of it do think that God is well pleased therewith, because you, as you are religious men, do do the same. Upon this mistake was Paul himself in danger of being destroyed; for he thought, because he was zealous, and one of the strictest sects for religion, therefore God would have been good unto him, and have accepted his doings, as it is clear, for he counted them his gain (Philippians 3:4-8). Now this is done thus—When a man doth think that because he thinks he is more sincere, more liberal, with more difficulty, or to the weakening of his estate; I say, if a man, because of this doth think that God accepteth his labor, it is done from an old-covenant spirit.

Again; some men think that they shall be heard because they have prayer in their families, because they can pray long, and speak excellent expressions, or express themselves excellently in prayer, that because they have great enlargements in prayer, I say, that therefore to think that God doth delight in their doings, and accept their works, this is from a legal spirit.

Again; some men think that because their parents have been religious before them, and have been indeed the people of God, they think if they also do as to the outward observing of that which they learned from their forerunners, that therefore God doth accept them; but this also is from a wrong spirit; and yet how many are there in England at this day that think the better of themselves merely upon that account; ay, and think the people of God ought to think so too, not understanding that it is ordinary for an Eli to have a Hophni and a Phinehas, both sons of Belial; also a good Samuel to have a perverse offspring; likewise David an Absalom. I say, their being ignorant of, or else negligent in regarding this, they do think that because they do spring from such and such, as the Jews in their generation did, that therefore they have a privilege with God more than others, when there is no such thing; but for certain, if the same faith be not in them which was in their forerunners, to lay hold of the Christ of God in the same spirit as they did, they must utterly perish, for all their high conceits that they have of themselves (John 8:33-35; Matthew 3:7-9).

SECOND. When people come into the presence of God without having their eye upon the Divine Majesty, through the flesh and blood of the Son of Mary, the Son of God, then also do they come before God, and do whatsoever they do from a legal spirit, an old-covenant spirit. As, for instance, you have some people, it is true, they will go to prayer, in appearance very fervently, and will plead very hard with God that He would grant them their desires, pleading their want, and the abundance thereof; they will also plead with God His great mercy, and also His free promises; but yet they neglecting the aforesaid body or Person of Christ, the righteous Lamb of God, to appear before Him in, I say, in thus doing they do not appear before the Lord no otherwise than in an old-covenant spirit; for they go to God as a merciful Creator, and they themselves as His creatures; not as He is, their Father in the Son, and they His children by regeneration through the Lord Jesus. Ay, and though they may call God their Father, in the notion—not knowing what they say, only having learned such things by tradition—as the Pharisees did, yet Christ will have His time to say to them, even to their faces, as He did once to the Jews, Your father, for all this your profession, is the devil, to their own grief and everlasting misery (John 8:44).

THIRD. The third thing that is to be observed, if we would not be under the Law, or do things in a legal spirit, is this—to have a care that we do none of the works of the holy Law of God for life, or acceptance with Him; no, nor of the Gospel neither. To do the works of the law to the end we may be accepted of God, or that we may please Him, and to have our desires of Him, is to do things from a legal or old-covenant spirit, and that is expressly laid down where it is said, "To him that worketh is the reward not reckoned of grace, but of debt"; that is, he appears before God through the Law, and his obedience to it (Romans 4:4-5). And again, though they be in themselves Gospel-ordinances, as baptism, breaking of bread, hearing, praying, meditating, or the like; yet, I say, if they be not done in the right spirit, they are thereby used as a hand by the devil to pull thee under the Covenant of Works, as in former times he used circumcision, which was no part of the Covenant of Works, the Ten Commands, but a seal of the righteousness of faith; yet, I say, they being done in a legal spirit, the soul was thereby brought under the Covenant of Works, and so most miserably destroyed unawares to itself, and that because there was not a right understanding of the nature and terms of the said covenants. And so it is now; souls being ignorant of the nature of the old covenant, do even by their subjecting to several Gospel ordinances, run themselves under the old covenant, and fly off from Christ, even when they think they are a-coming closer to him. O, miserable! If you would know when or how this is done, whether in one particular or more, I shall show you as followeth:

1.) That man doth bring himself under the Covenant of Works, by Gospel ordinances, when he can not be persuaded that God will have mercy upon him except he do yield obedience to such or such a particular thing commanded in the Word. This is the very same spirit that was in the false brethren (spoken of Acts 15; Galatians, the whole Epistle), whose judgment was, that unless such and such things were done, "they could not be saved." As now-a-days we have also some that say, Unless your infants be baptised they can not be saved;[23] and others say, unless you be rightly baptised, you have no ground to be assured that you are believers, or members of churches; which is so far off from being so good as a legal spirit, that it is the spirit of blasphemy, as is evident, because they do reckon that the Spirit, righteousness, and faith of Jesus, and the confession thereof, is not sufficient to declare men to be members of the Lord Jesus; when, on the other side, though they be rank hypocrites, yet if they do yield an outward subjection to this or that, they are counted presently communicable members, which doth clearly discover that there is not so much honor given to the putting on the righteousness of the Son of God as there is given to that which a man may do, and yet go to Hell within an hour after; nay, in the very doing of it doth shut himself for ever from Jesus Christ.

2.) Men may do things from a legal or old-covenant spirit when they content themselves with their doing of such and such a thing, as prayers, reading, hearing, baptism, breaking of bread, or the like; I say, when they can content themselves with the thing done, and sit down at ease and content because the thing is done. As, for instance, some men being persuaded that such and such a thing is their duty, and that unless they do do it, God will not be pleased with them, nor suffer them to be heirs of His kingdom, they from this spirit do rush into and do the thing, which being done, they are content, as being persuaded that now they are without doubt in a happy condition, because they have done such things, like unto the Pharisee, who, because he had done this and the other thing, said therefore, in a bragging way, "Lord, I thank thee that I am not as this publican"; for I have done thus and thus; when, alas! the Lord give him never a good word for his labor, but rather a reproof.

3.) That man doth act from a legal spirit who maketh the strictness of his walking the ground of his assurance for eternal life. Some men, all the ground they have to believe that they shall be saved, it is because they walk not so loose as their neighbors, they are not so bad as others are, and therefore they question not but that they shall do well. Now this is a false ground, and a thing that is verily legal, and savors only of some slight and shallow apprehensions of the old covenant. I call them shallow apprehensions, because they are not right and sound, and are such as will do the soul no good, but beguile it, in that the knowledge of the nature of this covenant doth not appear to the soul, only some commanding power it hath on the soul, which the soul endeavoring to give up itself unto, it doth find some peace and content, and especially if it find itself to be pretty willing to yield itself to its commands. And is not this the very ground of thy hoping that God will save thee from the wrath to come? If one should ask thee what ground thou hast to think thou shalt be saved, wouldst thou not say, Truly, because I have left my sins, and because I am more inclinable to do good, (Do not think that I am against the order of the Gospel). and to learn, and get more knowledge; I endeavor to walk in church order, as they call it, and therefore I hope God hath done a good work for me, and I hope will save my soul. Alas, alas! this is a very trick of the devil to make souls build the ground of their salvation upon this their strictness, and abstaining from the wickedness of their former lives, and because they desire to be stricter and stricter. Now, if you would know such a man or woman, you shall find them in this frame—namely, when they think their hearts are good, then they think also that Christ will have mercy upon them; but when their corruptions work, then they doubt and scruple until again they have their hearts more ready to do the things contained in the law and ordinances of the Gospel. Again, such men do commonly cheer up their hearts, and encourage themselves still to hope all shall be well, and that because they are not so bad as the rest, but more inclinable than they, saying, I am glad I am not as this publican, but better than he, more righteous than he (Luke 18:11).

4.) This is a legal and old-covenant spirit that secretly persuades the soul that if ever it will be saved by Christ, if must be fitted for Christ by its getting of a good heart and good intentions to do this and that for Christ; I say, that the soul when it comes to Christ may not be rejected or turned off; when in deed and in truth this is the very way for the soul to turn itself from Jesus Christ, instead of turning to Him; for such a soul looks upon Christ rather to be a painted Savior or a cypher than a very and real Savior. Friend, if thou canst fit thyself, what need hast thou of Christ? If thou cant get qualifications to carry to Christ that thou mightst be accepted, thou dost not look to be accepted in the Beloved. Shall I tell thee? Thou art as if a man should say, I will make myself clean, and then I will go to Christ that He may wash me; or like a man possessed, that will first cast the devils out of himself, and then come to Christ for cure from Him. Thou, must, therefore, if thou wilt so lay hold of Christ as not to be rejected by Him; I say, thou must come to Him as the basest in the world, more fit to be damned, if thou hadst thy right, than to have the least smile, hope, or comfort from Him. Come with the fire of Hell in thy conscience, come with thy heart hard, dead, cold, full of wickedness and madness against thy own salvation; come as renouncing all thy tears, prayers, watchings, fastings; come as a blood-red sinner; do not stay from Christ till thou hast a greater sense of thy own misery, nor of the reality of God's mercy; do not stay while thy heart is softer and thy spirit in a better frame, but go against thy mind, and against the mind of the devil and sin, throw thyself down at the foot of Christ, with a halter about thy neck, and say, Lord Jesus, hear a sinner, a hard-hearted sinner, a sinner that deserveth to be damned, to be cast into Hell; and resolve never to return, or to give over crying unto Him, till thou do find that He hath washed thy conscience from dead works with His blood virtually, and clothed thee with His own righteousness, and make thee complete in Himself; this is the way to come to Christ.

THE USE OF THE NEW COVENANT

Now a few words to the second doctrine, and so I shall draw towards a conclusion.

FIRST USE. The doctrine doth contain in it very much comfort to thy (The use, for the second doctrine.) soul who art a new-covenant man, or one of those who are under the new covenant. There is, *First*, pardon of sin; and, *Second*, the manifestation of the same; and, *Third*, as power to cause thee to persevere through faith to the very end of thy life.

1.) There is, first, pardon of sin, which is not in the old covenant; for in that there is nothing but commands; and if not obeyed, condemned. O, but there is pardon of sin, even of all thy sins, against the first and second covenant, under which thou art, and that freely upon the account of Jesus Christ the righteousness, He having in thy name, nature, and in the room of thy person, fulfilled all the whole law in Himself for thee, and freely giveth it unto thee. O, though the law be a ministration of death and condemnation, yet the Gospel, under which thou art, is the ministration of life and salvation (2 Corinthians 3:6-9). Though they that live and die under the first covenant, God regardeth them not (Hebrews 8:9). Yet they that are under the second are as the apple of His eye (Deuteronomy 32:10; Psalms 17:8; Zechariah 2:8). Though they that are under the first, the Law, are "called to blackness, and darkness, and tempest, the sound of a trumpet," and a burning mountain, which sight was so terrible, that Moses said, "I exceedingly fear and quake" (Hebrews 12:18-22). "But ye are come unto Mount Sion, and unto the city of the living God, the heavenly Jerusalem, and to an innumerable company of angels, to the general assembly and church of the firstborn," whose names "are written in Heaven, and to God the Judge of all, and to the spirits of just men made perfect, and to Jesus," to blessed Jesus, "the Mediator of the new covenant, and to the blood of sprinkling, that speaketh better things than that of Abel" (Hebrews 12:22-24). Even forgiveness of sins (Ephesians 1:7).

2.) The covenant that thou art under doth allow of repentance in case thou chance to slip or fall by sudden temptation; but the law allows of none (Revelation 2:5; Galatians 3:10). The covenant that thou art under allows thee strength also; but the law is only a sound of words, commanding words, but no power is given by them to fulfil the things commanded (Hebrews 12:19). Thou that art under this second, art made a son; but they that art under that first, are slaves and vagabonds (Genesis 4:12). Thou that art under this, hast a Mediator, that is to stand between justice and thee; but they under the other, their mediator is turned an accuser, and speaketh most bitter things against their souls (1 Timothy 2:5; John 5:45). Again; the way that thou hast into Paradise is a new and living way—

mark, a living way; but they that are under the old covenant, their way into Paradise is a killing and destroying way (Hebrews 10:20; Genesis 3:24). Again; thou has the righteousness of God to appear before God withal; but they under the old covenant have nothing but the righteousness of the Law, which Paul counts dirt and dung (Philippians 3:7-9). Thou hast that which will make thee perfect, but the other will not do so—"The law made nothing perfect, but the bringing in of a better hope did," which is the Son of God, "by the which we draw nigh unto God" (Hebrews 7:19).

3.) The new covenant promiseth thee a new heart, as I said before; but the old covenant promiseth none; and a new spirit, but the old covenant promiseth none (Ezekiel 36:26). The new covenant conveyeth faith, but the old one conveyeth none (Galatians 3). Through the new covenant the love of God is conveyed into the heart; but through the old covenant there is conveyed none of it savingly through Jesus Christ. Romans 5. The new covenant doth not only give a promise of life, but also with that the assurance of life, but the old one giveth none; the old covenant wrought wrath in us and to us, but the new one worketh love (Romans 4:15; Galatians 5:6). Thus much for the first use.

SECOND USE. As all these, and many more privileges, do come to thee through or by the new covenant, and that thou mightst not doubt of the certainty of these glorious privileges, God hath so ordered it that they do all come to thee by way of purchase, being obtained for thee, ready to thy hand, by that one Man Jesus, who is the Mediator, or the Person that hath principally to do both with God and thy soul in the things pertaining to this covenant; so that now thou mayst look on all the glorious things that are spoken of in the new covenant, and say, All these must be mine; I must have a share in them; Christ hath purchased them for me, and given them to me. Now I need not to say, O! but how shall I come by them? God is holy, I am a sinner; God is just, and I have offended. No; but thou mayst say, Though I am vile, and deserve nothing, yet Christ is holy, and He deserveth all things; though I have so provoked God by breaking His law that He could not in justice look upon me, yet Christ hath so gloriously paid the debt that now God can say, Welcome, soul, I will give thee grace, I will give thee glory, thou shalt lie in My bosom, and go no more out; My Son hath pleased Me, He hath satisfied the loud cries of the Law and justice, that called for speedy vengeance on thee; He hath fulfilled the whole Law, He hath brought in everlasting righteousness (Daniel 9:24-25). He hath overcome the devil, He hath washed away thy sins with His most precious blood, He hath destroyed the power of death, and triumphs over all the enemies. This He did in His own Person, as a common Jesus, for all persons in their stead, even as for so many as shall come in to Him; for His victory I give to them, His righteousness I give to them, His merits I bestow on them, and look upon them holy, harmless, undefiled, and for ever comely in my eye, through the victory of the Captain of their salvation (1 Corinthians 15:55-57).

And that thou mayest, in deed and in truth, not only hear and read this glorious doctrine, but be found one that hath the life of it in thy heart, thou must be much in studying of the two covenants, the nature of the one, and the nature of the other, and the conditions of them that are under them both. Also, thou must be well-grounded in the manner of the victory, and merits of Christ, how they are made thine.

1.) And here thou must, in the first place, believe that the babe that was born of Mary, lay in a manger at Bethlehem, in the time of Caesar Augustus; that He, that babe, that child, was the very Christ.

2.) Thou must believe that in the days of Tiberius Caesar, when Herod was tetrarch of Galilee, and Pontius Pilate governor of Judea, that in those days He was crucified, or hanged on a tree between two thieves, which by computation, or according to the best account, is above sixteen hundred years since.[24]

3.) Thou must also believe that when He did hang upon that cross of wood on the Mount Calvary, that then He did die there for the sins of those that did die before He was crucified; also for their sins that were alive at the time of His crucifying, and also that He did by that one death give satisfaction to God for all those that should be born and believe in Him after His death, even unto the world's end. I say, this thou must believe, upon pain of eternal damnation, that by that one death, that when He did die, He did put an end to the curse of the Law and sin (This is the doctrine that I will live and die by, and be willing to be damned if it saves me not. I am not ashamed of the Gospel of Christ, for it is the power of God to salvation; therefore I preach Christ crucified, to the Jews a stumbling block, and to the Greeks foolishness (Romans 1:16; 1 Corinthians 1:23).) and at that time by His death on the Cross, and by His resurrection out of Joseph's sepulchre, He did bring in a sufficient righteousness to clothe thee withal completely—"For by one offering He hath perfected for ever them that are sanctified." Not that He should often offer Himself—"for then must He often have suffered since the foundation of the world; but now ONCE in the end of the world hath He appeared to put," or do, "away sin by the sacrifice of Himself"—namely, when He hanged on the Cross. For it is by the offering up of the body of this blessed Jesus Christ ONCE for all. Indeed, other priests may offer oftentimes sacrifices and offerings which can never take away sins; but this Man, this Jesus, this anointed and appointed sacrifice, when He had offered ONE sacrifice for sins, for ever sat down on the right hand of God (Hebrews 10:14; 9:24-25).

A WORD OF ADVICE

But because thou in thy pursuit after the faith of the Gospel wilt be sure to meet with devils, heretics, particular corruptions, as unbelief, ignorance, the spirit of works animated on by suggestions, false conclusions, with damnable doctrines, I shall therefore briefly, besides what hath been already said, speak a word or two before I leave thee of further advice, especially concerning these two things. First, How thou art to conceive of the Savior. Second, How thou art to make application of Him.

FIRST. For the Savior. 1.) Thou must look upon Him to be very God and very Man; not man only, nor God only, but God and Man in one Person, both natures joined together, for the putting of Him in a capacity to be a suitable Savior; suitable, I say, to answer both sides and parties, with whom He hath to do in the office of His Mediator-ship and being of a Savior. 2.) Thou must not only do this, but thou must also consider and believe that even what was done by Jesus Christ, it was not done by one nature without the other; but thou must consider that both natures, both the Godhead and the manhood, did gloriously concur and join together in the undertaking of the salvation of our bodies and souls; not that the Godhead undertook anything without the manhood, neither did the manhood do anything without the virtue and union of the Godhead; and thou must of necessity do this, otherwise thou canst not find any sound ground and footing for thy soul to rest upon.

For if thou look upon any of these asunder—that is to say, the Godhead without the manhood, or the manhood without the Godhead—thou wilt conclude that what was done by the Godhead was not done for man, being done without the manhood; or else, that that which was done with the manhood could not answer Divine justice, in not doing what it did by the virtue and in union with the Godhead; for it was the Godhead that gave virtue and value to the suffering of the manhood, and the manhood being joined therewith, that giveth us an interest into the heavenly glory and comforts of the Godhead.

What ground can a man have to believe that Christ is his Savior, if he do not believe that He suffered for sin in his nature? And what ground also can a man have to think that God the Father is satisfied, being infinite, if he believe not also that He who gave the satisfaction was equal to Him who was offended?

Therefore, beloved, when you read of the offering of the body of the Son of Man for our sins, then consider that He did it in union with, and by the help of, the eternal Godhead. "How much more shall the blood of Christ, who, through the eternal Spirit, offered Himself without spot to God, purge your consciences from dead works," etc.

And when thou readest of the glorious works and splendour of the Godhead in Christ, then consider that all that was done by the Godhead, it was done as it had union and communion with the manhood. And then thou shalt see that the devil is overcome by God-man; sin, death, Hell, the grave, and all overcome by Jesus, God-man, and then thou shalt find them overcome indeed. They must needs be overcome when God doth overcome them; and we have good ground to hope the victory is ours, when in our nature they are overcome.

SECOND. The second thing is, how to apply, or to make application of this Christ to the soul. And for this there are to be considered the following particulars:

1.) That when Jesus Christ did thus appear, being born of Mary, He was looked upon by the Father as if the sin of the whole world was upon Him; nay, further, God did look upon Him and account Him the sin of man—"He hath made Him *to be* sin for us," (2 Corinthians 5:21) that is, God made His Son Jesus Christ our sin, or reckoned Him to be, not only a sinner, but the very bulk of sin of the whole world, and condemned Him so severely as if He had been nothing but sin. "For what the law could not do, in that it was weak through the flesh, God sending His own Son in the likeness of sinful flesh, and for sin, condemned sin in the flesh"— that is, for our sins condemned His Son Jesus Christ; as if He had in deed and truth been our very sin, although altogether "without sin" (Romans 8:3; 2 Corinthians 5:21). Therefore, as to the taking away of thy curse, thou must reckon Him to be made sin for thee. And as to His being thy justification, thou must reckon Him to be thy righteousness; for, saith the Scripture, "He," that is, God, "hath made HIM *to be* SIN for us, though He knew no sin, that we might be made the RIGHTEOUSNESS of God in HIM."

2.) Consider for whose sakes all this glorious design of the Father and the Son was brought to pass; and that you shall find to be for man, for sinful man (2 Corinthians 8:9).

3.) The terms on which it is made ours; and that you will find to be a free gift, merely arising from the tender-heartedness of God— you are "justified freely by His grace, through the redemption that is in Christ, whom God hath set forth to be a Propitiation through faith in His blood," etc. (Romans 3:25).

4.) How men are to reckon it theirs; and that is, upon the same terms which God doth offer it, which is freely, as they are worthless and undeserving creatures, as they are without all good, and also

The Doctrine of Law and Grace Unfolded 189

unable to do any good. This, I say, is the right way of applying the merits of Christ to thy soul, for they are freely given to thee, a poor sinner, not for anything that is in thee, or done by thee, but freely as thou art a sinner, and so standest in absolute need thereof.

And, Christian, thou art not in this thing to follow thy sense and feeling, but the very Word of God. The thing that doth do the people of God the greatest injury, it is their too little hearkening to what the Gospel saith, and their too much giving credit to what the Law, sin, the devil, and conscience saith; and upon this very ground to conclude that because there is a certainty of guilt upon the soul, therefore there is also for certain, by sin, damnation to be brought upon the soul. This is now to set the Word of God aside, and to give credit to what is formed by the contrary; but thou must give more credit to one syllable of the written Word of the Gospel than thou must give to all the saints and angels in Heaven and earth; much more than to the devil and thy own guilty conscience.

Let me give you a parable: There was a certain man that had committed treason against his king; but forasmuch as the king had compassion upon him, he sent him, by the hand of a faithful messenger, a pardon under his own hand and seal; but in the country where this poor man dwelt, there were also many that sought to trouble him, by often putting of him in mind of his treason, and the law that was to be executed on the offender. Now which way should this man so honor his king, but as by believing his handwriting, which was the pardon. Certainly he would honor him more by so doing than to regard all the clamours of his enemies continually against him.

Just thus it is here: thou having committed treason against the King of Heaven, He through compassion, for Christ's sake, hath sent thee a pardon; but the devil, the Law, and thy conscience do continually seek to disturb thee by bringing thy sins afresh into thy remembrance. But now, wouldst thou honor thy King? Why then, he that believeth "the record that God hath given of His Son," hath set to his seal that God is true. "And this is the record, that God hath given to us eternal life, and this life is in His Son" (1 John 5:11). And therefore, my brethren, seeing God our Father hath sent us damnable traitors a pardon from Heaven, even all the promises of the Gospel, and also hath sealed to the certainty of it with the heart-blood of His dear Son, let us not be daunted, though our enemies, with terrible voices, do bring our former life never so often into our remembrance.

OBJECTION: But, saith the soul, how, if after I have received a pardon, I should commit treason again? What should I do then?

ANSWER: Set the case: thou hast committed abundance of treason, He hath by Him abundance of pardons—"Let the wicked forsake his way, and the unrighteous man his thoughts: and let him return unto the LORD, and He will have mercy upon him; and to our God, for He will abundantly pardon" (Isaiah 55:7).

Sometimes I myself have been in such a strait that I have been almost driven to my wit's ends with the sight and sense of the greatness of my sins; but calling to mind that God was God in His mercy, pity, and love, as well as in His holiness, justice, etc.; and again, considering the ability of the satisfaction that was given to holiness and justice, to the end there might be way made for sinners to lay hold of this mercy; I say, I considering this, when tempted to doubt and despair, I have answered in this manner:

"Lord, here is one of the greatest sinners that ever the ground bare; a sinner against the Law, and a sinner against the Gospel. I have sinned against light, and I have sinned against mercy. And now, Lord, the guilt of them breaks my heart. The devil also he would have me despair, telling of me that Thou art so far from hearing my prayers in this my distress, that I can not anger Thee worse than to call upon Thee; for saith he, Thou art resolved for ever to damn, and not to grant me the least of Thy favor; yet, Lord, I would fain have forgiveness. And Thy Word, though much may be inferred from it against me, yet it saith, If I come unto Thee, Thou will in nowise cast me out. Lord, shall I honor Thee most by believing Thou canst pardon my sins, or by believing Thou canst not? Shall I honor Thee most by believing Thou wilt pardon my sins, or by believing Thou wilt not? Shall I honor the blood of Thy Son also by despairing that the virtue thereof is not sufficient, or by believing that it is sufficient to purge me from all my blood-red and crimson sins? Surely, Thou that couldst find so much mercy as to pardon Manasseh, Mary Magdalene, the three thousand murderers, persecuting Paul, murderous and adulterous David, and blaspheming Peter—Thou that offeredst mercy to Simon Magus, a witch, and didst receive the astrologers and conjurors in the 19th of Acts—Thou hast mercy enough for one poor sinner. Lord, set the case: my sins were bigger than all these, and I less deserved mercy than any of these, yet Thou hast said in Thy Word that he that cometh to thee Thou wilt in "nowise cast out." And God hath given comfort to my soul, even to such a sinner as I am. And I tell you, there is no way so to honor God, and to beat out the devil, as to stick to the truth of God's Word and the merits of Christ's blood by believing. When Abraham believed—even against hope and reason—he gave glory to God (Romans 4). And this is our victory, even our faith (1 John 5:4). Believe, and all things are possible to you. He that believeth shall be saved. He that believeth on the Son hath everlasting life, and shall never perish, neither shall any man pluck them out of Christ's Father's hands.

And if thou dost indeed believe this, thou wilt not only confess Him as the Quakers do—that is, that He was born at Bethlehem of Mary, suffered on Mount Calvary under Pontius Pilate, was dead and buried, rose again, and ascended, etc.; for all this they confess, and in the midst of their confession they do verily deny that His death on that Mount Calvary did give satisfaction to God for the sins of the world, and that His resurrection out of Joseph's sepulchre is the cause of our justification in the sight of God, angels, and devils; but, I say, if thou dost believe these things indeed, thou dost believe that then, so long ago, even before thou wast born, He did bear thy sins in His own body, which then was hanged on the tree, and never before nor since; that thy old man was then crucified with Him, namely, in the same body then crucified (See 1 Peter 2:24; and Romans 6:6). This is nonsense to them that believe not; but if thou do indeed believe, thou seest it so plain, and yet such a mystery, that it makes thee wonder. But,

THIRD. In the third place, this glorious doctrine of the new covenant, and the Mediator thereof, will serve for the comforting, and the maintaining of the comfort, of the children of the new covenant this way also—that is, that He did not only die and rise again, but that He did ascend in His own Person into Heaven to take possession thereof for me, to prepare a place there for me, standeth there in the second part of His surety-ship to bring me safe in my coming thither, and to present me in a glorious manner, without spot or wrinkle, or any such thing; that He is there exercising of His priestly office for me, pleading the perfection of His own righteousness for me, and the virtue of His blood for me; that He is there ready to answer the accusations of the Law, devil, and sin for me. Here thou mayst through faith look the very devil in the face, and rejoice, saying, O Satan! I have a precious Jesus, a soul-comforting Jesus, a sin-pardoning Jesus. Here thou mayst hear the biggest thunder-crack that the Law can give, and yet not be daunted. Here thou mayst say, O Law! thou mayst roar against sin, but thou canst not reach me; thou mayst curse and condemn, but not my soul; for I have righteous Jesus, a holy Jesus, a soul-saving Jesus, and He hath delivered me from thy threats, from thy curses, from thy condemnations; I am out of thy reach, and out of thy bounds; I am brought into another covenant, under better promises, promises of life and salvation, free promises to comfort me without my merit, even through the blood of Jesus, the satisfaction given to God for me by Him; therefore, though thou layest my sins to my charge, and sayest thou wilt prove me guilty, yet so long as Christ is above ground, and hath brought in everlasting righteousness, and given that to me, I shall not fear thy threats, thy charges, thy soul-scarring denunciations; my Christ is all, hath done all, and will deliver me from all that thou, and whatsoever else can bring an accusation against me. Thus also thou may say when death assaulteth thee—O death, where is thy sting? Thou mayst bite indeed, but thou canst not devour; I have comfort by and through the one Man Jesus; Jesus Christ, He hath taken thee captive, and taken away thy strength; He hath pierced thy heart, and let out all thy soul-destroying poison; therefore, though I see thee, I am not afraid of thee; though I feel thee, I am not daunted; for thou hast lost thy sting in the side of the Lord Jesus; through Him I overcome thee, and set foot upon thee. Also, O Satan! though I hear thee grumble, and make a hellish noise, and though thou threaten me very highly, yet my soul shall triumph over thee, so long as Christ is alive and can be heard in Heaven; so long as He hath broken thy head, and won the field of thee; so long as thou are in prison, and canst not have thy desire. I, therefore, when I hear thy voice, do pitch my thoughts on Christ my Savior, and do hearken when He will say, for He will speak comfort; He saith, He hath got the victory, and doth give to me the crown, and causeth me to triumph through His most glorious conquest.

Nay, my brethren, the saints under the Levitical Law, who had not the new covenant sealed or confirmed any further than by promise that it should be; I say, they, when they thought of the glorious privileges that God had promised should come, though at that time they were not come, but seen afar off, how confidently were they persuaded of them, and embraced them, and were so fully satisfied as touching the certainty of them, that they did not stick at the parting with all for the enjoying of them. (Shall not we then that see all things already done before us make it a strong argument to increase our faith (Hebrews 11).) How many times doth David in the Psalms admire, triumph, and persuade others to do so also, through the faith that he had in the thing that was to be done? Also Job, in what faith doth he say he should see his Redeemer, though He had not then shed one drop of blood for him, yet because He had promised so to do; and this was signified by the blood of bulls and goats. Also Samuel, Isaiah, Jeremiah, Zechariah, etc., how gloriously in confidence did they speak of Christ, and His death, blood, conquest, and everlasting priesthood, even before He did manifest Himself in the flesh which He took of the Virgin. (For they were so many sure promises, with a remembrance in them, also for the better satisfaction of them that believed them). We that have lived since Christ, have more ground to hope than they under the old covenant had, though they had the word of the just God for the ground of their faith. Mark, they had only the promise that He should and would come; but we have the assured fulfilling of those promises, because He is come; they were told that He should spill His blood, but we do see He hath spilt His blood; they ventured all upon His standing Surety for them, but we see He hath fulfilled, and that faithfully too, the office of His Surety-ship, in that, according to the engagement, He hath redeemed us poor sinners; they ventured on the new covenant, though not actually sealed, only "because He judged Him faithful who had promised" (Hebrews 11:11). But we have the covenant sealed, all things are completely done, even as sure as the heart-blood of a crucified Jesus can make it.

There is a great difference between their dispensation and ours for comfort, even as much as there is between the making of a bond with a promise to seal it, and the sealing of the same. It was made indeed in their time, but it was not sealed until the time the blood was shed on the Mount Calvary; and that we might indeed have our faith mount up with wings like an eagle, he showeth us what encouragement and ground of faith we have to conclude we shall be everlastingly delivered, saying, "For where a testament" or covenant "*is*, there must also of necessity be the death of the testator. For a testament *is* of force after men are dead: otherwise it is of no strength at all while the testator liveth. Whereupon neither the first *testament* was dedicated without blood" (Hebrews 9:16-18). As Christ's blood was the confirmation of the new covenant, yet it was not sealed in Abraham, Isaac, or Jacob's days to confirm the covenant that God did tell them of, and yet they believed; therefore we ought to give the more earnest heed to believe the things that we have heard, and not in any wise to let them be questioned; and the rather, because you see the testament is not only now made, but confirmed; not only spoken of and promised, but verily sealed by the death and blood of Jesus, who is the Testator thereof.

My brethren, I would not leave you ignorant of this one thing, that though the Jews had the promise of a sacrifice, of an everlasting High Priest that should deliver them, yet they had but the promise; for Christ was not sacrificed, and was not then come a high priest of good things to come; only the type, the shadow, the figure, the ceremonies they had, together with Christ's engaging as Surety to bring all things to pass that were promised should come, and upon that account received and saved.

It was with them and their dispensation as this similitude gives you to understand: Set the case that there be two men who make a covenant that the one should give the other ten thousand sheep on condition the other give him two thousand pound; but forasmuch as the money is not to be paid down presently, therefore if he that buyeth the sheep will have any of them before the day of payment, the creditor requesteth a surety; and upon the engagement of the surety there is part of the sheep given to the debtor even before the day of payment, but the other at and after. So it is here; Christ covenanted with His Father for His sheep—"I lay down My life for My sheep," saith He—but the money was not to be paid down so soon as the bargain was made, as I have already said, yet some of the sheep were saved even before the money was paid, and that because of the Surety-ship of Christ; as it is written, "Being justified," or saved, "freely by His grace through the redemption," or purchase, "that is in Christ Jesus. Whom God hath set forth *to be* a propitiation through faith in His blood, to declare His righteousness for the remission of sins that are past," or the sinners who died in the faith before Christ was crucified, through God's forbearing till the payment was paid; to declare, I say, at this time His righteousness; "that He might be just, and the justifier of him which believeth in Jesus" (Romans 3:24-26).

The end of my speaking of this is, to show you that it is not wisdom now to doubt whether God will save you or no, but to believe, because all things are finished as to our justification: the covenant not only made, but also sealed; the debt paid, the prison doors flung off of the hooks, with a proclamation from Heaven of deliverance to the prisoners of hope, saying, "Turn you to the stronghold, ye prisoners of hope, even today do I declare," saith God, "*that* I will render double unto thee" (Zechariah 9:12). And, saith Christ, when He was come, "The Spirit of the Lord is upon me, because He hath anointed Me to preach the Gospel," that is, good tidings "to the poor," that their sins should be pardoned, that their souls shall be saved. "He hath sent Me to heal the broken-hearted, to preach deliverance to the captives, and recovering of sight to the blind, to set at liberty them that are bruised," and to comfort them that mourn, "to preach the acceptable year of the Lord" (Luke 4:18-19).

Therefore here, soul, thou mayst come to Jesus Christ for anything thou wantest, as to a common treasure-house, being the principal Man for the distributing of the things made mention of in the new covenant, He having them all in His own custody by right of purchase; for He hath bought them all, paid for them all. Dost thou want faith? then come for it to the Man Christ Jesus (Hebrews 12:2). Dost thou want the Spirit? then ask it of Jesus. Dost thou want wisdom? Dost thou want grace of any sort? Dost thou want a new heart? Dost thou want strength against thy lusts, against the devil's temptations? Dost thou want strength to carry thee through afflictions of body, and afflictions of spirit, through persecutions? Wouldst thou willingly hold out, stand to the last, and be more than a conqueror? then be sure thou meditate enough on the merits of the blood of Jesus, how He hath undertaken for thee, that He hath done the work of thy salvation in thy room, that He is filled of God on purpose to fill thee, and is willing to communicate whatsoever is in Him or about Him to thee. Consider this, I say, and triumph in it.

Again; this may inform us of the safe state of the saints as touching their perseverance, that they shall stand though Hell rages, though the devil roareth, and all the world endeavoreth the ruin of the saints of God, though some, through ignorance of the virtue of the offering of the body of Jesus Christ, do say a man may be a child of God today, and a child of the devil tomorrow, which is gross ignorance; for what? Is the blood of Christ, the death of Christ, the resurrection of Christ, of no more virtue than to bring in for us an uncertain salvation? or must the effectualness of Christ's merits, as touching our perseverance, be helped on by the doings of man? Surely they that are predestinated are also justified; and they that are justified, they shall be glorified (Romans 8:30). Saints, do not doubt of the salvation of your souls, unless you do intend to undervalue Christ's blood; and do not think but that He that hath begun the good work of His grace in you will perfect it to the second coming of our Lord Jesus (Philippians 1:6). Should not we, as well as Paul, say, I am persuaded that nothing shall separate us from the love of God, which is in Christ Jesus (Romans 8). O let the saints know, that unless the devil can pluck Christ out of Heaven, he can not pull a true believer out of Christ. When I say a true believer, I do mean such an one as hath the faith of the operation of God in his soul.

Lastly, Is there such mercy as this? such privileges as these? Is there so much ground of comfort, and so much cause to be glad? Is there so much store in Christ, and such a ready heart in Him to give it to me? Hath His bleeding wounds so much in them, as that the fruits thereof should be the salvation of my soul, of my sinful soul, as to save me, sinful me, rebellious me, desperate me? What then? Shall not I now be holy? Shall not I now study, strive, and lay out myself for Him that hath laid out Himself soul and body for me? Shall I now love ever a lust or sin? Shall I now be ashamed of the cause, ways, people, or saints of Jesus Christ? Shall I now yield my members as instruments of righteousness, seeing my end is everlasting life? (Romans 6). Shall Christ think nothing too dear for me? and shall I count anything too dear for Him? Shall I grieve Him with my foolish carriage? Shall I slight His counsel by following of my own will? Thus, therefore, the doctrine of the new covenant doth call for holiness, engage to holiness, and maketh the children of that covenant to take pleasure therein. Let no man, therefore, conclude on this, that the doctrine of the Gospel is a licentious doctrine; but if they do, it is because they are fools, and such as have not tasted of the virtue of the blood of Jesus Christ; neither did they ever feel the nature and sway that the love of Christ hath in the hearts of His. And thus also you may see that the doctrine of the Gospel is of great advantage to the people of God that are already come in, or to them that shall at the consideration hereof be willing to come in, to partake of the glorious benefits of this glorious covenant. But, saith the poor soul,

OBJECTION: Alas! I doubt this is too good for me.

INQUIRER: Why so, I pray you?

OBJECTION: Alas! because I am a sinner.

REPLY: Why, all this is bestowed upon none but sinners, as it is written, While we were ungodly, Christ died for us (Romans 5:6, 8). "He came into the world to save sinners" (1 Timothy 1:15).

OBJECTION: O, but I am one of the chief of sinners.

REPLY: Why, this is for the chief of sinners—"Christ Jesus came into the world to save sinners, of whom I am chief," saith Paul (1 Timothy 1:15).

OBJECTION: O, but my sins are so big, that I can not conceive how I should have mercy.

REPLY: Why, soul? Didst thou ever kill anybody? Didst thou ever burn any of thy children in the fire to idols? Hast thou been a witch? Didst thou ever use enchantments and conjuration? (You that are resolved to go on in your sins, meddle not with this). Didst thou ever curse, and swear, and deny Christ? And yet if thou hast, there is yet hopes of pardon; yea, such sinners as these have been pardoned, as appears by these and the like Scriptures, 2 Chronicles 33:1-10, compared with verses 12-13. Again, Acts 19:19-20; 8:22, compared with verse 9; Matthew 26:74-75.

OBJECTION: But though I have not sinned in such kind of sins, yet it may be I have sinned as bad.

ANSWER: That can not likely be; yet though thou hast, still there is ground of mercy for thee, forasmuch as thou art under the promise (John 6:37).

The Unpardonable Sin

OBJECTION: Alas! man, I am afraid that I have sinned the unpardonable sin, and therefore there is no hope for me.

ANSWER: Dost thou know what the unpardonable sin, the sin against the Holy Ghost, is? and when it is committed?

REPLY: It is a sin against light.

ANSWER: That is true; yet every sin against light is not the sin against the Holy Ghost. REPLY: Say you so?

ANSWER: Yea, and I prove it thus—If every sin against light had been the sin that is unpardonable, then had David and Peter and others sinned that sin; but though they did sin against light, yet they did not sin that sin; therefore every sin against light is not the sin against the Holy Ghost, the unpardonable sin.

OBJECTION: But the Scripture saith, "If we sin wilfully after that we have received the knowledge of the Truth, there remaineth no more sacrifice for sins; but a certain fearful looking for of judgment and fiery indignation, which shall devour the adversaries."

ANSWER: Do you know what that wilful sin is?

REPLY: Why, what is it? Is it not for a man to sin willingly after enlightening?

ANSWER: 1. Yes; yet doubtless every willing sin is not that; for then David had sinned it when he lay with Bathsheba; and Jonah, when he fled from the presence of the Lord; and Solomon also, when he had so many concubines. 2. But that sin is a sin that is of another nature, which is this—For a man after he hath made some profession of salvation to come alone by the blood of Jesus, together with some light and power of the same upon his spirit; I say, for him after this knowingly, wilfully, and despitefully to trample upon the blood of Christ shed on the Cross, and to count it an unholy thing, or no better than the blood of another man, and rather to venture his soul any other way than to be saved by this precious blood. And this must be done, I say, after some light (Hebrews 6:4-5) despitefully (Hebrews 10:29) knowingly (2 Peter 2:21) and wilfully (Hebrews 10:26, compared with verse 29) and that not in a hurry and sudden fit, as Peter's was, but with some time beforehand to pause upon it first, with Judas; and also with a continued resolution never to turn or be converted again; "for *it is* impossible to renew such again to repentance," they are so resolved and so desperate (Hebrews 6).

QUESTION: And how sayest thou now? Didst thou ever, after thou hadst received some blessed light from Christ, wilfully, despitefully, and knowingly stamp or trample the blood of the Man Christ Jesus under thy feet? and art thou for ever resolved so to do?

ANSWER: O no; I would not do that wilfully, despitefully, and knowingly, not for all the world.

INQUIRY: But yet I must tell you, now you put me in mind of it, surely sometimes I have most horrible blasphemous thoughts in me against God, Christ, and the Spirit. May not these be that sin I trow?

ANSWER: Dost thou delight in them? Are they such things as thou takest pleasure in?

REPLY: O no; neither would I do it for a thousand worlds. O, methinks they make me sometimes tremble to think of them. But how and if I should delight in them before I am aware?

ANSWER: Beg of God for strength against them, and if at any time thou findest thy wicked heart to give way in the least thereto, for that is likely enough, and though thou find it may on a sudden give way to that Hell-bred wickedness that is in it, yet do not despair, forasmuch as Christ hath said, "All manner of sins and blasphemies shall be forgiven to the sons of men. And whosoever speaketh a word against the Son of man," that is Christ, as he may do with Peter, through temptation, yet upon repentance, "it shall be forgiven him" (Matthew 12:31-32).

OBJECTION: But I thought it might have been committed all on a sudden, either by some blasphemous thought, or else by committing some other horrible sin.

ANSWER: For certain, this sin and the commission of it doth lie in a knowing, wilful, malicious, or despiteful, together with a final trampling the blood of sweet Jesus under foot (Hebrews 10).

OBJECTION: But it seems to be rather a resisting of the Spirit, and the motions thereof, than this which you say; for, first, its proper title is the sin against the Holy Ghost; and again, "They have done despite unto the Spirit of grace"; so that it rather seems to be, I say, that a resisting of the Spirit, and the movings thereof, is that sin.

ANSWER #1: For certain, the sin is committed by them that do as before I have said—that is, by a final, knowing, wilful, malicious trampling under foot the blood of Christ, which was shed on Mount Calvary when Jesus was there crucified. And though it be called the sin against the Spirit, yet as I said before, every sin against the Spirit is not that; for if it were, then every sin against the light and convictions of the Spirit would be unpardonable; but that is an evident untruth, for these reasons—First, Because there be those who have sinned against the movings of the Spirit, and that knowingly too, and yet did not commit that sin; as Jonah, who when God had expressly by His Spirit bid him go to Nineveh, he runs thereupon quite another way. Secondly, Because the very people that have sinned against the movings of the Spirit are yet, if they do return, received to mercy. Witness also Jonah, who though he had sinned against the movings of the Spirit of the Lord in doing contrary there-unto, "yet when he called," as he saith, "to the Lord," out of the belly of Hell, "the LORD heard him, and gave him deliverance, and set him again about his work." Read the whole story of that Prophet. But:

ANSWER #2: I shall show you that it must needs be wilfully, knowingly, and a malicious rejecting of the Man Christ Jesus as the Savior—that is, counting His blood, His righteousness, His intercession in His own Person, for he that rejects one rejects all, to be of no value as to salvation; I say, this I shall show you is the unpardonable sin, and then afterwards in brief show you why it is called the sin against the Holy Ghost.

Must Be a Wilfully and Maliciously Rejecting the Savior

1.) That man that doth reject, as aforesaid, the blood, death, righteousness, resurrection, ascension, and intercession of the Man Christ, doth reject that sacrifice, that blood, that righteousness, that victory, that rest, that God alone hath appointed for salvation—"Behold the Lamb," or sacrifice, "of God" (John 1:29). "We have redemption through His blood" (Ephesians 1:7). That I may "be found in Him"—to wit, in Christ's righteousness, with Christ's own personal obedience to His Father's will (Philippians 3:7-10). By His resurrection comes justification (Romans 4:25). His intercession now in His own Person in the Heavens, now absent from His saints, is the cause of the saints' perseverance (Romans 8:33-39).

2.) They that reject this sacrifice, and the merits of this Christ, which He by Himself hath brought in for sinners, have rejected Him through whom alone all the promises of the New Testament, together with all the mercy discovered thereby, doth come unto poor creatures—"For all the promises of God in Him *are* yea, and in Him amen, unto the glory of God" (2 Corinthians 1:20). And all spiritual blessings are made over to us through Him; that is, through and in this Man, which is Christ, we have all our spiritual, heavenly, and eternal mercies (Ephesians 1:3-4).

3.) He that doth knowingly, wilfully, and despitefully reject this Man for salvation doth sin the unpardonable sin, because there is never another sacrifice to be offered. "There is no more offering for sin.—There remaineth no more sacrifice for sin," (Hebrews 10:18-26); namely, than the offering of the body of Jesus Christ a sacrifice once for all (Hebrews 10:10, 14, compared with 18, 26). No; but they that shall, after light and clear conviction, reject the first offering of His body for salvation, do crucify Him the second time, which irrecoverably merits their own damnation—"For *it is* impossible for those who were once enlightened, and have tasted of the heavenly gift, and were made partakers of the Holy Ghost, and have tasted the good Word of God, and the powers of the world to come, if they shall fall away, to renew them again unto repentance; seeing they crucify to themselves the Son of God afresh, and put *Him* to an open shame" (Hebrews 6:4-6). "If they shall fall away, to renew them again unto repentance." And why so? Seeing, saith the Apostle, they do crucify to themselves the Son of God afresh, and do put *Him* to an open shame. O, then, how miserably hath the devil deceived some, in that he hath got them to reject the merits of the first offering of the body of Christ, which was for salvation, and got them to trust in a fresh crucifying of Christ, which unavoidably brings their speedy damnation.

4.) They that do reject this Man, as aforesaid, do sin the unpardonable sin, because in rejecting Him they do make way for the justice of God to break out upon them, and to handle them as it shall find them; which will be, in the first place, sinners against the first covenant; and also despising of, even the life, and glory, and consolations, pardon, grace, and love, that is discovered in the second covenant, forasmuch as they reject the Mediator and priest of the same, which is the Man Jesus. And the man that doth so, I would fain see how his sins should be pardoned, and his soul saved, seeing the means, which is the Son of Man, the Son of Mary, and His merits, are rejected; "for," saith He, "if you believe not that I am He, you shall," mark, "you shall," do what you can; "you shall," appear where you can; "you shall," follow Moses' law, or any holiness whatsoever, "ye shall die in your sins" (John 8:24). So that, I say, the sin that is called the unpardonable sin is a knowing, wilful, and despiteful rejecting of the sacrificing of the Son of Man the first time for sin.

Why it is Called the Sin Against the Holy Ghost

And now to show you why it is called the sin against the Holy Ghost, as in these Scriptures, (Matthew 12; Hebrews 10; Mark 3).

1.) Because they sin against the manifest light of the Spirit, as I said before; it is a sin against the light of the Spirit—that is, they have been formerly enlightened into the nature of the Gospel and the merits of the Man Christ, and His blood, righteousness, intercession, etc.; and also professed and confessed the same, with some life and comfort in and through the profession of Him; yet now against all that light, maliciously, and with despite to all their former profession, turn their backs and trample upon the same.

2.) It is called the sin against the Holy Ghost because such a person doth, as I may say, lay violent hands on it; one that sets himself in opposition to, and is resolved to resist all the motions that do come in from the Spirit to persuade the contrary. For I do verily believe that men, in this very rejecting of the Son of God, after some knowledge of Him, especially at their first resisting and refusing of Him, they have certain motions of the Spirit of God to dissuade them from so great a soul-damning act. But they, being filled with an overpowering measure of the spirit of the devil, do despite unto these convictions and motions by studying and contriving how they may answer them, and get from under the convincing nature of them, and therefore it is called a doing despite unto the Spirit of Grace (Hebrews 10:29). And so:

3.) In that they do reject the beseeching of the Spirit, and all its gentle entreatings of the soul to tarry still in the same doctrine.

4.) In that they do reject the very testimony of the Prophets and Apostles with Christ Himself; I say, their testimony, through the Spirit, of the power, virtue, sufficiency, and prevalence of the blood, sacrifice, death, resurrection, ascension, and intercession of the Man Christ Jesus, of which the Scriptures are full both in the Old and New Testament, as the Apostle saith, for all the Prophets from Samuel, with them that follow after, have showed of these days—that is, in which Christ should be a sacrifice for sin (Acts 3:24, compared with verses 6, 13-15, 18, 26). Again, saith, he, "He therefore that despiseth not man, but God; who hath also given unto us His Holy Spirit" (1 Thessalonians 4:8); that is, he rejecteth or despiseth the very testimony of the Spirit.

5. It is called the sin against the Holy Ghost, because he that doth reject and disown the doctrine of salvation by the Man Christ Jesus, through believing in Him, doth despise, resist, and reject the wisdom of the Spirit; for the wisdom of God's Spirit did never more appear than its finding out a way for sinners to be reconciled to God by the death of this Man; and therefore Christ, as He is a sacrifice, is called the wisdom of God. And again, when it doth reveal the Lord Jesus it is called the "Spirit of wisdom and revelation in the knowledge of Him" (Ephesians 1:17).

OBJECTION: But, some may say, the slighting or rejecting of the Son of Man, Jesus of Nazareth, the Son of Mary, can not be the sin that is unpardonable, as is clear from that Scripture in Matthew 12:32, where He Himself saith, "Whosoever speaketh a word against the Son of Man, it shall be forgiven him; but whosoever speaketh against the Holy Ghost, it shall not be forgiven him, neither in this world, neither in the *world* to come." Now by this it is clear that the sin that is unpardonable is one thing, and the sin against the Son of Man another; that sin that is against the Son of Man is pardonable; but if that was the sin against the Holy Ghost, it would not be pardonable; therefore the sin against the Son of Man is not the sin against the Holy Ghost, the unpardonable sin.

ANSWER: 1.) I do know full well that there are several persons that have been pardoned, yet have sinned against the Son of Man, and that have for a time rejected Him, as Paul (1 Timothy 1:13-14) also the Jews (Acts 2:36-37). But there was an ignorant rejecting of Him, without the enlightening, and taste, and feeling of the power of the things of God, made mention in Hebrews 6:3-6.

2.) There is and hath been a higher manner of sinning against the Son of Man, which also hath been, and is still, pardonable; as in the case of Peter, who in a violent temptation, in a mighty hurry, upon a sudden denied Him, and that after the revelation of the Spirit of God from Heaven to him, that He, Jesus, was the Son of God (Matthew

16:16-18). This also is pardonable, if there be a coming up again to repentance. O, rich grace! O, wonderful grace! that God should be so full of love to His poor creatures, that though they do sin against the Son of God, either through ignorance, or some sudden violent charge breaking loose from Hell upon them, but yet take if for certain that if a man do slight and reject the Son of God and the Spirit in that manner as I have before hinted—that is, for a man after some great measure of the enlightening by the Spirit of God, and some profession of Jesus Christ to be the Savior, and His blood that was shed on the mount without the gates of Jerusalem to be the Atonement; I say, he that shall after this knowingly, wilfully, and out of malice and despite reject, speak against, and trample that doctrine under foot, resolving for ever so to do, and if he there continue, I will pawn my soul upon it, he hath sinned the unpardonable sin, and shall never be forgiven, neither in this world, nor in the world to come; or else these Scriptures that testify the truth of this must be scrabbled out, and must be looked upon for mere fables, which are these following—"For if after they have escaped the pollutions of the world, through the knowledge of our Lord and Savior Jesus Christ," which is the Son of Man (Matthew 16:13) "and are again entangled therein, and overcome," which must be by denying this Lord that brought them (2 Peter 2:1) "the latter end is worse with them than the beginning," (2 Peter 2:20). For *it is* impossible for those who were once enlightened, and have tasted of the heavenly gift—and have tasted the good Word of God, and the powers of the world to come; if they shall fall away," not only fall, but fall away, that is, finally (Hebrews 10:29) "it is impossible to renew them again unto repentance"; and the reason is rendered, "seeing they crucify to themselves the Son of God," which is the Son of Man, "afresh, and put *Him* to an open shame" (Hebrews 6:4-6). Now if you would further know what it is to crucify the Son of God afresh, it is this—for to undervalue and trample under foot the merits and virtue of His blood for remission of sins, as is clearly manifested in Hebrews 10:26-28, where it is said, "For if we sin wilfully after that we have received the knowledge of the Truth, there remaineth no more sacrifice for sins, but a certain fearful looking for of judgment and fiery indignation, which shall devour the adversaries. He that despised Moses' law died without mercy—of how much sorer punishment, suppose ye, shall he be thought worthy, who hath trodden under foot the Son of God," there is the second crucifying of Christ, which the Quakers think to be saved by, "and hath counted the blood of the covenant, wherewith he was sanctified, an unholy thing"—and then followeth—"and hath done despite unto the Spirit of Grace?" (verse 29). All that Paul had to keep him from this sin was, his ignorance in persecuting the Man and merits of Jesus Christ (Acts 9). But I obtained mercy, saith he, because I did *it* ignorantly (1 Timothy 1:13). And Peter, though he did deny Him knowingly, yet he did it unwillingly, and in a sudden and fearful temptation, and so by the intercession of Jesus escaped that danger. So, I say, they that commit this sin, they do it after light, knowingly, wilfully, and despitefully, and in the open view of the whole world reject the Son of Man for being their Lord and Savior, and in that it is called the sin against the Holy Ghost. It is a name most fit for this sin to be called the sin against the Holy Ghost, for these reasons but now laid down; for this sin is immediately committed against the motions, and convictions, and light of the Holy Spirit of God that makes it its business to hand forth and manifest the truth and reality of the merits and virtues of the Lord Jesus, the Son of Man. And therefore beware, Ranters and Quakers, for I am sure you are the nearest that sin by profession, which is, indeed, the right committing of it, of any persons that I do know at this day under the whole heavens, forasmuch as you will not venture the salvation of your souls on the blood shed on Mount Calvary, out of the side of that Man that was offered up in sacrifice for all that did believe (Luke 23:33). In that His offering up of His body at that time, either before He offered it, or that have, do, or shall believe on it for the time since, together with that time that He offered it, though formerly you did profess that salvation was wrought out that way, by that sacrifice then offered, and also seemed to have some comfort thereby; yea, insomuch that some of you declared the same in the hearing of many, professing yourselves to be believers of the same. O, therefore, it is sad for you that were once enlightened, and have tasted these good things, and yet, notwithstanding all your profession, you are now turned from the simplicity that is in Christ to another doctrine, which will be your destruction, if you continue in it; for without blood there is no remission (Hebrews 9:22).

Many other reasons might be given, but that I would not be too tedious; yet I would put in this caution, that if there be any souls that be but now willing to venture their salvation upon the merits of a naked Jesus, I do verily for the present believe they have not sinned that sin, because there is still a promise holds forth itself to such a soul where Christ saith, "Him that cometh to me, I will in nowise," for nothing that he hath done, "cast him out" (John 6:37). That promise is worth to be written in letters of gold.

Objections Answered for their Comfort Who Would Have Their Part in the New Covenant

OBJECTION: But, alas, though I should never sin that sin, yet I have other sins enough to damn me.

ANSWER: What though thou hadst the sins of a thousand sinners, yet if thou come to Christ, He will save thee (John 6:37; see also Hebrews 7:25).

OBJECTION: Alas, but how shall I come? I doubt I do not come as I should do? My heart is naught and dead; and, alas! then how should I come?

ANSWER: Why, bethink thyself of all the sins that ever thou didst commit, and lay the weight of them all upon thy heart, till thou art down loaded with the same, and come to Him in such a case as this, and He will give thee rest for thy soul (Matthew 11:28-30). And again; if thou wouldst know how thou shouldst come, come as much undervaluing thyself as ever thou canst, saying, Lord, here is a sinner, the basest in all the country; if I had my deserts, I had been damned in Hell-fire long ago; Lord, I am not worthy to have the least corner in the Kingdom of Heaven; and yet, O that Thou wouldst have mercy! Come like Benhadad's servants to the king of Israel, with a rope about thy neck (1 Kings 20:31-32) and fling thyself at Christ's feet, and lie there a while, striving with Him by thy prayers, and I will warrant thee speed (Matthew 11:28-30; John 6:37).

OBJECTION: O, but I am not sanctified.

ANSWER: He will sanctify thee, and be made thy sanctification also (1 Corinthians 1:30; 6:10-11).

OBJECTION: O, but I cannot pray.

ANSWER: To pray is not for thee to down on thy knees, and say over a many Scripture words only; for that thou mayest do, and yet do nothing but babble. But if thou from a sense of thy baseness canst groan out thy heart's desire before the Lord, He will hear thee, and grant thy desire; for He can tell what is the meaning of the groanings of the Spirit (Romans 8:26-27).

OBJECTION: O, but I am afraid to pray, for fear my prayers should be counted as sin in the sight of the great God.

ANSWER: That is a good sign that thy prayers are more than bare words, and have some prevalence at the Throne of Grace through Christ Jesus, or else the devil would never seek to labor to beat thee off from prayer by undervaluing thy prayers, telling thee they are sin; for the best prayers he will call the worst, and the worst he will call the best, or else how should he be a liar?

OBJECTION: But I am afraid the day of grace is past; and if it should be so, what should I do then?

ANSWER: Truly, with some men indeed it doth fare thus, that the day of grace is at an end before their lives are at end. Or thus, the day of grace is past before the day of death is come, as Christ saith, "If thou hadst known, even thou, at least in this thy day, the things *which belong* unto thy peace," that is, the word of grace or reconciliation, "but now they are hid from thine eyes" (Luke 19:41-42). But for the better satisfying of thee as touching this thing, consider these following things:

First, Doth the Lord knock still at the door of thy heart by His Word and Spirit? If so, then the day of grace is not past with thy soul; for where He doth so knock, there He doth also proffer and promise to come in and sup, that is, to communicate of His things unto them, which he would not do was the day of grace past with his soul (Revelation 3:20).

The Doctrine of Law and Grace Unfolded 209

OBJECTION: But how should I know whether Christ do so knock at my heart as to be desirous to come in? That I may know also, whether the day of grace be past with me or no?

ANSWER: Consider these things—1.) Doth the Lord make thee sensible of thy miserable state without an interest in Jesus Christ, and that naturally thou hast no share in Him, no faith in Him, no communion with Him, no delight in Him, or love in the least to Him? If He hath, and is doing this, He hath, and is knocking at thy heart. 2.) Doth He, together with this, put into thy heart an earnest desire after communion with Him, together with holy resolutions not to be satisfied without real communion with Him. 3.) Doth He sometimes give thee some secret persuasions, though scarcely discernible, that thou mayest attain, and get an interest in Him? 4.) Doth He now and then glance in some of the promises into thy heart, causing them to leave some heavenly savor, though but for a very short time, on thy spirit? 5.) Dost thou at some time see some little excellency in Christ? And doth all this stir up in thy heart some breathing after Him? If so, then fear not, the day of grace is not past with thy poor soul; for if the day of grace should be past with such a soul as this, then that Scripture must be broken where Christ saith, "Him that cometh to Me, I will in nowise," for nothing, by no means, upon no terms whatsoever, "cast out. (John 6:37).

OBJECTION: But surely, if the day of grace was not past with me, I should not be so long without an answer of God's love to my soul; that therefore doth make me mistrust my state the more is, that I wait and wait, and yet am not delivered.

ANSWER: 1. Hast thou waited on the Lord so long as the Lord hath waited on thee? It may be the Lord hath waited on thee these twenty, or thirty, yes, forty years or more, and thou hath not waited on Him seven years. Cast this into thy mind, therefore, when Satan tells thee that God doth not love thee, because thou hast waited so long without an assurance, for it is his temptation, for God did wait longer upon thee, and was fain to send to thee by His ambassadors time after time; and, therefore, say thou, I will wait to see what the Lord will say unto me; and the rather, because He will speak peace, for He is the Lord thereof. But, 2. Know that it is not thy being under trouble a long time that will be an argument sufficiently to prove that thou art past hopes; nay, contrariwise, for Jesus Christ did take our nature upon Him, and also did undertake deliverance for those, and bring it in for them who "were all their LIFETIME subject to bondage" (Hebrews 2:14-15).

OBJECTION: But alas! I am not able to wait, all my strength is gone; I have waited so long, I can wait no longer.

ANSWER: 1.) It may be thou hast concluded on this long ago, thinking thou shouldst not be able to hold out any longer; no, not a year, a month, or a week; nay, it may be, not so long. It may be in the morning thou hast thought thou shouldst not hold out till night; and at night, till morning again; yet the Lord hath supported thee, and kept thee in waiting upon Him many weeks and years; therefore that is but the temptation of the devil to make thee think so, that he might drive thee to despair of God's mercy, and so to leave off following the ways of God, and to close in with thy sins again. O therefore do not give way unto it, but believe that thou shalt "see the goodness of the Lord in the land of the living. Wait on the Lord, be of good courage, and He shall strengthen thine heart; wait, I say, on the Lord" (Psalms 28:13-14). And that thou mayest so do, consider these things—a.) If thou, after thou hast waited thus long, shouldst now give over, and wait no longer, thou wouldst lose all thy time and pains that thou hast taken in the way of God hitherto, and wilt be like to a man that, because he sought long for gold, and did not find it, therefore turned back from seeking after it, though he was hard by it, and had almost found it, and all because he was loath to look and seek a little further. b.) Thou wilt not only lose thy time, but also lose thy own soul, for salvation is nowhere else but in Jesus Christ (Acts 4:12). c.) Thou wilt sin the highest sin that ever thou didst sin before, in drawing finally back, insomuch that God may say, My soul shall have no pleasure in him (Hebrews 10:38). But, 2.) Consider, thou sayest, all my strength is gone, and therefore how should I wait? Why, at that time when thou feelest and findest thy strength quite gone, even that is the time when the Lord will renew and give thee fresh strength. "The youths shall faint and be weary, and the young men shall utterly fall: but they that wait upon the Lord shall renew their strength: they shall mount up with wings as eagles; they shall run and not be weary; they shall walk, and not faint" (Isaiah 40:30-31).

OBJECTION: But though I do wait, yet if I be not elected to eternal life, what good will all my waiting do me? "For *it is* not of him that willeth, nor of him that runneth, but of God that showeth mercy." Therefore, I say, if I should not be elected, all is in vain.

ANSWER #1: 1.) Why in the first place, to be sure thy backsliding from God will not prove thy election, neither thy growing weary of waiting upon God. But, 2.) Thou art, it may be, troubled to know whether thou art elected; and, sayest thou, If I did but know that, that would encourage me in my waiting on God.

ANSWER #2: I believe thee; but mark, thou shalt not know thy election in the first place, but in the second—that is to say, thou must first get acquaintance with God in Christ, which doth come by thy giving credit to His promises, and records which He hath given of Jesus Christ's blood and righteousness, together with the rest of His merits—that is, before thou canst know whether thou are elected, thou must believe in Jesus Christ so really, that thy faith laying hold of, and drinking and eating the flesh and blood of Christ, even so that there shall be life begotten in thy soul by the same; life from the condemnings of the Law; life from the guilt of sin; life over the filth of the same; life also to walk with God in His Son and ways; the life of love to God the Father, and Jesus Christ His Son, saints and ways and that because they are holy, harmless, and such that are altogether contrary to iniquity.

For these things must be in thy soul as a forerunner of thy being made acquainted with the other; God hath these two ways to show His children their election—a.) By testimony of the Spirit— that is, the soul being under trouble of conscience and grieved for sin, the Spirit doth seal up the soul by its comfortable testimony; persuading of the soul that God, for Christ's sake, hath forgiven all those sins that lie so heavy on the conscience, and that do so much perplex the soul, by showing it that that Law, which doth utter such horrible curses against it, is by Christ's blood satisfied and fulfilled

(Ephesians 1:13-14). b.) By consequence—that is, the soul finding that God hath been good unto it, in that He hath showed it its lost state and miserable condition, and also that He hath given it some comfortable hope that He will save it from the same; I say, the soul, from a right sight thereof, doth, or may, draw this conclusion, that if God had not been minded to have saved it, He would not have done for it such things as these. But for the more sure dealing with thy soul, it is not good to take any of these apart—that is, it is not good to take the testimony of the Spirit, as thou supposest thou hast, apart from the *fruits* thereof, so as to conclude the testimony thou hast received to be a sufficient ground without the other; not that it is not, if it be the testimony of the Spirit, but because the devil doth also deceive souls by the workings of his spirit in them, pretending that it is the Spirit of God. And again; thou shouldst not satisfy thyself, though thou do find some seekings in thee after that which is good, without the testimony of the other—that is to say, of the Spirit—for it is the testimony of two that is to be taken for the truth; therefore, say I, as thou shouldst be much in praying for the Spirit to testify assurance to thee, so also thou shouldst look to the end of it when thou thinkest thou hast it; which is this, to show thee that it is alone for Christ's sake that thy sins are forgiven thee, and also thereby a constraining of thee to advance Him, both by words and works, in holiness and righteousness all the days of thy life. From hence thou mayst boldly conclude thy election—"Remembering without ceasing your work of faith, and labor of love, and patience of hope in our Lord Jesus Christ, in the sight of God and our Father. Knowing, brethren," saith the Apostle, "beloved, your election of God." But how? why by this, "For our Gospel came not unto you in word only, but also in power, and in the Holy Ghost, and in much assurance. And ye became followers of us, and of the Lord, having received the word in much affliction, with joy of the Holy Ghost: so that ye were examples to all that believe in Macedonia and Achaia. And to wait for His Son from Heaven, whom He raised from the dead, *even* Jesus, which" hath "delivered us from the wrath to come" (1 Thessalonians 3:4-6, 10).

OBJECTION: But alas, for my part, instead of finding in me anything that is good, I find in me all manners of wickedness, hard-heartedness, hypocrisy, coldness of affection to Christ, very great unbelief, together with everything that is base and of an ill savor. What hope therefore can I have?

ANSWER: If thou wast not such an one, thou hadst no need of mercy. If thou wast whole, thou hadst no need of the physician. Dost thou therefore see thyself in such a sad condition as this? Thou hast the more need to come to Christ, that thou mayst be not only cleansed from these evils, but also that thou mayst be delivered from that wrath they will bring upon thee, if thou dost not get rid of them, to all eternity.

QUESTION: But how should I do? and what course should I take to be delivered from this sad and troublesome condition?

ANSWER: Dost thou see in thee all manner of wickedness? The best way that I can direct a soul in such a case is, to pitch a steadfast eye on Him that is full, and to look so steadfastly upon Him by faith, that thereby thou mayst even draw down of His fullness into thy heart; for that is the right way, and the way that was typed out, before Christ came in the flesh, in the time of Moses, when the Lord said unto him, "Make thee a fiery serpent" of brass, which was a type of Christ "and set it upon a pole; and it shall come to pass" that when a serpent hath bitten any man, "when he looketh upon it, shall live" (Numbers 21:8). Even so now in Gospel times, when any soul is bitten with the fiery serpents—their sins—that then the next way to be healed is, for the soul to look upon the Son of Man, who, as the serpent was, was hanged on a pole, or tree, that whosoever shall indeed look on Him by faith may be healed of all their distempers whatever (John 3:14-15).

As now to instance in some things. 1. Is thy heart hard? Why, then, behold how full of bowels and compassion is the heart of Christ towards thee, which may be seen in His coming down from Heaven to spill His heart-blood for thee. 2. Is thy heart slothful and idle? Then see how active the Lord Jesus is for thee in that He did not only die for thee, but also in that He hath been ever since His ascension into Heaven making intercession for thee (Hebrews 7:25). 3. Dost thou see and find in thee iniquity and unrighteousness? Then look up to Heaven, and see there a righteous Person, even thy righteous Jesus Christ, now presenting thee in His own perfection before the throne of His Father's glory (1 Corinthians 1:30). 4. Dost thou see that thou art very much void of sanctification? Then look up, and thou shalt see that thy sanctification is in the presence of God a complete sanctification, representing all the saints as righteous, as sanctified ones in the presence of the great God of Heaven. And so whatsoever thou wantest, be sure to strive to pitch thy faith upon the Son of God, and behold Him steadfastly, and thou shalt, by so doing, find a mighty change in thy soul. For when we behold Him as in a glass, even the glory of the Lord, we are changed, namely, by beholding, "from glory to glory, *even* as by the Spirit of the Lord" (2 Corinthians 3:18). This is the true way to get both comfort to thy soul, and also sanctification and right holiness into thy soul.

Poor souls that are under the distemper of a guilty conscience, and under the workings of much corruption, do not go the nearest way to Heaven if they do not in the first place look upon themselves as cursed sinners by Law; and yet at that time they are blessed, for ever blessed saints by the merits of Jesus Christ. "O wretched man that I am," saith Paul; and yet, O blessed man that I am, through my Lord Jesus Christ; for that is the scope of the Scripture (Romans 7:24-25).

OBJECTION: Alas, I am blind, and cannot see; what shall I do now?

ANSWER: Why, truly, thou must go to Him that can make the eyes that are blind to see, even to our Lord Jesus, by prayer, saying, as the poor blind man did, "Lord, that I might receive my sight"; and so continue begging Him, till thou do receive sight, even a sight of Jesus Christ, His death, blood, resurrection, ascension, intercession, and that for thee, even for thee. And the rather, because, 1.) He hath invited thee to come and buy such eye-salve of Him that may make thee see (Revelation 3:18). 2.) Because thou shalt never have any true comfort till thou dost thus come to see and behold the Lamb of God that hath taken away thy sins (John 1:29). 3.) Because that thereby thou wilt be able through grace, to step over and turn aside from the several stumbling-blocks that Satan, together with his instruments, hath laid in our way, which otherwise thou wilt not be able to shun, but will certainly fall when others stand, and grope and stumble when others go upright, to the great prejudice of thy poor soul.

OBJECTION: But, alas, I have nothing to carry with me; how then should I go?

ANSWER: Hast thou no sins? If thou hast, carry them, and exchange them for His righteousness; because He hath said, "Cast thy burden upon the Lord, and He shall sustain thee" (Psalms 54:22); and again, because He hath said, though thou be heavy laden, yet if thou do but come to Him, He will give thee rest (Matthew 11:28).

OBJECTION: But, you will say, Satan telleth me that I am so cold in prayers, so weak in believing, so great a sinner, that I do go so slothfully on in the way of God, that I am so apt to slip at every temptation, and to be entangled therewith, together with other things, so that I shall never be able to attain those blessed things that are held forth to sinners by Jesus Christ; and therefore my trouble is much upon this account also, and many times I fear that will come upon me which Satan suggesteth to me—that is, I shall miss of eternal life.

ANSWER: 1.) As to the latter part of the objection, that thou shalt never attain to everlasting life, that is obtained for thee already, without thy doing, either thy praying, striving, or wrestling against sin. If we speak properly, it is Christ that hath in His own body abolished death on the Cross, and brought light, life, and glory to us through this His thus doing. But this is the thing that thou aimest at, that thou shalt never have a share in this life already obtained for so many as do come by faith to Jesus Christ; and all because thou art so slothful, so cold, so weak, so great a sinner, so subject to slip and commit infirmities. 2.) I answer, Didst thou never learn for to outshoot the devil in his own bow, and to cut off his head with his own sword, as David served Goliath, who was a type of him.

QUESTION: O how should a poor soul do this? This is rare, indeed.

ANSWER: Why, truly thus—Doth Satan tell thee thou prayest but faintly, and with very cold devotion? Answer him thus, and say, I am glad you told me, for this will make me trust the more to Christ's prayers, and the less to my own; also I will endeavor henceforth to groan, to sigh, and to be so fervent in my crying at the Throne of Grace, that I will, if I can, make the heavens rattle again with the mighty groans thereof. And whereas thou sayest that I am so weak in believing, I am glad you mind me of it; I hope it will henceforward stir me up to cry the more heartily to God for strong faith, and make me the more restless till I have it. And seeing thou tellest me that I run so softly, and that I shall go near to miss of glory, this also shall be, through grace, to my advantage, and cause me to press the more earnestly towards the mark for the prize of the high calling of God in Christ Jesus. And seeing thou dost tell me that my sins are wondrous great, hereby thou bringest the remembrance of the insupportable vengeance of God into my mind, if I die out of Jesus Christ, and also the necessity of the blood, death, and merits of Christ to help me; I hope it will make me fly the faster, and press the harder after an interest in Him; and the rather, because, as thou tellest me, my state will be unspeakably miserable without Him. And so all along, if he tell thee of thy deadness, dullness, coldness, or unbelief, or the greatness of thy sins, answer him, and say, I am glad you told me, I hope it will be a means to make me run faster, seek more earnestly, and to be the more restless after Jesus Christ. If thou didst but get this art as to outrun him in his own shoes, as I may say, and to make his own darts to pierce himself, then thou mightst also say, how doth Satan's temptations, as well as all other things, work together for my good, for my advantage (Romans 8:28).

OBJECTION: But I do find many weaknesses in every duty that I do perform, as when I pray, when I read, when I hear, or any other duty, that it maketh me out of conceit with myself, it maketh me think that my duties are nothing worth.

ANSWER: I answer, it may be it is thy mercy that thou art sensible of infirmities in thy best things thou doest; ay, a greater mercy than thou art aware of.

QUESTION: Can it be a mercy for me to be troubled with my corruptions? Can it be a privilege for me to be annoyed with my infirmities, and to have my best duties infected with it? How can it possibly be?

ANSWER: Verily, thy sins appearing in thy best duties, do work for thy advantage these ways—1. In that thou findest ground enough thereby to make thee humble; and when thou hast done all, yet to count thyself but an unprofitable servant. And, 2. Thou by this means art taken off from leaning on anything below a naked Jesus for eternal life. It is like, if thou wast not sensible of many by-thoughts and wickednesses in thy best performances, thou wouldst go near to be some proud, abominable hypocrite, or a silly, proud dissembling wretch at the best, such an one as would send thy soul to the devil in a bundle of thy own righteousness. But now, thou, through grace, seest that in all and everything thou doest there is sin enough in it to condemn thee. This, in the first place, makes thee have a care of trusting in thy own doings; and, secondly, showeth thee that there is nothing in thyself which will do thee any good by working in thee, as to the meritorious cause of thy salvation. No; but thou must have a share in the birth of Jesus, in the death of Jesus, in the blood, resurrection, ascension, and intercession of a crucified Jesus. And how sayest thou? Doth not thy finding of this in thee cause thee to fly from a depending on thy own doings? And doth it not also make thee more earnestly to groan after the Lord Jesus? Yea, and let me tell thee also, it will be a cause to make thee admire the freeness and tender heartedness of Christ to thee, when He shall lift up the light of His countenance upon thee, because He hath regarded such an one as thou, sinful thou; and therefore, in this sense, it will be mercy to the saints that they do find the relics of sin still struggling in their hearts. But this is not simply the nature of sin, but the mercy and wisdom of God, who causeth all things to work together for the good of those that love and fear God (Romans 8). And, therefore, whatever thou findest in thy soul, though it be sin of never so black a soul-scarring nature, let it move thee to run the faster to the Lord Jesus Christ, and thou shalt not be ashamed—that is, of thy running to Him.

But when thou dost apprehend that thou art defiled, and also thy best duties annoyed with many weaknesses, let that Scripture come into thy thoughts which saith, "Of Him are ye in Christ Jesus, who of God is made unto us wisdom, and righteousness, and sanctification, and redemption"; and if thou shalt understand that, what thou canst not find in thyself thou shalt find in Christ. Art thou a fool in thyself? then Christ is made of God thy wisdom. Art thou unrighteous in thyself? Christ is made of God thy righteousness. Dost thou find that there is but very little sanctifying grace in thy soul? still here is Christ made thy sanctification; and all this in His own Person without thee, without thy wisdom, without thy righteousness, without thy sanctification, without in His own Person in thy Father's presence, appearing there perfect wisdom, righteousness, and sanctification in His own Person; I say, as a public Person for thee; so that thou mayest believe, and say to thy soul, My soul, though dost find innumerable infirmities in thyself, and in thy actions, yet look upon thy Jesus, the Man Jesus; He is wisdom, and that for thee, to govern thee, to take care for thee, and to order all things for the best for thee. He is also thy righteousness now at God's right hand, always shining before the eyes of His glory; so that there it is unmovable, though thou art in never such a sad condition, yet thy righteousness, which is the Son of God, God-man, shines as bright as ever, and is as much accepted of God as ever. O this sometimes hath been life to me; and so, whatever thou, O my soul, findest wanting in thyself, through faith thou shalt see all laid up for thee in Jesus Christ, whether it be wisdom, righteousness, sanctification, or redemption. Nay, not only so, but, as I said before, He is all these in His own Person without thee in the presence of His Father for thee.

OBJECTION: But now, if any should say in their hearts, O, but I am one of the old-covenant men, I doubt—that is, I doubt I am not within this glorious Covenant of Grace. And how if I should not?

ANSWER: Well, thou fearest that thou are one of the old covenant, a son of the bond-woman.

1.) In the first place, know that thou wast one of them by nature, for all by nature are under that covenant; but set the case that thou art to this day under that, yet let me tell thee, in the first place, there are hopes for thee; for there is a gap open, a way made for souls to come from under the Covenant of Works, by Christ, "for He hath broken down the middle wall of partition *between us*" and you (Ephesians 2:14). And therefore, if thou wouldst be saved, thou mayest come to

Christ; if thou wantest a righteousness, as I said before, there is one in Christ; if thou wouldst be washed, thou mayest come to Christ; and if thou wouldst be justified, there is justification enough in the Lord Jesus Christ. That is the first.

2.) And thou canst not be so willing to come to Christ as He is willing thou shouldst come to Him. Witness His coming down from Heaven, His humiliation, His spilling of His blood from both His cheeks, by sweat under the burden of sin (Luke 22:44) and His shedding of it by the spear when He hanged on the Cross. It appears also by His promises, by His invitations, by His sending forth His messengers to preach the same to poor sinners, and threateneth damnation upon this very account, namely, the neglect of Him; and declares that all the thousands and ten thousands of sins in the world should not be able to damn those that believed in Him; that He would pardon all, forgive and pass by all, if they would but come unto Him; moreover, promiseth to cast out none, no, not the poorest, vilest, contemptiblest creature in the whole world. "Come unto Me all," every one, though you be never so many, so vile, though your load be never so heavy and intolerable, though you deserve no help, not the least help, no mercy, not the least compassion, yet "cast your burden upon Me, and you shall find rest for your souls." Come unto Me and I will heal you, love you, teach you, and tell you the way to the Kingdom of Heaven. Come unto Me, and I will succour you, help you, and keep you from all devils and their temptations, from the Law and its curses, and from being for ever overcome with any evil whatever. Come unto Me for what you need, and tell Me what you would have, or what you would have Me do for you, and all My strength, love, wisdom, and interest that I have with My Father shall be laid out for you. Come unto Me, your sweet Jesus, your loving and tender-hearted Jesus, your everlasting and sin-pardoning Jesus. Come unto Me, and I will wash you, and put My righteousness upon you, pray to the Father for you, and send My Spirit into you, that you might be saved. Therefore,

Consider, besides this, what a privilege thou shalt have at the Day of Judgment above thousands, if thou do in deed and in truth close in with this Jesus and accept of Him; for thou shalt not only have a privilege in this life, but in the life everlasting, even at the time of Christ's second coming from Heaven; for then, when there shall be the whole world gathered together, and all the good angels, bad angels, saints, and reprobates, when all thy friends and kindred, with thy neighbors on the right hand and on the left shall be with thee, beholding of the wonderful glory and majesty of the Son of God; then shall the Son of Glory, even Jesus, in the very view and sight of them all, smile and look kindly upon thee; when a smile or a kind look from Christ shall be worth more than ten thousand worlds, then thou shalt have it. You know it is counted an honor for a poor man to be favorably looked upon by a judge, or a king, in the sight of lords, earls, dukes, and princes; why, thus it will be with thee in the sight of all the princely saints, angels, and devils, in the sight of all the great nobles in the world; then, even thou that closest in with Christ, be thou rich or poor, be thou bond or free, wise or foolish, if thou close in with Him, He will say unto thee, "Well done, good and faithful servant," even in the midst of the whole world; they that love thee shall see it, and they that hate thee shall all to their shame behold it; for if thou fear Him here in secret, He will make it manifest even at that day upon the house-tops.

Secondly, Not only thus, but thou shalt also be lovingly received and tenderly embraced of Him at that day, when Christ hath thousands of gallant saints, as old Abraham, Isaac, Jacob, David, Isaiah, Jeremiah, together with all the Prophets, and Apostles, and martyrs, attending on Him; together with many thousands of glittering angels ministering before Him; besides, when the ungodly shall appear there with their pale faces, with their guilty consciences, and trembling souls, that would then give thousands and ten thousands of worlds, if they had so many, if they could enjoy but one loving look from Christ. I say, then, then shalt thou have the hand of Christ, reached to thee kindly to receive thee, saying, Come, thou blessed, step up hither; thou was willing to leave all for Me, and now will I give all to thee; here is a throne, a crown, a kingdom, take them; thou wast not ashamed of Me when thou wast in the world among my enemies, and now will not I be ashamed of thee before thine enemies, but will, in the view of all these devils and damned reprobates promote thee to honor and dignity. "Come, ye blessed of My Father, inherit the kingdom prepared for you from the foundation of the world." Thou shalt see that those who have served Me in truth shall lose nothing by the means. No; but ye shall be as pillars in My temple, and inheritors of My glory, and shall have place to walk in among My saints and angels (Zechariah 3:7). O! who would not be in this condition? who would not be in this glory? It will be such a soul-ravishing glory, that I am ready to think the whole reprobate world will be ready to run mad, to think that they should miss of it (Deuteronomy 28:34). Then will the vilest drunkard, swearer, liar, and unclean person willingly cry, "Lord, Lord, open to us," yet be denied of entrance; and thou in the meantime embraced, entertained, made welcome, have a fair mitre set upon thy head, and clothed with immortal glory (Zechariah 3:5). O, therefore, let all this move thee, and be of weight upon thy soul to close in with Jesus, this tender-hearted Jesus. And if yet, for all what I have said, thy sins do still stick with thee, and thou findest thy hellish heart loath to let them go, think with thyself in this manner—Shall I have my sins and lose my soul? Will they do me any good when Christ comes? Would not Heaven be better to me than my sins? and the company of God, Christ, saints, and angels, be better than the company of Cain, Judas, Balaam, with the devils in the furnace of fire? Canst thou now that readest or hearest these lines turn thy back, and go on in your sins? Canst thou set so light of Heaven, of God, of Christ, and the salvation of thy poor, yet precious soul? Canst thou hear of Christ, His bloody sweat and death, and not be taken with it, and not be grieved for it, and also converted by it? If so, I might lay thee down several considerations to stir thee up to mend thy pace towards Heaven; but I shall not; there is enough written already to leave thy soul without excuse and to bring thee down with a vengeance into Hell-fire, devouring fire, the Lake of Fire, eternal everlasting fire; O to make thee swim and roll up and down in the flames of the furnace of fire!

FOOTNOTES

1. These words are quoted from the Genevan or Breeches Bible (Mark 2:17).

2. This quotation is from the Genevan translation (Ephesians 2:3).

3. It is observable that the reason given for the punishment of the murderer with death (Genesis 9:6) is taken from the affront he offers to God, not from the injury he does to man.—Scott.

4. The reader need scarcely be reminded, that by "public person" is meant the Savior, in whom all His people have an equal right. "For He made Him, who knew no sin, to be sin for us." (2 Corinthians 5:21)

5. Bunyan's first sight of the spiritual, inward, and extensive requirements of the law filled his heart with despair; see "Grace Abounding," No. 28. It was like the alarming sound of the drum Diabolus mentioned in the "Holy War," which caused Mansoul to shake with terror and dismay. Thus the soul is stripped of self-righteousness, and flies to Christ, whose blood alone cleanseth from all sin.

6. "Crank," brisk, jolly, lusty, spiritful, buxom.

7. From the Puritan or Genevan version.

8. These nine particulars are very methodically arranged, and are all deeply interesting. Very few of those who read the scriptural law of sacrifices see how clearly they pointed as types to Christ the great Antitype.

9. It is a mark of prying and dangerous, if not wicked curiosity to inquire whether God could have found any other way of salvation than by the atoning death of our blessed Lord. Instead of such vain researches, how much more consistent would it be to call upon our

souls, and all that is within us, to bless His name, who hath thus provided abundant pardon, full remission, even to the chief of sinners.

10. The duty of the priests, under the law, led them to be familiar with the most loathsome and catching diseases; and doubtless they took every precaution to avoid contagion. Poor sin-sick soul, do you consider your state more loathsome and dangerous than the leprosy? Fly to Christ, our High Priest and Physician; He will visit you in the lowest abyss of misery, without fear of contagion, and with full powers to heal and save.

11. שאול (sheol) in the Psalms 16:10, and ᾅδην (hades) in Acts 2:31, usually translated as "hell" in the two verses means the unseen place of the dead, the invisible world, or the grave.

12. How awful and vast must have been the sufferings of the Savior, when He paid the redemption price for the countless myriads of His saints; redeemed "out of every kindred, and tongue, and people, and nation." How magnificent His glory when "ten thousand times ten thousands, and thousands of thousands, shall sing with a loud voice, Worthy is the Lamb that was slain to receive power, and riches, and wisdom, and strength, and honor, and glory, and blessing, for ever and ever." Such were the ecstatic vision which Bunyan enjoyed, drawn from the unerring pages of eternal truth.

13. This singular use of the law term "praemunire," meaning that the soul has trusted in a foreign jurisdiction, incurred God's anger, and forfeited its liberty and all its goods.

14. These are solemn truths, in homely, forcible language. Let the soul be convinced that by the obedience of Christ it is released from the law, it has no fear of Satan or of future punishment; Christ is all and in all.

15. "Indenture"; a written agreement, binding one party to reward the other for specified services. As man is by nature bound to love God with all his soul, he can not be entitled to any reward for anything beyond his duty. When he feels that he has failed in his obedience, he must fly to Christ for that mercy which he can never obtain by indenture of service or merit and reward.

16. Same as 15

17. Same as 15

18. For a deeply affecting account of the author's experience about this period read Grace Abounding, No. 259-261.

19. "Scrabble"; to go on the hands and feet or knees. See a remarkable illustration of the word "scrabble" in Grace Abounding, No. 335.

20. As Bunyan was a Baptist, this is full proof that his friends did not ascribe regeneration to water baptism. It is an awful delusion to suppose that immersion in or sprinkling with water can effect or promote the new birth or spiritual regeneration of the soul.

21. This is one of the very thrilling circumstances described by Bunyan in his Grace Abounding, No. 24: Sunday sports were then allowed by the State, and after hearing a sermon on the evil of Sabbath-breaking, he went as usual to his sport. On that day it was a game at cat, and as he was about to strike, "a voice did suddenly dart from Heaven into my soul, which said, Wilt thou leave thy sins and go to Heaven, or have thy sins and go to Hell?"

22. The word Man was essential in Bunyan's days, as an antidote to the jargon of the Ranters, who affirmed that Jesus only existed in the heart of the believer.

23. Same as 20

24. Same as 22

THE MISSION OF GREAT CHRISTIAN BOOKS

The ministry of Great Christian Books was established to glorify The Lord Jesus Christ and to be used by Him to expand and edify the kingdom of God while we occupy and anticipate Christ's glorious return. Great Christian Books will seek to accomplish this mission by publishing Gospel literature which is biblically faithful, relevant, and practically applicable to many of the serious spiritual needs of mankind upon the beginning of this new millennium. To do so we will always seek to boldly incorporate the truths of Scripture, especially those which were largely articulated as a body of theology during the Protestant Reformation of the sixteenth century and ensuing years. We gladly join our voice in the proclamations of— Scripture Alone, Faith Alone, Grace Alone, Christ Alone, and God's Glory Alone!

Our ministry seeks the blessing of our God as we seek His face to both confirm and support our labors for Him. Our prayers for this work can be summarized by two verses from the Book of Psalms:

"...let the beauty of the LORD our God be upon us, And establish the work of our hands for us; Yes, establish the work of our hands." —Psalm 90:17

"Not unto us, O LORD, not unto us, but to your name give glory." —Psalm 115:1

Great Christian Books appreciates the financial support of anyone who shares our burden and vision for publishing literature which combines sound Bible doctrine and practical exhortation in an age when too few so-called "Christian" publications do the same. We thank you in advance for any assistance you can give us in our labors to fulfill this important mission. May God bless you.

For a catalog of other great
Christian books including
additional titles by
John Bunyan
contact us in
any of the following ways:

write us at:
Great Christian Books
160 37th Street
Lindenhurst, NY 11757

call us at:
631. 956. 0998

find us online:
www.greatchristianbooks.com

email us at:
mail@greatchristianbooks.com

www.ingramcontent.com/pod-product-compliance
Lightning Source LLC
LaVergne TN
LVHW041249080426
835510LV00009B/661